KILL 'EM AND LEAVE

By James McBride

Fiction

Miracle at St. Anna
Song Yet Sung
The Good Lord Bird

Non-fiction

The Color of Water
Kill 'Em and Leave

KILL 'EM AND LEAVE

SEARCHING FOR THE REAL JAMES BROWN

James McBride

WEIDENFELD & NICOLSON

First published in the United States in 2016
by Spiegel & Grau
First published in Great Britain in 2016
by Weidenfeld & Nicolson

10 9 8 7 6 5 4 3 2 1

A CIP catalogue record for this book is
available from the British Library.

ISBN 978-1-474-60363-8 (HB)
ISBN 978-1-474-60364-5 (TPB)

Printed in Great Britain by CPI Group (UK) Ltd,
Croydon, CR0 4YY

The Orion Publishing Group's policy is to use papers
that are natural, renewable and recyclable and made
from wood grown in sustainable forests. The logging
and manufacturing processes are expected to conform
to environmental regulations of the country of origin.

Weidenfeld & Nicolson
The Orion Publishing Group Ltd
Carmelite House
50 Victoria Embankment
London EC4Y 0DZ

An Hachette UK Company

www.orionbooks.co.uk

Dedicated to Professor Logan

and his late wife, Bettye

If you're not about the truth, you're not qualified to play

any kind of music.

—Professor Wendell Logan (November 24, 1940–June 15, 2010),
founder of the Jazz Department, Oberlin Conservatory of Music

Contents

Part II. Hit It!

Part III. Quit It!

The Buzz

The statue sits smack in the middle of downtown Augusta, Georgia, face high, because the old man never wanted to be standing above anybody else. He wanted to be down with the people. And as you stand before it on this deserted stretch of cheap stores and old theaters on a hot August afternoon, you say to yourself, "This is what they don't teach you in journalism school": to walk through the carcass of a ruined, destroyed life—this broken life and the one behind it, and the one behind that—to navigate the maze of savage lawyers who lined up to feed at the carcass; to listen to the stories of the broke musicians who traveled the world in glory only to come home with a pocket full of nothing; to make sense of the so-called music experts who helped themselves to a guy's guts and history trying to make a dollar change pockets. Everybody's got a hustle in this world. Meanwhile the guy who made the show, he's deader than yesterday's beer, his legacy scattered everywhere but where he wanted it.

James Brown, the Godfather of Soul, America's greatest soul singer, left most of his wealth, conservatively estimated at $100 million, to educate poor children in South Carolina and Georgia. Nine years after his death on December 25, 2006, not a dime of it had reached a single kid. Untold millions have been frittered away by lawyers and politicians who have been loosed on one another by various factions of his destroyed family.

It's a sad end to an extraordinary yet tragic life, though you figure with thousands of poor kids in South Carolina and Georgia needing a good education, somebody would have the integrity to figure the whole thing out. But that's a long shot these days because, in part, that would mean we've figured out James Brown. And that's impossible. Because to figure him out, we'd have to figure ourselves out. And that's like giving an aspirin to a two-headed baby.

It's an odd thing. They're big on him here in Augusta, his adopted hometown. They named an arena after him and a street, held a James Brown Day, all of that tribute jazz. But the truth is, other than this weird statue, there's not a wisp of James Brown in this place. There's no feeling of him here. He's a vapor now, just another tragic black tale, his story bought and sold and bought again, just like the slaves that were once sold at the Haunted Pillar just two blocks from where his statue stands. Brown's saga is an industrial-strength story, a big-box store of a life filled with cheap goods for any writing hack looking for the equivalent of the mandatory five-minute gospel moment you see in just about every Broadway show these days. Lousy story, great music. And everybody's an expert: a documentary here, a book there, a major motion picture, all produced by folks who "knew" and "loved" him, as if that were possible. The fact is, it really doesn't matter whether they knew him or not, or loved him or hated his guts and hoped somebody would tie him to a pickup truck and drag his body across the quit line. The worst has already happened. The guy is finished. Gone. Perfect dead. Paying him homage now doesn't cost anyone a thing. He's like John Coltrane, or Charlie Parker, or Louis Jordan, or any other of the dozens of black artists whose music is immortalized while the communities that produced them continue to suffer. James Brown is forgotten in Augusta, really. The town is falling apart, just like his memory. He's history. Safely dead.

But over in Barnwell County, just across the state line in South Carolina, the place where Brown was born and was living when he died, there's no uncertainty about who James Brown is. He is not a vapor there, but rather a living, breathing thing.

There used to be an old black-run soul food joint on Allen Street in the town of Barnwell, not far from James Brown's birthplace, called Brooker's. Every time I would go to that town to pick around the bones of James Brown's story—what's left of it—I would head to Brooker's and eat pork and grits and collards and whatever else Miss Iola and her sister Miss Perry Lee were serving. I had a lot of fun goofing off in that joint. I'd sit at a table and watch the people come in— young, old, some quiet as bedbugs, others talkative and friendly, a few suspicious, folks of all types: small businessmen, local workers, farmers, an undertaker, hairdressers. I'd always leave the place laughing and saying to myself, "They don't teach you this in journalism school either"—to stand in somebody's hometown and still hear the laughter and the pride. They love James Brown in Barnwell. They don't see his broken life; they don't care about the bottom-feeder lawyers who lined up to pick at his bones, or his children fighting over the millions Brown left to the poor instead of them. They've seen enough evil in their own lives, going back generations, to fill their own book of sad tales. So why talk about it? Laugh and be happy in the Lord! James Brown died on top. The white man can say whatever he wants. Put that down in your little old notebook, kid: We don't care. We know who James Brown was. He was one of us. He sleeps with the Lord now. In good hands! Now, here, have some more pie.

They laugh and smile and make you feel good. But behind the laughter, the pie, the howdies, and the second helpings, behind the huge chicken dinners and the easy chuckles, there's a silent buzz. If you put your ear to a table, you can almost hear it; it's a churning kind of grind, a rumble, a growl, and when you close your eyes and listen, the noise is not pleasant. It's nothing said, or even seen, for black folks in South Carolina are experts at showing a mask to the white man. They've had generations of practice. The smile goes out before their faces like a radiator grille. When a white customer enters Brooker's, they act happy. When the white man talks, they nod before the man finishes his sentences. They say "yes sir" and "right on" and laugh and joke and say "I declare!" and "Is that right?" and howdy 'em and yes 'em to death. And you stand there dumbfounded, because you're hearing something different, you're hearing that buzz, and you don't know if it's coming from the table or the bottom of your feet, or if it's the speed of so much history passing between the two of them, the black and the white, in that moment when the white man pays for his collard greens with a smile that ties you up, because you can hear the roar of the war still being fought—the big one, the one the northerners call the Civil War and southerners call the War of Northern Aggression, and the more recent war, the war of propaganda, where the black guy in the White House pissed some people off no matter what he did. It's all about race. Everybody knows it. And there's no room to breathe. So you sit there, suffocating, watching this little transaction over your own plate of collard greens, as these two people laugh and small-talk over the chasm that divides them, and you stare in amazement, feeling like you're sitting on a razor blade, waiting for one or the other to pull out a gun and blow the other's face off. You think you're losing your mind as the buzz in your ears grows louder; it morphs into a kind of electricity that builds until it's no longer a buzz but an unseen roar of absolute fury and outrage, marked only by an occasional silent glance of unsaid understanding, one that slips between you and the rest of the blacks in the room like the silent dollar bill that leaves that white customer's hand and slips into Miss Iola's old cash register, which closes with a silent click.

If you wait till the white man leaves and ask about that space, the space between white and black folks in South Carolina, the black folks say, "Oh, it ain't nothing. Such-and-so is my friend. I've known him forty years. We all get along here." Only at night, when they get home, when the lights are down and all the churchin' is done and the singing is over and the TV is off and the wine is flowing and tongues are working freely, only within the safety of home and family does the talk change, and then the buzz is no longer a buzz. It's a roaring cyclone of fury laced with distaste and four hundred years of pent-up bitterness.

There is not a single marker for James Brown in this place, they say. No spot to commemorate his birth, no building named after him, no school, no library, no statue, no nothing. And even when they do name something after him, or celebrate him in the state legislature or some such thing, it doesn't matter. They smile about it during the day, but at night they cuss that thing so hard it'll curl up on its own and crawl away like a snake. There's not even a marker at the spot where the greatest soul singer this country ever knew came from. Why would they put one there? They hate him. There was a sign at the state line, but after Brown got arrested the last time, they did away with it. The white man in this state will forgive his own sin a million times. He will write history any way he wants to down here. And when it's all over, them witches in suits down at the courthouse will rob every cent Mr. Brown earned, you'll see. Poor folks ain't got a chance with them, no matter what their color, and any fool 'round here stupid enough to stand up and open their mouth on that subject, they'll bust down on them so hard, pus will come out their ears.

That whole thing came crashing down on me one hot afternoon when I was sitting inside Brooker's, joking around with Miss Perry Lee, and a big fella I'd met named Joe Louis Thomas wandered in. Joe is a well-built, handsome, brown-skinned man who worked in New York as a professional wrestler. Tired of being told to throw matches intentionally for a few dollars, he returned home to Blackville, South Carolina, got married, sent two of his three kids to college—one of whom, Joe Thomas, Jr., joined the Green Bay Packers in 2014. Then Joe went back to college himself at South Carolina State University and joined the track and football team—at age fifty-one. He'd grown up hauling cotton off a white man's field in Blackville with all eleven of his siblings. For most of his life, he was considered deaf. Only his outstanding skill as a football player—he ran a 40-yard dash in 4.35 seconds in high school—kept him in school. One day when he was seventeen, a doctor stuck a probe in Joe's ear. The doc pulled out seventeen years' worth of trash: cotton, junk, dirt. Now that Joe Thomas could hear again, he heard things he'd never heard before. He saw things he'd never seen before.

Joe sat down across from me. Miss Perry Lee said, "Hey Joe, your buddy's back."

Joe looked at me. "You still working on that book?" he asked.

I said I was. I gave him the whole deal: Having a hard time telling the real story. Terrible court case. A lot of fighting. Got a bunch of questions with no answers, trying to get to the bottom of things, blah, blah, blah.

Joe listened silently, holding his fork loosely. It hung in the air as I spoke. When I was done, he still held his fork over his plate of liver and collards.

"You watch yourself out here," he said softly.

"I haven't done anything wrong," I said. "It's just a book."

He looked at me, steady, silent. He pointed his fork at me and said, "You watch yourself out here, young man."

Part I

Countin' Off

Chapter 1

Mystery House

Back in the 1960s, when I was a kid living in St. Albans, Queens, in New York City, there was a huge, forbidding, black-and-gray house that sat on a lovely street not far from my home. The house was located across a set of Long Island Rail Road tracks that basically split my neighborhood in half. My side of the tracks was the poor side— tightly clumped, small, exhausted-looking homes, some with neat lawns and manicured flower beds; others were like mine, in total disarray. The neighborhood was mostly working-class blacks, post office and city transit workers from America's South who had moved to the relative bliss of Queens from the crowded funk of Brooklyn, Harlem, and the Bronx. It was a proud crowd. We had moved up. We were living the American dream.

But on the other side of the railroad tracks was the high life. Big, sumptuous homes with luscious lawns; long, shiny Cadillacs that eased down smooth, silent streets. A gigantic all-glass church, a beautiful park, and a glistening, brand-new Steak N Take diner run by the Nation of Islam that stayed open twenty-four hours on weekends. The Nation scared the shit out of everybody in my neighborhood back in those days, by the way. Not even the worst, most desperate junkie would stalk into a Steak N Take and pull out his heater. He'd be dead before he hit the door. Many of the Nation of Islam Muslims who worked in Steak N Take were ex-cons, serious, easygoing men in clean white shirts and bow ties who warned you about the ills of pork as they served you all the cheesesteaks you wanted. That place was smooth business. And then there were the celebs who had bought homes nearby: Roy Campanella. Lena Horne. Count Basie. Ella Fitzgerald. Fats Waller. Milt Hinton. All stars. Big time.

But none of them lived in the huge, forbidding house on Murdock Avenue, with vines creeping onto the spiraled roof and a moat that crossed a small built-in stream, with a black Santa Claus illuminated at Christmas, and a black awning that swooped down from the front yard in the shape of a wild hairdo.

None of them was James Brown.

We used to stand outside his house and dream, me and my best friend, Billy Smith. Sometimes crowds of us would stand around: kids from my neighborhood, kids from other neighborhoods. A kid from nearby Hollis named Al Sharpton used to stand out there sometimes, but I didn't know him in those days. Billy had moved from my side of the tracks into a house just down the street from James Brown, and in the summer I would cross the Long Island Rail Road tracks alone, a dangerous piece of business, just to hang with him. We'd linger outside the forbidding black-and-gray mansionlike home for days at a time, waiting for the Godfather of Soul to emerge. Sometimes other kids from Billy's crowd came: Beanie, Buckie, Pig, Marvin, Emmitt, Roy Bennett, son of the great singer Brooke Benton, who lived right across the street from James Brown. Kids came from all over, from South Jamaica and Hollis and Far Rockaway. The rumor was—and this went on for years—that the Godfather of Soul would slip out of his house at night, walk around the corner to nearby Addisleigh Park, sit down and talk to the kids, and just *give out* money—give it out by the twenties and fifties—if you promised him you'd stay in school.

We hung out in the park and waited and waited. We waited for months, all summer, all winter, our promises ready. He never showed.

I knew of no one in my neighborhood who'd actually met the great man until my sister Dotty, age eleven, fell into our house one afternoon breathless, sweaty, and screaming. "Oh my God! Oh my God! You won't believe it! *Ohhh my Goooood!!! Helennnnnnn!*"

Helen, the sister above Dotty in age and Dot's guru in those days, came running, and the rest of us gathered around. It took several minutes for Dotty to compose herself. Finally she blurted out her story:

She and her best friend, Shelly Cleveland, had slipped across the railroad tracks to linger outside James Brown's house after school like all the kids did. Of course he didn't come out. But that afternoon, Dotty and Shelly decided to do something no kid in my neighborhood, no kid in New York City—no kid in the world that I knew of at that point in my eight-year-old life—had ever done or even thought to do.

They went up to the front door and knocked.

A white maid answered. She said, "What do you want?"

"Can we speak to Mr. Brown?" Dotty asked.

"Wait a minute," the maid said. She disappeared.

A few moments later, James Brown himself appeared at the door, with two white women, one on each arm, both dressed in sixties wear, complete with beehive hairdos.

Dotty and Shelly nearly fainted. The Godfather of Soul seemed tickled. He greeted them warmly. He asked Dotty, "What's your name?"

"Dotty . . ."

"Stay in school, Dotty. Don't be no fool!" He shook her hand and shook Shelly's hand and the two girls fled.

We listened, breathless, as Dotty recounted it. It seemed unbelievable. Even my mother was impressed. "See that?" she barked. "Listen to James Brown. Stay in school!" But who cared about what she said.

What was important was that *James Brown said it!* Dotty's star soared. She'd always been a total James Brown fanatic, but in a house of twelve kids where food was scarce and attention scarcer, where ownership of the latest James Brown 45 rpm was like owning the Holy Grail, Dotty morphed from underling to holding a kind of special status—ambassador to famedom, chosen member of the tribe, a button man, a made member of the mob. In other words, a Big Kid with Gold Star standing.

The shine lasted months. She would stand in our freezing living room on cold winter nights when there was nothing to eat and nowhere to go and no money to go there anyway, and play out the scenario. "He's so small," she'd declare. "He's a little guy." She'd leap up, whip her hair back in James Brown style, thrust out her jaw, and holler in a southern accent, *"Stay in school, Dot-tay! Don't be no fool! Hah!"* We howled. Visitors, neighbors, even my gruff stepfather and the serious people from church asked her to relive the moment, which she did, giving a blow-by-blow account of how the Hardest Working Man in Show Business—Mr. Dynamite himself—had come to the door of his house and given it to her straight: *"Stay in school, Dot-tay!"* The grumpy old church folks listened and nodded stern approval. James Brown was right. *Stay in school, Dotty, stay in school.*

I watched all this in grim silence. My crummy sister had beat me to the punch. She had kissed the black stone. She'd met James Brown. My jealousy lasted years.

Every man or woman in this life has a song, and if you're lucky you can remember it. The song of your wedding, the song of your first love, the song of your childhood. For African Americans, the song of our life, the song of our entire history, is embodied in the life and times of James Brown.

He is easily one of the most famous African Americans in the world, and arguably the most influential African American in pop music history. His picture hangs on the walls of African homes and huts where people don't even know what he did for a living. His imprint has been felt throughout Western Europe, Asia, the Far East. His dances, his language, his music, his style, his pioneering funk, his manner of speaking are stamped into the American consciousness as deeply as that of any civil rights leader or sports hero, including Muhammad Ali, Michael Jordan, Martin Luther King, and Malcolm X. He is also arguably the most misunderstood and misrepresented African American figure of the last three hundred years, and I would speculate that he is nearly as important and as influential in American social history as, say, Harriet Tubman or Frederick Douglass. When his 2006 funeral procession steered slowly through Harlem, men rushed out of barbershops with shaving cream on their faces, children stayed home from school, old people wept openly. The Apollo Theater crowds lined the streets for five city blocks, thousands of people, from 125th up to 130th Street. Black America from front to back took a knee and bowed. The King of Pop himself, Michael Jackson, flew to Augusta for the funeral service, a coronation *from* a king *to* a king. Black Americans loved Michael, too, but while he was black America's child—abandoned at times, forsaken, adopted again, in, out, black, white, not sure—there was no question about who James Brown was. James Brown was our soul. He was unquestionably black. Unquestionably proud. Unquestionably a man. He was real and he was funny. He was the uncle from down South who shows up at your house, gets drunk, takes out his teeth, embarrasses you in front of your friends, and grunts, "Stay in school!" But you love him. And you know he loves you.

But there is more, and here is where the story grows extra body parts. During the course of his forty-five-year career, James Brown sold more than 200 million records, recorded 321 albums, 16 of them hits, wrote 832 songs, and made 45 gold records. He revolutionized American music: he was the very first to fuse jazz into popular funk; the very first to record a "live" album that became a number-one record. His influence created several categories of music now tabulated by *Billboard*, *Variety*, *Downbeat*, and *Rolling Stone;* he sang with everyone from hip-hop creator Afrika Bambaataa to Pavarotti to pioneer jazz arranger Oliver Nelson. His band was revolutionary—it was made up of outstanding players and vocalists, among the best in popular music this nation has ever produced. His opening performance that preceded the Rolling Stones' appearance at the T.A.M.I. concert from Santa Monica in 1964 was so hot that Keith Richards later confessed that following James Brown was the worst decision of the Rolling Stones' career. Yet James Brown never once made the cover of *Rolling Stone* magazine during his lifetime. To the music world, he was an odd appendage, a kind of freak, a large rock in the road that you couldn't get around, a clown, a black category. He was a super talent. A great dancer. A real show. A laugher. A drug addict, a troublemaker, all hair and teeth. A guy who couldn't stay out of trouble. The man simply defied description.

The reason? Brown was a child of a country in hiding: America's South.

There is nowhere in the USA quite like America's South; there is no place more difficult to fully understand or fully capture. No one book can get close to the man because he comes from a land that no one book can explain, a land shaped by a history of slavery and oppression and misunderstanding, whose self-definition defies simple explanation and pushes out any impression you may try to lay upon it. The South is simply a puzzle. It's like the quaint, loyal housewife who, after forty years of watching her husband spend Sunday afternoons sprawled on the couch watching football, suddenly blurts out, "I never did like your daddy," pulls out a knife, and ends Hubby's football season for good. To even get close to the essence of the reasoning behind that act is like trying to touch the sun with your bare hand: why bother. You cannot understand Brown without understanding that the land that produced him is a land of masks. The people who walk that land, both black and white, wear masks and more masks, then masks beneath those masks. They are tricksters and shape-shifters, magicians and carnival barkers, able to metamorphize right before your eyes into good old boys, respectable lawyers, polite society types, brilliant scholars, great musicians, history makers, and everything's-gonna-be-all-right Maya Angelou look-alikes—when in fact nothing's gonna be all right. This land of mirage produces characters of outstanding talent and popularity—Oprah Winfrey being the shining example. It is peopled by a legion of ghosts that loom over it with the same tenacity and electric strength that propelled a small group of outnumbered and outgunned poor white soldiers to kick the crap out of the northern Union army for three years running during the Civil War 150 years ago.

The South almost won the Civil War, and maybe they should have, because America's southerners play-act and pretend with a brilliance that is unmatched. They obstruct your view with a politeness and deference that gives slight clue to the power within. Outside the looking glass, they are chameleons, whistling "Dixie" and playing slow and acting harmless and goofy. But behind their aw-shucks veneer, behind the bowing and scraping and moon pies and cigarettes and chitchat about the good old Alabama Crimson Tide and hollering for the Lord, the unseen hand behind them is a gnarled, loaded fist prepped for a diesel-powered blow. If that hand is coming in your direction, get out of the way or you're likely to find yourself spending the rest of your life sucking your meals through a straw.

No one is more aware of the power of America's southerners than the blacks who walk among them. There's an old slave saying, "Go here, go there, do nothing," and the descendants of those slaves are experts at that task. They do whatever needs to be done, say whatever needs to be said, then cut for the door to avoid the white man's evil, which they feel certain will, at some point, fall on them like raindrops. Brown, who grew up in a broken home and spent three years in a juvenile prison before he was eighteen, was an expert at dodging the white man's evil. He had years of practice covering up, closing down, shutting in, shutting out, locking up, locking out, placing mirrors in rooms, hammering up false doorways and floorboards to trap all comers who inquired about his inner soul. He did the same with his money. From the time he was a boy who bought his own ball and bat with money earned from dancing and shining shoes for colored soldiers at nearby Fort Gordon, Brown kept his money close. When he became a star, he had a secret room for cash in his house. He buried money in distant hotel rooms, carried tens of thousands, even hundreds of thousands, around in a suitcase; he kept wads of cashier's checks in his wallet. He always had a back door, a quick exit, a way of getting out, because behind the boarded-up windows of his life, the Godfather's fear of having nothing was overwhelming in its ability to swallow him whole and send him into a series of wild behaviors. I once asked his personal manager, Charles Bobbit, who for forty-one years knew James Brown as well as any man on this earth, what Brown's truest, deepest feeling about the white man was.

Bobbit paused for a moment, looking at his hands, then said simply, "Fear."

That fear—the knowledge that a single false step while wandering inside the maze of the white man's reality could blast you back home with the speed of a circus artist being shot out of a cannon—is the kryptonite that has lain under the bed of every great black artist from 1920s radio star Bert Williams to Miles Davis to Jay Z. If you can't find a little lead-lined room where you can flee that panic and avoid its poisonous rays, it will control your life. That's why Miles Davis and James Brown, who had similar reputations for being cantankerous and outrageous, seem so much alike. Each admired the other from a distance. Those who knew them describe them similarly: hard men on the outside, but, behind the looking glass, sensitive, kind, loyal, proud, troubled souls working to keep pain out, using all kinds of magic tricks, sleights of hand, and cover-up jobs to make everyone think "the cool" was at work when in fact the cool was eating them alive. Keeping the pain out was a full-time job, and Brown worked harder at it than any black star before or after. "You did not get to know James Brown," says his lawyer Buddy Dallas, "because he did not want to be known. In twenty-four years of working with him, I have never known a person who worked harder at keeping people from knowing who he was."

I still drive by that old house in Queens. I don't know who lives there now. Word is that four different people owned it before Brown did. One of them was said to be Cootie Williams, trumpet player in Duke Ellington's orchestra. All four owners, I'm told, lost the house, till Brown got hold of it. James Brown, however, did not lose that house. He owned it for nearly ten years and sold it at a profit in 1968, three years after he shook my sister Dotty's hand.

For years, that house was a mystery to me. For years, I wanted to set foot in it, to know what went on inside there. Now I don't want to know anymore. Because I already know.

Chapter 2

Cussin' and Fussin'

James Brown used to tell this joke: There was a lawyer who worked the same case for twenty-five years. While working the case, the lawyer had a son. He bought his son toys at Christmas. He bought him a bicycle, a train set, books. Later on, he bought the kid a car. He sent the son to college. When the son got out of college, the lawyer sent him to law school. His dream was that his son would someday join his law firm. The son followed his father's wishes. He joined the firm right after he got his law degree. The father was delighted. "This is great, son!" he said. "Now I don't have to work so hard." He went on vacation, leaving the business to his son. While he was away, the son took a look at the case that the father was working. When the father returned from vacation, the son said, "Dad, I have a surprise for you. I solved the case. It's finished."

The father said, "You fool! We've been living off that case for twenty-five years. Now we're broke."

So it was with the life of the greatest soul singer to grace modern American history.

James Brown lived off the "case," the high moral ground, of African American life.

During the civil rights movement, which was his heyday, he epitomized that striving and pride of the African American struggle. Yet since his sad, dispirited death in an Atlanta hospital in 2006, the facts of his life have become twisted like a pretzel beyond recognition, which is how, sadly, a lot of black history ends up—on the cutting room floor of some Hollywood filmmaker, filed under the heading of "black rage" or simply "black story." There's no room for so many of the details that really make up a man or woman when you hide them under those headings. The legacy of caring, insight, trust, and sophistication that makes up black American Christian life and culture is fragile compost for the American storytelling machine, which grinds old stereotypes and beliefs into a kind of mush porridge best served cold, if at all.

Today, at the dawn of the twenty-first century, Brown, one of the most recognizable entertainers in American history, is tumbling toward history as an enigma. The public—especially poor children of all colors and backgrounds, to whom he left his fortune—has no idea who he is. The story of his life as told in the plethora of films, books, and documentaries serves more as a feeding ground for the entertainment industry, which plays out his history as a strange blend of fiction and nonfiction rather than as a true reflection of the troubled soul who lived underneath the pompadour hairdo. But then again, why try to get it right? Black history in the United States is low-hanging fruit for anyone who wants to play Tarzan and swing down into the open jungle of African American life to pluck the easy pickings. You can make a few dollars in the storytelling world that way. It's free money.

Case in point is the Big Kahuna, Hollywood, which weighed in on Brown in 2014 with the biopic *Get On Up*. In an opening scene, James Brown, clad in a sweat suit and bearing a shotgun, strides into an Augusta, Georgia, office building he owns, interrupting a meeting of white insurance executives who had rented one of the conference rooms for a seminar. They stare in terror as he launches into a tirade that ends with, "Which one of you gentlefolk hung a number two in my commode?" Then his shotgun accidentally discharges into the ceiling—BLAM! Brown stares at the ceiling and mutters, "Good God." Then he scans the quaking executives and spots the offender, a cowering, quivering white woman trembling on the floor in terror. Brown approaches. He tells her to sit up, pats her paternally on the knee, and gives her a stern lecture, saying, "You did right by yourself." Then he hears a police siren and says, "Awww shit . . . I got to go!" He then leads the police on a wild, high-speed car chase, in which he drives through two Georgia state police cars set as a barricade across the road, destroying them both.

It's a funny scene.

Problem is, it's mostly fiction.

According to FBI material concerning the 1988 incident, James Brown never discharged a rifle in that room. He walked in with an old hunting rifle that, his manager and attorney Buddy Dallas says, didn't even have a firing pin in it. He placed it in a corner, asked those in the room not to use his private bathroom, then turned to leave. As he was leaving, someone in the room reminded him that he'd left the old gun in a corner, and he said thank you, picked up the gun, and left. He didn't say, "Awww, shit . . . I gotta go!" James Brown rarely cursed. "I knew him more than forty years," said Charles Bobbit. "I heard him curse maybe three times." Adds Buddy Dallas: "In twenty-four years, I never heard Mr. Brown utter a curse word." And James Brown driving through a police barricade and destroying two Georgia state police cars? Not in Georgia he didn't. Brown was a black man from the South. He wasn't stupid. In fact, it was the other way around. The cops destroyed *his* pickup truck. They caught him after a low-speed "chase" not far away and reportedly fired seventeen bullets into the truck, two of which entered the gas tank—with Brown still inside the truck. Brown was terrified. He later complained that after he was taken into custody, a cop in plain clothes—nobody ever did figure out

who—walked up to him while he was cuffed and seated in the station
and punched him in the jaw, knocking out one of his teeth.

The police were mad. And I understand. Years ago, when I was a
cub reporter at the Wilmington, Delaware, *News Journal,* a friendly
Delaware state trooper gave me a piece of advice about police car
chases. "We don't like them," he said. "Because we can get killed chasing down some idiot." That's the part they don't show on television:
the cop coming home, hands shaking, nerves shot, after running
down a drunk doing ninety miles per hour on a twenty-five-mile-per-
hour suburban street filled with kids. Brown was in the middle of a
bad run that year. His life had collapsed. His great band had disbanded.
The IRS had cleaned him out to the walls, twice. He had outrun his
own musical revolution. At fifty-five, he'd fallen into relative obscurity, and was smoking PCP, a hallucinogen, a habit he began in midlife
after years of eschewing drugs. He had turned to drugs because his
career had nose-dived and he was depressed. His marriage to his third
wife, Adrienne, also a reported drug addict, was a mess. His father, Joe
Brown, to whom Brown was very close, was in the hospital; when
Brown saw the cops following him after he left his office, he was, piti-
fully and desperately, trying to get to his father, one of the few people
in the world who loved him unconditionally. At that point in his life,
everybody he'd cared about, with the exception of a few close friends
and select family, had left or he'd driven away. He was a physical mess.
His knees were going—arthritis was killing him. His teeth, which had
required several operations, hurt so much he could hardly eat at times.
He'd arrived at his Augusta office building that day, portions of which
were rented out to other businesses, saw an unlocked door, and, according to his son Terry, recalled in his drug-addled memory that
someone had recently slipped into his office and stolen his wallet.
Thinking his office was being robbed again, he got mad and did what
many a country-born, God-fearing South Carolinian might do. He
walked in there with his rifle—and spent the next three years in jail
because of it.

But that's not in the movie. And why should it be? Movies are simple. And Brown's life was anything but that. Thus one of the most humiliating events of Brown's life was played for laughs in a movie distributed around the world for millions to see—a film of half-truths, implying that his beloved mother, for example, who left him when he was a child, was a whore and a drunk who bummed a hundred dollars off him at the Apollo after he became a star, leaving out the fact that he took his mother back into his Georgia home after discovering her and reunited her with his father; a film that depicts his father, a gentle, funny, country man who worked hard and deeply loved his son, as a stereotypical child-beating, wife-beating, cornpone country hick— a ticking time bomb of black fury, sitting at a forlorn table in a cabin in the woods with his son James, singing a song lifted straight from anthropologist Alan Lomax's collection of Mississippi chain-gang recordings. And the thing that would hurt James Brown most of all: the portrayal of James Brown himself, a proud man who spent his entire career trying to show, as southerners do, his best face; a guy who sat in a hair dryer for three hours after every show, because he always wanted the public to see him "clean and proper"; a man who'd spent his childhood so disheveled and dirty in appearance that for the rest of his life he kept a house as clean as a whistle and shined and cleaned himself to a tee, insisting that he be addressed as "Mr. Brown," and addressing others, even friends, by their surnames. Yet audiences around the world are treated to a full two hours of James Brown acting like a complete wacko in a film that is roughly 40 percent fiction and that shows not one iota of sophistication about black life or the black culture that spawned him. The film portrays the black church—in this case the United House of Prayer, one of the most unusual and beloved sects of twentieth-century black Christian life and an important source of African American music—as a kind of howling extravaganza, and shows the other usual stereotypical puff and smoke: the big black "aunt" announcing to young James Brown, "You special, boy!"; the good loyal white man as manager; and the black musicians who helped Brown create one of America's seminal art forms as a bunch of know-nothings and empty heads, including a scene showing

Alfred "Pee Wee" Ellis, a musical pioneer and co-creator of American soul music, making a complete fool of himself—a scene that Pee Wee says never happened. Tate Taylor, the white director of *Get On Up*, is also the director of the acclaimed *The Help*, yet another white version of black history. "I despise most everything that's been written about him," says Emma Austin, seventy, who knew Brown for more than forty years. "I can't stand to look at most of it."

But that's show business. And some of that public persona Brown created himself. But here's something only a musician might think about: that film was co-produced by Rolling Stones impresario Mick Jagger. More than forty years earlier, Brown and his band of nobodies—a bunch of unknown black sidemen called the Flames—smoked Jagger and the Rolling Stones on the T.A.M.I. show. Before the show, Brown was told by the producers that the Stones, the new rock band of the moment, a bunch of kids from England, would have the honor of closing the show. According to Charles Bobbit, the producers didn't even give Brown a dressing room. He had to rehearse his dancing on a sloped carpet on the auditorium floor. (The film *Get On Up* portrays Brown in a dressing room.) The snub charged Brown, and he hit the stage a man possessed: he and his high-stepping band left it in cinders. When Jagger and the Rolling Stones followed, they sounded like a garage band by comparison, with Jagger dancing around like the straw man in *The Wizard of Oz*. It's all online. You can see it.

Or you can see Jagger's version of it in the film *Get On Up*. Or hear Jagger's version of James Brown in the documentary *Mr. Dynamite: The Rise of James Brown* (2014), which he also co-produced. Today Jagger is rock royalty, James Brown is dead, and Inaudible Productions, which oversees the licensing of Jagger's Rolling Stones catalog, administers James Brown's music as well.

That's a bitter pill to swallow for those who knew the real James Brown. "Mr. Brown didn't even like Mick Jagger," fumes Charles Bobbit. "He had no love for Mick Jagger."

Chapter 3

American Jive

Here's how music history in America works: a trumpet player blows a solo in a Philly nightclub in 1945. Somebody slaps it on a record, and fifty years later that same solo is a final in a college jazz department, and your kid pays $60,000 a year to take the final, while the guy who blew the solo out of his guts in the first place is deader than yesterday's rice and beans, his family is suffering from the same social illness that created his great solo, and nobody gave two hoots about the guy when he died and nobody gives two hoots about his family now. They call that capitalism, the Way of the World, Showbiz, You Gotta Suck It Up, an upcoming Movie About Diversity, and my favorite term, Cultural History. I call it fear, and it has lived in the heart of every black American musician for the last hundred years.

That fear is nearly impossible to explain if you are not a musician who understands the sweat involved in making music. It's rarely talked about in the music press, which plays along in pretending there are no race problems in the music business. Why shouldn't it? Musicians of all colors get snookered by the biz. We all leave our blood on the floor for the Big Corporation, Big Brother, the Record Label, the Country & Western Community—whatever you want to call it. The difference is this: Most of us don't walk through department stores buzzing with background music that plays ninth chords borrowed from our history. Most of us don't know the feeling of sweating for hours over your music, then watching a foreigner from, say, England or Australia cop that music, ape their version of it, make a million, then call you a genius while they're living high and you're barely living. Most of us don't understand the ache of hearing blues great Robert Johnson called "a legend," knowing that poor Mr. Johnson is nothing more than a 1920s version of, say, Afrika Bambaataa or Kool Herc, the rap pioneers from the South Bronx who fell into relative obscurity after the recording industry took their music—originally written to empower poor kids and working-class women from communities in the South Bronx—and transformed it into chants that encourage kids to clobber their neighbor, pillage women, drink as much booze as possible, and blow each other's brains out over tennis shoes. Most of us are not privy to the silent suffering of the classically trained black performers who spend their careers watching the major opera companies and orchestras in America leave port without them, knowing that nearly the same paucity of black faces that existed on board those ships fifty years ago still exists today, while hearing the same fifty-year-old excuses about why there's no space for them in those hotbeds of nepotism and cronyism.

It's a trick bag. You open your mouth on the subject and you're a racist and a malcontent. You close your mouth on it and you're a fool, because when the coin flips the other way—and it does a lot these days—you find that when blacks or other minorities climb to the top rail in show business or the arts, some are just as bad—sometimes horrifically worse—than their white counterparts.

The fact is, Brown, one of America's greatest "cultural" creations, was a terrible businessman. And a terrible person at times, in part because he was afraid of the very world from which his music emerged. In Brown's world, the white man—whatever that phrase means these days—defined reality. From Brown's point of view, nothing happened in this world—the sun did not rise, the moon did not crest, red traffic lights did not turn green—unless white folks said they did. The white man's view of history, his laughs, his money, his record business was all that counted. Without this understanding, you cannot understand James Brown or the world that spawned him, or the world that would one day forget his history and seek only his money.

But history has its own life. It moves like an erupted volcano, spreading lava that sets fires in places far distant because of the enormous heat contained within it. In Brown's story, that heat is the business of race. Brown's rags-to-riches Horatio Alger story has helped mushroom the lawsuits surrounding his valuable estate into a toxic cloud, creating—years after his 2006 death—exactly what he predicted it would. "A mess," is what he told his manager. "Mr. Bobbit, when I die, it's gonna be a big mess."

And with forty-seven lawsuits comprising more than four thousand pages of litigation, an estimated ninety lawyers—most of whom never knew James Brown—and nine years of court fighting, a mess it is.

Here's the known-world material: Brown was born in a house in Barnwell, South Carolina, in May 1933 or thereabouts. He was an only child. His mother left his father when Brown was four, five, or six, depending on whom you ask. Whether she was driven away or departed on her own is an open question, as she is dead and no one can seem to remember—though his close friends insist that his parents had a bad fight and she was driven off. Young James gathered coal, picked cotton, and hunted squirrels with his father, Joe Brown, a former sharecropper, who raised James with the help of extended family in the Ellenton, South Carolina, area, with female cousins who were more like sisters to Joe than cousins. Joe later took young James, nicknamed Junior, to nearby Augusta, Georgia, to stay with one of those female cousins—a cousin James called Aunt Honey—when Brown was still in grade school. Her Augusta home was filled with relatives and boarders and functioned, at times, as a brothel. "I was nine before I got my first pair of underwear from a store," Brown recalled. "All my clothes were made from sacks and things like that."

He attended segregated schools in Augusta until the seventh or eighth grade, and at fifteen was busted for stealing car parts and given an eight-to-sixteen-year sentence, of which he served three years and a day in a juvenile prison in Toccoa in northeast Georgia. He was released at age nineteen on ten years' probation, provided he stay out of Augusta, so he stayed in Toccoa, where he began to sing in churches for a local gospel group that eventually called themselves the Famous Flames. Their first record, "Please, Please, Please," recorded as a demo in a radio station, was rerecorded and released nationally by Cincinnati-based King Records under the name James Brown and the Famous Flames, and it launched Brown's career in 1955. After nine straight bombs and two years on the "chitlin circuit," the string of theaters and eating joints that constituted black entertainment life in the forties and fifties for black bands, he resurfaced and rose to stardom as, basically, a solo act with a hit called "Try Me," in October 1958, and entered the 1960s as a bona fide soul master.

Brown was a way-out star from the start, a guy with a pushed-in face, a hoarse voice, and a style of music seen by some white critics as the same song sung over and over again. The late Albert Goldman, a talented music critic of that era, writing in *The New York Times,* called him "The greatest demagogue in the history of Negro entertainment . . . dragging out the oldest Negro dances, the most basic gospel shouts, the funky low down rhythms of black history . . . playing the shoeshine genius, the poor boy who rose from polish rags to riches."

But it's not that simple, really. Nothing is simple when you're poor. Poverty, for example, is very loud. It's full of traffic, cussing, drinking, fisticuffs, wrong sex, anguish, embarrassments, and psychic wounds that feed all sorts of inner ailments and create lots of loose ends. For

Brown, those loose ends made great grist for the entertainment rags, especially after his career tanked in his middle years and his marriages ended up a public mess.

But beneath all that complexity was resolve. Brown propelled himself to the top of a vicious business that swallowed many groundbreaking black artists of supreme if not greater skill, most notably Louis Jordan, the 1940s star after whom Brown patterned himself. Jordan vanished into obscurity after the fifties. Brown, with lesser musical skill but arguably more creativity, hit the chitlin circuit nearly alone after "Please, Please, Please" vanished from the charts after 1955, hiring pickup bands and working as a one-man howling show, even after his record label essentially had given up on him as a one-hit wonder. Those were dark years, moving about the circuit from roughly 1956 to 1960, clawing his way up the greasy pole back to radio, black fans, and eventually white listeners, where the big money was. As a black child growing up in the South, he was an expert at knowing what white people expected of him, secure in the knowledge that white folks didn't care enough about him, or black history, or black music, to even pay attention to what he said. As long as you could dance and sing and entertain them, they didn't care what you did or did not do. Sell yourself and get paid. They were going to believe whatever they wanted to about you anyway. So tell 'em anything.

And he did. The first few lines of Brown's autobiography, *The Godfather of Soul*, written with the capable white biographer Bruce Tucker, is a good example. Here is Brown on his family history: "When I look at my family tree," he wrote, "the hardest thing to figure out is where the African came in." He describes his father as half Indian and part white, and his mother as "Asian-Afro, but she was more Asian." This from a guy who was stone-cold black American. *The* black man. Said Bobbit, who was there when Brown did his autobiography, "I was laughing because Brown didn't even want to do that book. He just told the guy anything he wanted." This is the same man whose few words scrawled on a napkin in 1968, "Say it loud, I'm black and I'm proud" (with music penned by his musical director Pee Wee Ellis), would in one fell swoop change the self-image of an entire Negro nation. Hell, I was ten years old with a black father and white mother and I figured out where the African came in: it came in the form of James Brown! *"Say it loud! I'm black and I'm proud!"* I loved that song. As a kid, I dreamed of being in his band. Who cared that my mother was white! Brown's sax man, Maceo Parker, was *the* saxophonist, the coolest, and James would holler for him, "Maceo! C'mon blow!" Here Maceo would come, grooving with pure D soul. The guys in the band were gods, and James Brown was their Supreme Leader of Cool and Funk. That feeling lasted in my mind for years.

And it wasn't just me. Some years back I did a recording session with the late saxophonist Grover Washington, Jr. Grover is the unsung pioneer of the "smooth jazz" sound, an underrated stylist and a very versatile player—his last record was an album full of arias—and in terms of R&B groove, Grover was a master. I asked him, "You ever play with James Brown?" Grover laughed and said, "You kidding? I wasn't funky enough." And Grover, believe me, was plenty funky.

It wasn't "funkiness" that makes Brown important, though. That word is overused, misunderstood, and misrepresented anyway. The true substitute for it, really, is the term *sound,* or *influence.* Brown's musical sound—acknowledged as supreme among the greats in African American music, from Miles Davis to the avant-garde Art Ensemble of Chicago to the fabulously talented bassist Christian McBride—is what sets him apart, as well as the longevity he achieved in a tough musical world. Brown arguably outlasted or overshadowed every single major black star of the fifties, sixties, and seventies, a period that birthed some of the mightiest figures that American music had ever seen and will likely ever see: Little Richard, Ruth Brown, Hank Ballard and the Midnighters, Screamin' Jay Hawkins, Little Willie John, Ray Charles, Jackie Wilson, Otis Redding, Aretha Franklin, Wilson Pickett, Joe Tex, Isaac Hayes, Earth, Wind & Fire, Sly and the Family Stone, and of course the Motown heavy hitters of the seventies, to name just a few. It could be argued that the only two stars out of the brilliant cadre of Motown artists who equaled or bettered Brown creatively are Michael Jackson and Stevie Wonder, and both had to push past the boundaries of soul music to do it, rewriting the genre to create their own brand. Jackson redefined pop music. Wonder, an underrated musical genius with perfect pitch and instant music recall, is a genre unto himself.

There are other great American pop-music wonders of those years whose work will stand up to history: the extraordinary team of Donald Fagen and Walter Becker of Steely Dan and Prince come to mind, along with several others. But there is little question that Brown stands unique among them, in part because the man nicknamed Mr. Dynamite, the Hardest Working Man in Show Business, Soul Brother Number One, and the Godfather of Soul stitched into his work an element that still has bone and muscle in this Internet age overflowing with flabby musical jive posing as "product," where every high school kid with a trumpet is walking around with a self-recorded compact disc or online links to their own original music:

Content. Plain old content.

His unique blend of hollers, grunts, and squeals did little in his early years to move white critics, who saw Brown as a scream at the end of the radio dial, where most of the black radio stations lived. But it was catnip to black listeners, who understood Brown's inner struggle and loved him as a member of the family. Twice during the urban upheavals following Martin Luther King's 1968 murder he quelled riots in entire cities, first in Boston, later in Washington, DC, both at the requests of the mayors of those towns. His message to his followers at those fabled events was an intensified version of what he preached to his mostly black audiences over the years: *I'm like you. If I can succeed, so can you. Educate yourself. Be somebody.* During the 1960s, his concerts featured ninety-nine-cent tickets for kids ten and under. Howard Burchette, a radio DJ who grew up in the New York City area, remembers seeing Brown at a 1971 Apollo Christmas concert dressed as Santa Claus. "He always gave out free bicycles and prizes to kids in the audience," Burchette recalls. "He talked about education. And bettering yourself. I'm glad I saw it all with my own eyes." It's hard to imagine seeing many of today's major African American stars comporting themselves that way onstage, or staying so close to the communities that produced them.

In Brown's adopted hometown of Augusta, and in adjacent South Carolina, blacks remember Brown in his later years as relentlessly generous: He handed out free turkeys and Christmas gifts till just days before he died, even giving away his coat and working in the cold, shivering. He provided scholarships, furnished local football teams with uniforms, bought dozens of new computers for community centers, talked high school dropouts back into school, supported black businesses, bought cars for fellow churchgoers, and took care of old friends and acquaintances, even taking into his home for a time Clint Brantley, the manager who discovered him in the early years, paying Brantley's nursing-home costs, according to Brown's son Terry. My late sister Jack worked in a dry cleaners around the corner from the Apollo in the 1960s, and Jack said James Brown used to sometimes venture outside the Apollo when he was headlining and serve coffee, chat, and give autographs to fans who were lined up in the cold, waiting to see his show. Says Al Sharpton, who spent nearly two decades with Brown, "I remember times he would play in the South and kids would ride up to the airport just to look at his jet. I've seen kids in the middle of the night standing behind the gate while we was getting ready to take off, crying, looking at this black man with this jet. That's how inspiring he was. You gotta remember, you're talking about times when we wasn't three years, four years into voting, and this man's flying into little towns in Alabama and Georgia in a private jet, owning radio stations." Black fans simply loved Brown.

And he loved them back. Even during his worst years, in the mid-eighties, when he was broke, his great band having fled, his personal life in shambles, his three radio stations sold or losing money, his plane repossessed, with no record deal and not enough cash to pay his band or even his utility bills at home, Brown refused to do sneaker or beer commercials. "Children need education," he told Buddy Dallas. "They don't need sneakers and beer."

Behind the looking glass Brown was, like many older blacks, deeply disappointed with the direction that some of black America had taken in the post–civil rights era. His accountant David Cannon tells the story of Brown being approached in an Augusta parking lot in the nineties by two kids, both dressed in hip-hop style, wearing their pants down around their butts and their baseball caps twisted backward. "Mr. Brown, we need a break," one of them said. "It's hard out here. We can't get a job."

"If you pull your britches up where they oughta be, and turn your cap around to the direction you're walking," Brown said, "you'll be a lot better off."

Yet, ironically, the same man who eschewed drugs and preached toeing the straight and narrow veered off it so badly at the end of his life that he became the subject of comedy routines. The film *Get On Up* shows a man who was once the essence of black American pride as a wild, crazy, torn-up mess, which is about right, I guess—except you could say that about a hungry three-year-old. It's a perfect storm of wrong history, offered up while the man's estate was still flung in the air for grabs, with lawyers gorging themselves on his musical carcass, which he left for the poor, not for them. The whole thing is a troubling metaphor for what the race discourse has become in America now. A troubled world, this new America, a disturbing world, where the n-word is verboten but the notion of poverty is not; a world with liars on both sides of the racial divide who will say anything and twist history any way they can in order to gain a percentage; a nation of private for-profit supermax prisons full of young men who desperately need help, guarded by other young men who once worked on farms and grew corn and raised cows in the very same places where those prisons now sit. A world of beer, cognac, guns, violence, nice cars, tennis shoes, and Super Bowl commercials. Jive. For Us. By Us. Sold to Us. By Ourselves.

The new cultural export: American Jive.

And today the lawyers argue about his estate while the guy who once gave us so much pride is buried in his daughter Deanna's front yard, his body having been deposited there while some of his children ponder the idea of his home becoming a museum someday.

By the time that "museum" opens, if it ever does, the cultural history will have shifted so much that the tundra will be unrecognizable. And there's not much more to look for in this story, really. Because the James Brown story is not about James Brown. It's about who's getting paid, whose interest is involved, who can squeeze the estate and black history for more. It's all in the hands of the executors, the lawyers, Brown's children, his ex-wives, his ex-friends. It's about how that whole pot gets passed around. It's reflective of the sad state of the American popular emporium these days, where for the last decade talent shows judged by stars whose names we'll forget five minutes past breakfast decide who has "talent" in America, while songs like "Bitch Better Have My Money" climb the charts. Maybe that's the kind of song we always wanted. Maybe it's the song we all deserve. But it wasn't the song Brown had in mind.

Part II

Hit It!

Chapter 4

The Vapors

The search for understanding begins here at the margins, at a field near midnight, off Seven Pines Road, deep in the South Carolina backwoods of Barnwell County. It's a pitch-black night. A few crumpled beer cans lie in the gravel. I make out what looks like a piece of a barrel. A pail. A thick fog seems to have wrapped itself around the weeping willows. A dog barks somewhere. All around, the forest is taking back the land: weeds as high as my head, vines hanging low. South Carolina is full of weeping willows. It's a land of beauty and sorrow—and for black folks from here to the lowland Gullah country like Hilton Head Island, where clever developers paid unwitting poor blacks relative pennies for thousands of acres of waterfront property that they later sold for millions, it's also a land of a thousand ghosts.

An old jeep with one headlight appears out of the black field ahead. It jumbles forward through the high grass, the headlight jouncing and bouncing, winking through the weeds as it approaches. The jeep stops near me and the door flings open. A muscular brown arm appears. A brown head, lit from the inside of the jeep, pops out of the window. He calls out.

"Edgar?"

"Yeah."

"What's up."

"Nothing, man." That's Edgar Brown talking. He's standing next to me. Edgar is a distant cousin of the late James Brown. Edgar's a tall, handsome, brown-skinned electrician in his fifties with a goatee. He's wide-shouldered and cool. The aim here is to find the true origins of the late James Brown.

Many have gone down this road and none, to my knowledge, have succeeded. The reason: James Brown didn't want you to know. Because if you did know, you wouldn't understand anyway. The house where he was born is one thing. That's easily found. It was a shack just up the road from where I'm standing. He showed the ruins of that old shack to friends all the time. I saw where it once sat myself—in a man's yard. A man with a big dog. That was close enough for me. The disappeared shack is part of the Brown mystery: keep 'em guessing. He told the Reverend Al Sharpton, whom he unofficially adopted when Sharpton was a teenager during the 1970s: "Don't let folks get too familiar, Rev. Don't stay in one place too long. Come important and leave important." Even with his audiences, Brown had that attitude. His band would arrive onstage and blow the doors down, knock 'em dead, while Brown waited backstage, occasionally smoking a Kool cigarette, watching the audience, figuring out the exact right time to hit the stage, when the audience was primed and greased, howling for him. Only when the fans were warmed up, ready to burst with anticipation, would he stride onstage with his pigeon-toed gait and send them howling into delirium. And after he'd charged 'em up, picked 'em up, and leveraged 'em to the moon, knocked 'em out with blasts of soulful levity, he'd leave the stage. Afterward, the important folks—celebrities, other stars who hung backstage waiting to congratulate

Brown—would wait for two or three hours while he sat under the hair dryer in his dressing room getting his pompadour redone, then he'd slip out without seeing anyone. "Why you leaving now?" Sharpton would say. "There's important people here! They want to see you!"

"Kill 'em and leave, Rev. Kill 'em and leave."

He did it for almost fifty years. James Brown was not common. James Brown was not easily found or discussed or discovered—by anyone. James Brown kept his distance.

But his past he could not kill and leave.

He didn't want people to know, and standing here in this vacant lot, I can see why. There's no glory in this area here. It's not forlorn, but if you're not from here, you'd think twice about being here. It's not ugly, but it's not pretty either. It's just . . . funky.

Brown was always foggy about his past. When asked by reporters, he weaved and bobbed. He told a biographer this, he told a reporter that. What difference did it make? Folks think what they want anyway. He'd say he was from "the Augusta / Barnwell / Williston area," where he lived in a "house with eighteen people" and no money. The story grew hair over the years: How his mother "ran off." How his father left him with his aunt Honey when he was seven or eight. There's lots of versions of the story: a white version, a black version, a historical version, a record-company version. There's even an official version in his biography.

Charles Bobbit says of the biography, "A lot of that stuff is the writer. Mr. Brown didn't talk that way. He had a lot of stuff in his family, his family life, that he didn't want to come out. I'm probably the only one who knows what's real and what's not."

So what's real?

Finding out became a question of angles, then more angles. I spun round in circles for months trying to find out what was real, only to find more angles. But one angle did check out. That was Edgar, a distant cousin of Brown. I met Edgar through a guy through a guy through a guy. It was a stroke of good luck, or bad luck, depending, since I'm standing on the edge of a dark field in the middle of nowhere feeling chickenhearted, looking like a hippie holding a peace sign at a gun convention, and this guy in the jeep is staring at me hard.

The jeep purrs. Edgar and I squint through the headlight at the driver. Edgar motions his head toward me:

"This is the guy I was telling you about."

As I approach the jeep, the driver, CR Gaines, a stout, brown-skinned man, looks me over suspiciously. "You bring me some ciga-rettes?"

"Yeah."

I hand him the pack of Kools, the long ones. That's what he wanted. Given what most folks have been asking for every time I show up to do an interview on the Godfather, a pack of Kools is cheap. That's one of the first things you learn when you write about James Brown. Everybody's got one hand in their pocket and the other in yours. And by the way, they're all writing books. And since you're not writing theirs, they want money, favors, meals, book contracts, edito-rial guidance, movie deals, or just plain old cash for the bit of history they claim to know. Every two-bit hustler who ever touched Brown's hand, or played second guitar with him, or served him chicken and black beans, or promoted a concert, or sucked his vapors one way or the other thinks their story is worth something and wants to be paid for it. And those are the small-timers. The big boys, the lawyers, politi-cians, and accountants down in Bamberg and Aiken Counties, the guys who took Brown's last will and testament to court and some of whom munched at his estate, scavenging the bones, charging his es-tate huge sums in legal fees while they argued about it and dissected it, passing the carcass to their friends for further gouging—they're an-other matter entirely. Industrial-strength hustlers.

"You ready?" CR says. He is staring at me.

I don't know this guy from Adam. In fact I didn't know any of the craziness surrounding this story when I first got snookered into this game. Edgar said he was a distant cousin of Brown and that this guy, a direct cousin of Brown's, was "okay." I'd only known Edgar twenty minutes and *he* seemed okay. But then again, so did the guy who stole my jalopy back in Brooklyn that time. I'm sure he was "okay"—to his momma.

CR sits there, glaring from the crappy-looking jeep with one head-light, in a barren field in the middle of nowhere, at near midnight, asking if I want to go for a ride into James Brown's history.

Nothing is okay.

But there is no choice to make. I've come a long way to get here. I've already taken my publisher's money. What else am I gonna do? I gotta go. I gotta take this ride.

I came down here on a bum steer. No need to lie or toss that in later. No need to slip that in with the old excuse, "I'm a musician too and I love the music," or "The public needs a guy like me who can really tell it," or whatever music critics say so that the corporate-music taste-makers can pump up the latest fifteen-year-old cuss artist while ignor-ing some real talent who's not good-looking or young enough. I needed the dough, plain and simple. The ex-wife dropped the ham-mer. Left two neat blue legal packets on the floor of the barren living room. The words said "McBride versus McBride," which is another way of saying that whatever you thought passed for love didn't. I never cheated on her, by the way. Never did any of those nasty things that James Brown supposedly did with some of the women in his life, like punching her out or sleeping around. She got tired of benign neglect, is one reason, and hit the eject button with both fists. When that hap-pens, you're sent flying, the explosion wrapping the whole sordid business around your nose like Saran Wrap. By the time you clear your nostrils to breathe and look for the rip cord, whatever half-truths are swirling in the air make every word you utter sound like a lie. En-emies appear. Friends are outraged. Neighbors shun you. And the lawyers charge.

I slept on a couch in a cold-water flat in Hell's Kitchen for a year and ate spaghetti and meatballs like one of those button men from *The Godfather*. When you blab that sob story to a divorce lawyer, by the way, their eyes roll to the back of their head and they look at their watch, wondering if there's an easier way to make a dollar change pockets. It's a skin game. Your skin, their game. My wife's attorney turned up for the contest wearing a crisp gray pinstripe suit and a yarmulke—which I took as an added jab, since my white, Jewish mom had closed her eyes in death just six months before. Call it what you want, but when I saw that guy walk into the room, I said to myself, "I better throw out those vacation folders."

I had a good attorney. I'm thankful for that. But I was still cleaned out. Not long after that I got an email, and later a call, from a guy who knew a guy who knew a guy. Some dude was bouncing about the Manhattan publishing scene peddling a whopper of a story. He was out of bounds, really. Nobody off the street hawks books to publishers these days except in the movies. Book agents sell books. But this guy was a kind-of guy. A kind-of record guy, kind-of filmmaker, kind-of documentary maker, kind-of agent, kind-of this and kind-of that, with flimflam written all over him. But he said the magic words: *"I got the James Brown story. The authentic one. From the family."*

Fourteen books on James Brown by some pretty good writers already on the deck, including two by Nelson George, the dean of R&B scribes, but I listened anyway. I should've faded out of the matter right then and there, or at least figured out where the mirrors were placed. But I agreed to meet him in Manhattan.

He showed up at my agent's office looking thoughtful, a middle-aged fellow in wire-rimmed glasses. When we sat down, the first thing I said to him was, "Gerri Hirshey is the writer you want. She knows James Brown better than any writer around." I needed the money, but I still knew she was the one to do the book.

"I need a black writer to do this," he snapped. This was a white guy talking. Right then I should have closed my raggedy notebook and headed back to my flophouse on Forty-Third Street to watch the tourists out the window and sip grape and feel sorry for myself. There was no one better for the job than Gerri. We'd walked a few miles together back at *The Washington Post*—and before that when she covered Mi-

chael Jackson's 1984 Victory Tour for *Rolling Stone* while I covered it
for *People* magazine. That tour was a six-month monster, the biggest
and most disorganized tour the music industry had ever seen. The
entertainment press covered that thing like a presidential campaign.
Time, Life, Newsweek, Life, USA Today, US Magazine, even my friend
Steve Morse, the highly respected rock critic from *The Boston Globe,*
showed up at opening night in Kansas City. We followed that circus
like the White House press corps follows the president, staggering
red-eyed from one city to the next, male reporters grumbling under
their breath about what a jerk Michael Jackson was because he refused to do interviews, the female reporters strutting around in jeans
tight enough to read the dates of the coins in their pockets.

Gerri didn't play that game. She was a slim, soft-spoken woman
who never raised her voice, never asked for favors, never threw a fit.
She was a smooth, silent assassin. She beat us all hands down. She
slipped into and out of backstage dressing rooms like a ghost. She
seemed to know the name of every tattooed techie and every one of
the thirty truck drivers. She knew the keyboard player's setup and the
guitar player's last gig. She knew other things too—important things—
like where the tour was going next. That tour gave every reporter fits.
No set itinerary. It had about six bosses and no one knew who was
supposed to do what. It was like one of those funeral extravaganzas
where all the third cousins who never cared about the dead guy are
hollering and tearing out their hair over the coffin while the funeral
director is in the back room squeezing the last pennies out of the poor
widow's pocket. Michael was *the* show. The guy was on fire. His
Thriller album had sold millions and flung the music industry and the
burgeoning MTV channel on its ear. Music videos were new back
then, and MTV had resisted showing videos with black artists. Michael blew that door off with a bazooka and changed the industry
forever, but, kindhearted soul that he was, he was trapped between
family, friends, and "professionals," all of whom seemed bent on sucking him dry. Every week the itinerary changed, which is no small thing
when you're traveling with two hundred support people, thirty trucks,

forty-five airport runway lights, and playing fifty-thousand-seat stadiums. The promoters played one city against another, with the winning city hollering "Bingo" and the loser screaming foul. I never knew what to tell the magazine when they asked where we were going next. If it weren't for Jay Lovinger, my editor at *People,* I would've quit. The Jacksons hated *People* magazine, by the way, which made matters worse. They saw it as a white man's rag that put only white stars on the cover. They were shocked when I appeared and identified myself as the magazine's reporter—they had never seen a black reporter from *People* before. They tagged me for an Uncle Tom and didn't speak to me for months. I was twenty-five years old. I'd just come from slinging my tenor sax through the Ivory Coast, a one-man wrecking crew trying to do my Alex Haley thing, find my "roots" and all that. I got sick with dysentery and something else. I'd have gotten off easier if I'd gone to Poland and checked on the roots of my Jewish mother, but I was a young, happy fool in those days. In any case, compared to tromping through the West African jungle and getting needles in the rear end for VD—okay, so that's what it was—the Jackson Victory Tour was cake icing. The food was great in LA. The fruit was fresh, there were incredible tacos everywhere. And I needed the dough. Which circles me back to my standing in a field with James Brown's cousin at near midnight in Barnwell, South Carolina. Twenty-five years later and I'm still in the dark, and I still need the dough.

Still, I tried to hand the gig over to Gerri. She could write her ass off. She was a top soul-music writer. She had been writing about black music back when few white writers had the stones to venture south to get near James Brown. James Brown was tough on writers—everyone knew that. But Brown respected Gerri. She wrote the *Rolling Stone* feature on him when he died—the first and last time he was on the cover of the magazine. She was the one to do his book, not me.

But this guy selling his "exclusive story," he didn't want her.

I was broke. I had three kids, two of them college-aged. The ex-wife was standing on my head. So I sat there and listened as Mr. Exclusive Story said this and that, dumped a few more candies on the floor, and pointed south. And I followed his pointed fingers and jumped on a plane and that's how I got here. Watching this jeep roll backward in the woods as I followed in my rental car. Feeling my eyelids getting sore from blinking too much. Sucking on the James Brown vapors just like every two-bit writer who's ever needed a contract. Fifty-five years old and going nowhere. And not feeling a bit of goodness in my heart toward James Brown either, that's the other thing. Six months in and I'm just like everybody else who lived off the Godfather. I'm sucking on his vapors, trying to get paid.

Chapter 5

Six Gaines

C R drove with his head out the door, backing up, gunning the motor.

The jeep whirred to the left and the right, its one headlight shooting from the weeds and into the sky as it rocketed over bumps and holes in the earth before it stopped at the shack. Junk was everywhere. Edgar followed us in his van. I guess he didn't like the look of that jeep neither.

I knew the place wasn't gonna be the kind of spot where the welcome mat was written in olde English, but still, I fell onto the porch of that old shack feeling like somebody had been picking at my guts with an icepick. A bare lightbulb illuminated old crates, chairs, kitchen items, an old moped, pieces of cars, all scattered about. The floor was thick with blue Budweiser beer cans. A dog barked furiously from inside the shack someplace. I couldn't see three feet past the porch into the field beyond. CR and I sat on the porch on crates while Edgar stood. CR lit a cigarette.

"What you do out here all day?" Edgar asked. I was glad he was there.

"Nothing," CR said.

All three of us laughed.

CR looked at me. "You didn't bring no beer?" he asked.

He had me there. When we'd talked on the phone earlier, he hadn't said a word about beer. I would've given him a beer if I'd had one, though I was low on cash at the moment, having dispensed huge chunks of money fooling around in nearby Augusta and in various parts of Georgia and western South Carolina, chasing the ghost of the Godfather of Soul. I'd run into more low-level hustlers in one month than I had back in the eighties when I played tenor in blues bands up and down New York's Bleecker Street in Greenwich Village. I slid from one chiseler to the next back then, trying to keep my pockets from remaining smooth, beautiful, and empty. But in this world, everybody's got an itchy palm, hollering about the white man's evil and chiseling their neighbor at the same time. You don't know who's telling the truth, even if you do grease them, which made it all pointless.

"You didn't say nothing about a beer," I said. "I would've brought a beer if you said something."

I was hoping CR wouldn't back out. It was so dark, I couldn't see his face clearly. This is what happens when you're chasing a guy who ended up in a crypt in his daughter's front yard, I thought. You're standing in the middle of nowhere, hoping you don't end up in an urn in somebody else's yard, waiting for answers that may never come.

CR's stern face broke into a grin. "I should've asked you to bring me one," he said.

Like any starving lowlife seeking a scoop, I promised him a beer the next time, knowing there likely wouldn't be one. "So did you know James Brown?" I asked.

"Surely did. He's my cousin."

"How's that?"

"His daddy and my grandma were first cousins."

"Say that again?"

"His daddy and my grandma, they were the children of two sisters."

CR's mutt was now roaring and snarling a few feet behind the worn screen door. I could hardly hear CR for all that howling. I moved toward the door to peek at the dog and to make sure the flimsy screen door was locked. That creature saw me and must've thought I was a basket of fish; he leaped and barked and snapped at the door, but the screen door held tight. Just in case, I held it shut anyway. I was feeling pretty wobbly. The guys were ignoring the barking, so after a minute of trying to look cool, I took my hand off the door and sat back down on my crate.

CR, sitting on his crate, looked over his shoulder at the snarling dog, and said, "Hush!" The dog ignored him. That mongrel was a distraction. He kept howling.

"Could you say that again?" I asked.

"His daddy and my grandma, they were children of two sisters."

"Was your grandma his aunt Honey? They say she raised him. He wrote that in his book."

"Aunt Honey did raise him. My grandma helped raise him too when he was little."

"Who was she?"

"My grandma?"

"No. Aunt Honey."

"James Brown's daddy's cousin."

"How's that again?"

CR looked at me out of the corner of his eye. "What college you say you went to?"

The three of us laughed.

He repeated what he'd said before, loud this time, as if saying it louder would make it more understandable. "My grandma and James Brown's daddy, they were *the children of two sisters.*"

I don't know if it was the dark, or that barking dog, or the late hour, or all that junk on that porch, or my own fatigue, but I didn't get it. People from down South have a gift for relations that us northerners don't. I have cousins like that in North Carolina. They twang so deep, you need a translator to understand what they're saying. But I love them, and they can reel off ten generations and have you related to John Quincy Adams like it's nobody's business. It took me months to find CR, and in seconds he'd reeled off some important characters in young James Brown's life. He was revealing something that no one, not even Brown's son Terry and Brown's first wife, Velma, knew. But I couldn't get it. So I went backward. I got a piece of paper out of my pad. "Let's draw a family tree," I said.

"All right."

I drew the tree, and CR talked, and as he did, he connected one relative to the next, going back decades: Shelleree Scott, Iveree Scott, Saree Scott, and Lydree Scott, James Brown's grandmother—James's granddaddy—said to be a man named Eddie Evans, who disappeared —and the two sisters Aunt Honey and Doll Baby. In the three or four hours he talked, the years peeled away and the descendants of the Gaines-Scott family appeared, a family of religious sharecroppers, long on laughs, trusting in God, and bent on a better life. They were tenant farmers and laborers for the white man, living in a town that no longer exists, a town sixteen miles away that vanished into thin air one day in 1951. He connected the lines, with Edgar pitching in what he knew, but CR had the floor, and as he talked, the mystery of the origins of the greatest soul singer in America's history unraveled before my eyes, right there on that porch, amid all that junk, in the dark. By the time he was done—and his brother Shelleree added crucial elements later—I wanted to reach over and hug him. I wanted to buy him ten beers. He had done what a dozen music writers and historians had not. He had unearthed James Brown's history. He'd given bone and substance to the history of a man who'd spent his entire life sprinting from his past until he could outrun it no more. He'd explained why no matter how much he said he loved America, James

Brown could not enjoy its fullest prosperity: because his own roots were bathed in the worst part of its history.

The tragedy of James Brown's history actually dates back to a story passed down in his extended family on his father's side for several generations, nearly back to the Civil War.

At the banks of the Savannah River in Augusta, Georgia, not long after the war ended, a group of white prison guards watching over a chain gang moved to silence one of the workers, a young black boy by the name of Oscar Gaines. It was a hot Georgia day, and young Gaines, who was doing short time for some kind of wrong—perceived or real, no one remembers what sin he'd committed to bring on the white man's punishment—had grown exhausted and asked to go back to his cell to rest. "I can't do no more," he said. "I'm just too hot."

The armed guards, who were mounted on horses, told him to keep quiet and keep working.

Gaines persisted, saying, "I'm hot. I got to cool off." A few terse words were exchanged, and the guards got down off their horses. They grabbed Gaines's hands and feet. "You hot? The river will cool you off," they told him.

They swung him like a pendulum back and forth while Gaines begged for his life. "Please, boss," Gaines pleaded. "Don't throw me in the river. I can't swim."

But throw him in they did.

Gaines flew into the river and disappeared. Then, to their surprise, his head popped to the surface. Young Gaines, who'd insisted he couldn't swim, in fact swam very well. As the guards watched, unable to reach him, Gaines did the backstroke. He did the front stroke. He threw in the breaststroke. He sidestroked some. He belly-stroked. He paddled his feet. He threw in the monkey stroke, the boogaloo stroke, the camel-walk stroke, and, finally, the see-you-later stroke. Before they knew it, Gaines was in the middle of the river and still stroking.

He swam clear across the Savannah, climbed out on the other side, and escaped into South Carolina. He never did come back to Georgia.

Young Oscar Gaines slipped into a small town called Ellenton, South Carolina, about sixteen miles from Barnwell, and got a job chopping cotton for a white man who didn't care what kind of history a colored had with those damned Georgians on the other side of the Savannah, and in fact hoped every one of them Georgians would drop dead from fever and go to hell on account of constant border and white-lightning disputes with them and their kind.

So Oscar Gaines got married, lived a long, full life, and begat three sons, Oscar, Shorty, and Cutter. Cutter was killed in the 1930s by a white mob that accused him of stalking a white woman. He was placed on the railroad tracks and the Atlantic Coast rail line eased his mind. Shorty died in prison. But Oscar Gaines, Jr. . . . Oscar, Jr., lived a long life.

Oscar had a son named John Gaines. John Gaines didn't walk until he was six years old, so they called him "Six" his entire life. Six Gaines.

Six Gaines had a wife named Iveree Scott. Iveree had a sister named Lydree Scott. Lydree Scott had a son.

That son's name was Joseph James Gardner Brown, James Brown's father.

Joe Brown was an only child. He was raised in an extended share-cropping household of the Gaines/Scott/Evans clan, a household full of stories, strong women, and lots of laughs. Joe's grandfather Eddie Evans had murdered his grandmother and fled to Florida, but the two had almost a dozen kids, so his mother, Lydree, and all his aunts were raised as a large family by various relatives. Monday they'd stay with this aunt, Tuesday they'd spend with another aunt. "We always knew who family was," says Shelleree Gaines, one of the many Gaines cousins who was told the story by his grandmother, Joe's aunt.

That style of raising children in extended family is how Joe Brown was raised. Joe Brown's father was never discussed, though Joe was the spitting image of a local sharecropper named Bill Evans. It didn't matter, because everyone was poor and everyone lived together—the Gaines/Scott/Evans family of Ellenton. They cared for one another's children, sharecropped the land, tended house for white folks, and over the years, worshipped at Book Creek Baptist, St. Paul Baptist, and St. Peter Baptist Church. They were a large, loving family, with lots of quirks. The Scott side, Joe's mother's side, was lighthearted. Their late mother, who was murdered, liked the sound, so all her children had *-ree* in their names. There was Iveree, Tyree, Zazaree, Lydiaree, and so on. To this day, there are *-rees* in the Gaines family tree in Barnwell County and beyond. The Gaines side, Joe's great-uncle by marriage, were serious, sharp thinkers, and, when riled, dangerous. They had long memories. If you crossed one of them, they did not forget. The story of Cutter Gaines's death on the railroad tracks was passed down through the family for years. The murderers were never tried, though everyone in Ellenton knew who they were. In 1971, decades after Cutter Gaines was killed, one of his murderers, then an old man, was lying in Barnwell Hospital when two Gaines boys, Johnny and Shelleree Gaines—Cutter's nephews—were working there as orderlies. They walked into the man's room to clean it. The old man, lying in the hospital bed, looked up, spied one of the Gaines boys, and thought he'd seen a ghost. "I thought I killed you," he said. Johnny Gaines leaped for him, and Shelleree had to pull Johnny out of the room.

Such was the family that raised Joseph James Brown, and later his son James Brown in James Brown's weaning years. They were hard people because the land made you hard. They were strong people because the land made you strong. They were religious people because only God could help you. "You had to be tough," Shelleree Gaines told me. As sharecroppers they were tied to laws that kept you always in debt to someone else, laws passed down from slavery and the brutal Reconstruction era that followed it. For generations.

Joe had no sisters, but his cousins Doll Baby and Honey were raised as his sisters, and because they were family and close in age and lived on the same land and, even at times, in the same house, they had similar dreams. The two strong-minded, practical girls didn't want to pull cotton. They had plans to move to Augusta. That was everyone's dream in those days. Getting out. Getting to Augusta, or Atlanta. All the young folks in the Gaines clan dreamed of it, but nobody dreamed of it more than Joe.

Joe Brown was a handsome, brown-skinned young man with a firm jaw and a quick smile. He was fast on his feet and a quick thinker, with a stutter that masked an intelligence that he learned to keep to himself in a world where a smartass black kid could find himself tossed in jail for thirty days for sassing a white man wrong—he'd seen that happen more than once. Joe saw those cotton fields of Ellenton and saw his future buried in its long rows. That wasn't for him. He liked to sing in local juke joints and wear fine clothing. He even joined a local singing group as a teenager and picked cotton in his one silk shirt—he liked fine things that much. He loved playing skin, a card game, and his quick wit made him a hit with the local young ladies. "Uncle Joe," says Shelleree, "was much of a man." Cocky and humorous, he liked to have fun, and later in life when his son became rich, Joe was never without a new Lincoln and his favorite things on the front seat: a cigar, a pack of cards for a game of skin, a bag of pork skins, and a jar of hot sauce. His grandson Terry would recall his grandfather Joe, whom everyone affectionately called Pop, ripping up the streets in Augusta in a new Lincoln that James had paid for, extinguishing his cigars on the plush leather front seat. "Pop, this is a new car!" Terry would protest. "I d-d-d-d-don't care about no d-d-d-damn car!" Pop would laugh, stubbing out the cigar and roaring down the street like a madman, speed limit be damned. He lived well because he'd grown up hard. Life without pulling cotton was gravy.

But Joe knew where he came from. He'd spent his young life hearing stories from his aunts about his great-great-uncle Oscar Gaines, who'd tricked the white man on the chain gang to toss him into the Savannah so he could escape, and his great-uncle Cutter who was murdered, and his uncle Shorty who was a hell-raiser who died in prison, and his grandmother who was murdered by his grandfather.

He slipped out of Ellenton as a young man and wandered over to the town of Bamberg, where he met a fine girl named Susie Behling. She was a small woman, barely five feet tall. Susie Behling was a stranger to the Gaines clan. Bamberg was forty-five miles away from Ellenton, and in the world of mules, wagons, and no telephones, it might as well have been the moon. Nobody knew much about Susie but that she was musical and religious. Her family could sing. She and Joe had a son named James Joseph Brown, born in Snelling. Joe called James "Junior."

James Brown later told the world that he was born in Barnwell, in a shack, and that his mother Susie left him when he was four or five or six years old. The bare truth is that Joe's marriage was fraught with problems. Handsome Joe Brown flirted with women all his life. When I asked about Joe in the Barnwell area twenty years after his 1993 death, I heard talk of the women he knew or reportedly chased after. The inside rumor, according to one James Brown friend who asked that her name not be used, was, "Joe and Susie had a fight, Joe pulled out his gun, and Susie jumped out the window and took off running and didn't stop till she got to New York."

However the split occurred, Joe was alone with a boy he knew he couldn't raise alone. Junior needed family. Joe had one. A big one. He didn't have one mother—he had five aunts who were all just like his mother, all those -rees: Iveree, Zazaree, Saree. He knew they would take care of James, just as they had taken care of him. These were the women James Brown was raised by before Joe took him to his "cousin" (read: sister) Honey's house in Augusta, the fabled "whorehouse" James talked of being raised in. During those young years among the Gaines, Scott, and Evans families in Ellenton, James Brown did what all the children of that family did: he picked cotton and walked barefoot, attending church on Sunday in his one pair of shoes, which he took off on the way home and stored for the next week's service, thanking God for the one pair that he did have. His great-aunts, Iveree, Saree, and the other Gaines women, saw to that. They understood Junior. His life was tough. He was the only son of an only son.

His ma and pa didn't get along and his pa was a stuttering rascal who left him for long stretches, but he left James in the right place: with family. A family that knew how to work, because the Gaineses pulled their own weight in the world. They loved Junior, and in the little time Joe spent with his son, he always reminded Junior of that—the importance of family.

But Junior did not always remember.

Fifty years later, when Joe Brown and his now-famous son James Brown pulled up to a gas station in Barnwell, Joe looked out the window and saw his cousin pumping gas into James Brown's Lincoln Town Car. Joe Brown rolled down the window and yelled, "CR! Come here!" He turned to James Brown and said excitedly, "Junior! This is one of your cousins. He's one of Uncle Six's grandkids."

CR watched as James Brown nodded a "howdy" and put his hand in his pocket.

"I thought he was gonna pull out a wad of money and peel off a five-dollar bill," CR told me, laughing.

Instead, the Godfather of Soul pulled out a handkerchief and blew his nose, started the car, and drove off.

CR laughed about it. "Maybe he blew his handkerchief because he didn't want me to shake his hand," CR said. But CR's father, Shelleree Gaines, never spoke of James Brown again. And when James Brown died in 2006 and the TV reporters came around to talk to Old Man Shelleree Gaines, wanting to interview folks from James Brown's family, Shelleree Gaines, son of Six Gaines and great-grandson of the Oscar Gaines who had fled the white man's injustice more than a hundred years before, Shelleree Gaines, who had never been on television in his life, most of which had been spent picking the white man's cotton, sawing his lumber, and dodging the white man's evil like his father and his grandfather before him, refused.

"Junior forgot where he came from," he said. "And look what it done for him. It done him no good."

Chapter 6

Leaving the Land

In the summer of 1950, the black farmers and sharecroppers of Ellenton who stopped in for supplies and feed at the general store
began to overhear whispers among the white farmers who gathered
there to gossip and pass on local news. Odd things were happening.
Strangers with measuring sticks were driving new-model cars straight
into white farmers' fields, digging holes near cow pastures, measuring
distances, taking pictures, sighting tree lines. Planes flew overhead.
Trucks arrived. Men piled out, took quick measurements, then piled
back in and left.

Plenty of the gossip passed from Ellenton, Dunbarton, Meyers
Mill, and the surrounding towns through the general store in Ellenton. Much of it was puff, some of it was meant for white ears only, but
in a small rural community, few secrets live long. Black folks and
whites lived together. They barbecued together in summer and con-
gregated in fall and winter during holidays. When there was nothing

to do, they watched the early-morning train they called Fido pass through the train depot. There were at least thirty-five churches in and around Ellenton, among them several black churches: Mt. Moriah, Four Mile, the Runs, Friendship Baptist, Steele Creek, St. Luke's, and St. Peter. In addition to the general store, the church was the telegraph of rural life in those days. And for black residents, many of whom had no phones or electricity and could barely read or write, it was the only pipeline to the world.

That fall, from Sunday to Sunday, among whites and blacks alike, terrible rumors began to spread:

Everybody got to leave this land.

That kind of talk sent everybody scrambling for information. Every single black minister from the black churches walked into the Ellenton General Store, called the Long Store, hat in hand, to check out the rumor with the white folks. The blacks who owned businesses around Ellenton—a gin mill, a cleaning business, a funeral home— poked for answers among their customers, black domestics who worked for white folks, white folks to whom some of those blacks were, in secret, related—for not every black family in those towns around Ellenton and Dunbarton was dark-skinned. (There was, as James Brown's cousin Shelleree Gaines says, "Plenty tipping going on.") There were eight thousand farmers in all, the majority of whom, the census notes, were African American sharecroppers—and not a single one of them had a bit of information on the rumor. Neither did the white farmers, many of them barely living above the poverty line themselves; not even the well-to-do farmers who owned cows, mules, wagons, and land that had been in their families for generations had information. That answer was a horrible blank.

Everybody got to leave this land.

The rumor traveled from ear to ear, from one plowed field to the neighboring field, from one kitchen to another, from one shanty to the next. It gnawed at every cotton picker, maid, cook, mule driver, and housewife, and at the workers who sweated out long hours at the banana crate company and sawed lumber for the International Paper

Company. It was too unsettling to be true. Too impossible to believe. But by late summer of 1950, the rumor began to gather steam. By fall, it grew teeth and bones. By December of 1950, it had blossomed into a horrible reality:

Everybody got to leave this land.

The announcement was made by the community leaders at a packed, segregated meeting held at the Ellenton High School auditorium, where five hundred people from the town assembled to hear it. The whites sat in chairs, the blacks were crowded into a single doorway.

Everybody got to leave this land.

The question was, Why?

The answer was simple.

The government says so.

There was more. It was to protect America. The Commies were coming. This was the Cold War. America needed to be strong. For that, there would have to be sacrifice. The government needed the land to make a bomb factory.

Why us? Why here?

That part was never made too clear. The backroom shenanigans of South Carolina's political machine were a mystery to the farmers of Ellenton and its surrounding areas. From 1932 into the 1970s, the state was basically run by four powerful politicians known as the Barnwell Ring: Senator Edgar A. Brown, state representatives Solomon Blatt, Sr., and Winchester Smith, Jr., and onetime governor Joseph Emile Harley. Wherever those four moved, so went the state of South Carolina. A deal had been struck, one so far over the heads of the good people of Ellenton that it might as well have been made on the moon; it was a deal struck between the state, the federal government, and its big-business partners. The nation needed Ellenton's land and water—big water, Savannah River water and its surrounding rivers, creeks, gullies, and tributaries—for its bomb factory. On November 28, 1950, the rumor became fact, and the fact became a heartbreaking reality that changed life in Ellenton forever, including the life of its most famous African American son.

Everybody got to leave this land.

And they did.

In 1951, everyone and everything—dogs, sheep, cows, horses, mules, carts, house keys, wagons, family photos, outhouses, had to go; 1,500 homes, 2,300 farms, 8,000 people, the majority of whom were African American. Entire cemeteries—more than 1,700 graves— were dug up and moved. Churches, schools, sawmills, icehouses, drugstores, cotton gins, factories, fifty-six businesses in Ellenton alone, all moved. Six towns in all—Dunbarton, Hawthorne, Meyers Mill, Robbins, Leigh, and Ellenton—gone. Scattered to the wind, so that the U.S. Atomic Energy Commission, General Electric, and the DuPont Company could construct the Savannah River Nuclear Site, the biggest bomb maker the world had ever seen: 310 square miles of government secrets, stretching into three rural counties; five nuclear reactors and a cooling tower; two chemical separation plants; management compounds; offices, labs, checkpoints; and security—a giant engine built to extract plutonium and uranium products from materials superheated in the reactors to make enough bombs to blow up the world one hundred times over. The Cold War had begun, and the people of Ellenton and its surrounding towns were among its first American victims.

Those who owned homes got new homes built elsewhere or their homes were moved. Those whose businesses were bought out were resettled elsewhere with new businesses. Their schoolhouses were moved or rebuilt elsewhere. They were all uprooted to new towns, where they were strangers.

There was no giant protest. No rally, no marchers picketing in circles chanting. But there were a slew of stories in the press. *Life* magazine bit off a touching piece by a white schoolteacher from one of the major families in the area. Other local papers wrote pieces depicting the sad, elderly white residents who tenaciously sat on their porches till the very last, watching in shock as their neighbors' homes, churches, and local business were literally picked up and carted past their front doors on the backs of trucks; stories about confused schoolchildren crying as their schoolhouses were lifted and carried off or destroyed, distraught farmers gnashing their teeth as their livestock was carted away and the churches where their families worshipped for generations went past like groceries on the back of trucks, to be relocated to "New Ellenton" or some nearby town, or simply destroyed. The press wrote of old people who kicked the headstones off their dearly departeds' graves so that their loved ones would not be exhumed. It was heartrending, powerful stuff.

But if there was a single tearful story about the majority of displaced people—the thousands of black sharecroppers from those largely black towns—if there was a single heart-tugging saga of black schoolchildren crying as their schoolhouses were torn down, or a touching story of a brokenhearted old black woman sitting on the tombstone of her beloved husband someplace, determined that he should lie forever in his resting place, I have not seen it. If there is a single stirring piece about an African American farmer whose children quit school at age twelve to pull cotton, who lived in a beaten shack owned by the same boss who came to him every Christmas bearing a contract and pen saying, "Sign your X here and your taxes will be paid for the year," I have not seen it. Even the Savannah River Archaeological Research Program confesses, "The story of African American displacement caused by the making of the site is little known." The thousands of blacks there simply vanished into history.

One of those vanquished was the Gaines family—all the -rees—the Evans family, the Scott family, the Washingtons; all the cousins, aunts, uncles, and relatives of James Brown: Aunt Millie, Aunt Honey, Doll Baby, Aunt Saree. They slipped into history, scattered. Some went to "New" Ellenton. Others went to Blackville, Elko, Barnwell, or Augusta. James Brown's father went to Barnwell. They went where they could. And most could not go far.

James Brown's family—the Gaines-Scott clan—is part of a lost tribe. Like their white counterparts, they would talk about the old country of Ellenton, Dunbar, and the surrounding towns for the rest of their lives: The nine-cent movie theater in town where they sat on barrels in the back; the passenger train, Fido, that chugged through town every day at 4:30; the kind white physician Dr. Finkley, who traveled back roads caring for poor farmers of any color, and whose fee was whatever you could pay—a piece of catfish, or a penny, or a smile would do. The long, hot summer days, the cool evenings watching the stars after the annual barbecues, the birthday gatherings, the funny relatives, the tall tales, the vicious white bosses, the kind white friends. Over the years, the displaced ones would seek each other out. They had annual reunions where they barbecued and drank beer and talked about the Big Move, about jobs that were promised but that never materialized; about the training that was supposed to happen that never happened; about the promises that were made and broken. So much was gone. Aunt Honey, for example, who had helped raise James Brown, would end up buried in Snelling, thirty-five miles from her old birthplace, in an unmarked grave, on a piece of land the family managed to get hold of after the Big Move.

Dunbarton, Ellenton, Hawthorne, Meyers Mill, Robbins, and Leigh: gone forever. Wiped from the map by the scratch of a distant pen. The only thing left of their homes were the curbs, streets, driveways, and walkways, all off-limits, behind signs marked KEEP OUT. GOVERNMENT PROPERTY. Because the government could do whatever they wanted. They could take everything you have, anytime. No matter what your color. All they had to do was walk into your house and hang their hat on the rack.

James Brown was long gone by then. He was just out of jail in 1951 and living in Toccoa, Georgia, starting his life as a janitor at Toccoa Elementary School and singing at night with a group of young guys who eventually became the Famous Flames. But the Ellenton area, Dunbarton, and its surrounding towns were always home country to James Brown. It was where he learned to pick cotton, skin a pig, and shoot squirrels; where he walked to church barefoot and prayed to

God under the careful eyes of great-aunts Iveree, Zazaree, and Saree—in fact, Brown joined his great-aunt Saree's church, St. Peter, in Elko in the years just before his death. He was baptized there and sang in the choir. He loved his great-aunt Saree. She was one of that extended family of women who understood him, who knew how to raise a motherless child, because they had grown up motherless themselves. "James is a handful," Aunt Honey would complain to her aunts. "He's always in trouble. I can't keep up with him." But she did her best.

When Brown was released after serving his juvenile prison term, the place where he might have retreated to, where he might have regrouped and recovered, learned to stay out of wrong and to create real relationships, learn to build something and trust people under the watch of his great-aunts, who were among the few people he did trust: that was wiped off the map. And in its place was a bomb factory.

We got to leave this land. Government says so.

It was a bitter lesson for the entire Brown family, and one that Brown—who during the course of his career was wiped out by the IRS twice—would never forget. For years, until his death, James Brown walked around with five or ten or even twenty three-thousand-dollar cashier's checks in his wallet—the equivalent of cash. His son Terry recalls that when his father handed him cash, often the bills were old and damp, the edges chewed off, like rats or vermin had been at them; they had been hidden in the dirt in his backyard. In one California hotel he hid $10,000 under a carpet, came back a year later, checked in to the same hotel room, pulled the carpet back, and retrieved his money. His accountant David Cannon recalls a "red room" in his Beech Island, South Carolina, house with two or three cardboard cartons full of hundred-dollar bills.

Toward the end of his life, Brown, who could have lived anywhere on earth he wanted, moved into the shadow of that bomb factory. He built a $3.5 million house on a sixty-acre stretch of Beech Island—which is not an island, just a stretch of land—not far from old Ellenton. From the front gate of that house, you can see the giant radio-antenna towers of the Savannah River Site, which reach high into the sky, their red lights blinking clear into east Georgia.

In the last years of his life, after he walled off the world, forcing his children and grandchildren to make appointments with him, after he'd driven off his great musicians, after his son Teddy, his third wife, Adrienne, and his father died, Brown, troubled by his tumultuous fourth marriage, would often look up at the two giant towers from the Savannah River Nuclear Site—towers that sit upon the only place his family truly knew as home—and tell Charles Bobbit, "You see those towers, Mr. Bobbit? The government's listening to me. They can hear everything I say. They're listening through my teeth."

Chapter 7

Bro

You can hear the church three blocks before you get there—the horns, the howling, the soaring music. The sound roars into the silent fog of the Augusta night each time the door opens, then quickly slices off as it shuts. You slip toward the sound in a hurry, walking down the dark street, looking over your shoulder. Only a fool walks south Augusta alone at night, unless of course you're strolling through the nearby Medical College of Georgia, whose grim, gray buildings will likely one day swallow this colorful black community whole. That's coming. But not yet. And certainly not tonight. This September night is special. The United House of Prayer is having its annual throwdown, which means God still rules the world.

I remember the House of Prayer from my own childhood. The adults called it "Daddy Grace's church," after its founder, a West African immigrant who died in 1960. When I was a kid, Daddy Grace, Reverend Ike, and Father Divine were like the big three automakers—

Ford, GM, and Chrysler—or at least in my house they were. My mother liked them all. Reverend Ike, with his fancy pompadour hairstyle, fine suits, and funny sermons about money—she thought he was hilarious. Father Divine's was a place I remember her dragging us to for free food; we had to wear a white shirt and shoes. Daddy Grace's House of Prayer she knew the least about, and now I realize why. The main difference between the three, frankly, is Jesus. For Baptists and Pentecostals, Jesus is the front, back, and middle. At the House of Prayer, they love Jesus too, but they consider their minister an apostle, a kind of prophet with a direct pipeline to God. He's "anointed" to carry a special message from God himself.

That would be the man I'm looking at right now.

His name is Daddy Bailey. He's two successors after Daddy Grace, and he sits behind a pulpit—called the Holy Mountain—in his massive church, waving to thousands who have come to see him from everywhere: Virginia, California, Alabama, South Carolina, Georgia, New York. They've come by car, truck, on foot, in yellow school buses, and in fourteen charter buses that cram an empty weeded lot two blocks away.

Daddy Bailey sits on a velvet-lined throne. He's an impressive, friendly looking man, tall and enormous. He has to weigh in the ballpark of three hundred pounds. He's impeccably dressed in a gorgeous gray three-piece suit, smiling like a benevolent king. A pretty young girl in a white usher dress fans him with a giant hand fan. Several ushers with stern faces, also dressed in white, patrol the aisles, looking like traffic cops, collecting money and then suddenly bursting out into smiles when they see a friend. Grim black men in white military caps and brown military uniforms, with medals and braided rope decorations on their shoulders, line the walls looking like Idi Amin soldiers on duty, and they, too, frequently burst into chuckles, cracking jokes with other congregants. The House of Prayer is a happy place. A teenage boy strutting down the aisle wearing a pair of butterfly wings for a praise dance he's about to do gets a warm clap on the back. A woman stands up and hollers that she's happy and gets a hearty hug and a drink of water from one of the "soldiers" on duty. Adults greet one another with smiles and hugs. You can eat all the food you want downstairs for practically nothing. They treat one another well here. The conversation is warm, genuine—and shouted, by the way, because you can't hear a thing. Not a word.

The reason? The shout band.

There is nothing in the world like them.

There must be at least thirty of them. They are squeezed between the pulpit and the front-row pews. They are mostly trombones, with a smattering of trumpets and a gigantic sousaphone. They blast with the power of a marching band, with the swing of a jazz or R&B group. They're backed by a full rhythm section of drums, keys, guitar, and bass. Their soulful blasts are topped by the gorgeous wail of a trombonist whose high notes—he's playing in the range of a flügelhorn—float above the ensemble. It's more reminiscent of a vocalist than any horn I've heard and gives the entire band a heavenly, supernatural feel that's eerie and mesmerizing. The band members are dressed in impeccable black suits with white shirts. They play and sway as one, continuously. Even as an assortment of ministers preach and admonish the congregation, the shout band never quite stops, burbling low underneath as someone speaks, then busting loose when the preachers finish talking, the bells of the trumpets and slides of the trombones swaying skyward. The effect of hearing these men blow and sway with such heart and soul, jamming with all their might, is like watching a Broadway show without the Broadway: it's raw soul. Electrifying. It lifts the room.

Behind them, Daddy Bailey seems in this world and out of it at the same time. As a young minister hollers, congregation members thrust dollar bills in the air. A silent usher dressed in white moves to the edge of the pew. The dollar is passed from one hand to the next until it reaches the usher in the aisle, who takes it, walks it to the front of the church, and hands it to another usher. That usher walks it up to Daddy Bailey. Daddy accepts the dollar—the dollar's a symbolic gesture, really—and hands it to yet another usher, who carefully places it in a big box. Then he waves to the donor of the dollar. It's a friendly wiggle—a kind of giggly, chatty, suburban-housewife peekaboo wiggle.

Squeezed between Daddy's pulpit and the first pew, the shout band, the engine of this whole bit, roars on, charging the room with music, while at the pulpit, a minister hollers out to the congregation: "Thank you, Daddy Bailey! We love Daddy!" And the congregation responds:

"Yes, Daddy!"

"We love Daddy!"

I once went to a funeral in a village in the Ivory Coast of West Africa, and it had this kind of electric drama and excitement: the continuous music, the tears, the celebration, the pounding, the nonstop drums, the continuous preaching, the laughing and dancing. It went on all night. If this event is anything like that one, we might be here till dawn.

I don't know if I'll make it that long. I groove in the frolic a while and raise a couple of my own dollar bills in the air for the ushers to collect for Daddy Bailey's pot—why not? I wanna get in that *long line* when I die, and I don't care how I get in or who gets me there. But after a couple of hours, they're still prayer frolicking and I'm hungry, so I slip downstairs to give my ears and soul a rest. A guy serving food in the cafeteria asks me, "What you doing down here in Augusta?"

Only then do I remember why I am here: this is the very church—on the very same street where James Brown found two of the most important constants in his life. One was music. The other was a man.

One brisk afternoon in 1941, Leon Austin, a tall, light-skinned eight-year-old boy who lived down the street from Daddy Grace's—he was at 1207, Daddy Grace's was 1269—and whose gift for playing piano was so great that he was occasionally corralled into playing for Daddy Grace's church even though he was the pianist for a different church, walked into his classroom at the all-colored Silas X. Floyd Elementary School and noticed a new kid sitting in the back. The boy was a dark-skinned and poorly clad country boy from South Carolina, just across the state line. He'd just moved to Augusta, to the poor side of town called the Terry. Little James Brown.

None of the other kids wanted to bother with little James. But Leon had a kind heart, and when he discovered that James loved music, Leon said, "C'mon home with me. I'll show you some music." James readily agreed.

Leon grew up playing for Macedonia Baptist, and like musicians the world over, he knew where the real special music could be found. In Augusta, the good stuff was just three doors away from his house. He dragged James to Daddy Grace's House of Prayer. It was there that James Brown saw his future: the blasting trombones, the pounding drums, the nonstop groove, the swaying, high-stepping musicians of the United House of Prayer's legendary shout band. He was awed.

"I've got to do that," James announced. Leon took James back to the piano at his house and showed him chords, the movement of the left hand, the boogie-woogie that was so popular back then.

That friendship, bound from those first days around the high-swinging shout band of Daddy Grace's House of Prayer, would last the rest of their lives. They became best friends. Leon had older brothers, but he'd been a sickly baby—his parents didn't think he'd survive when he was born—so he wasn't allowed to play and roughhouse like they were. He was a precocious child, tender and kindhearted, a loner who loved music, and James, whose parents had broken up and whose father had slipped off and left him with his aunt Honey, was equally lonely and, Leon later told his wife, "sensitive about things." They were inseparable, like brothers, so instead of calling each other by name, they called each other Bro, pronounced *Bra* in their southern twang.

"What you doin', Bra?"

"Waiting for you, Bra."

"You got any money, Bra?"

"Wouldn't know a nickel if I saw one, Bra."

Broke and having a ball. Broke and being a kid. *Bra* and *Bra*. They were an odd pair. James was a short, dark-skinned poor kid, an outsider at school; Leon was taller, light-skinned, middle-class, and goodlooking. Leon taught James two-handed boogie-woogie piano. James, a good boxer, taught Leon how to defend himself with his fists. They sang church songs together. They performed at the local Show Palace Theatre talent shows and at school. Leon enjoyed sneaking over to Aunt Honey's so-called whorehouse, which wasn't exactly a whorehouse but a place where poor folks struggled to live off nickels and dimes. There were a lot of people in that house—eighteen at one point—and while some of Aunt Honey's roomers turned tricks for the soldiers from nearby Fort Gordon, some of them also did what poor folks all over the South did in those days to survive: they sold moonshine and scrap metal; they sewed clothing, knitted blankets, and did odd carpentry and plumbing jobs; some washed white folks' laundry and cleaned their houses; a few made money playing skin, a card game; some went to church all day Sunday and ran numbers all day Monday. It was a busy house in a wild section of town, which made it perfect for two wild boys. James introduced Leon to his cousin Willie Glen—nicknamed Big Junior—and to his humorous, stuttering, cigar-smoking father, who appeared long enough to call James "Little Junior" but never seemed to call on Little Junior enough. James and Leon organized baseball games with neighborhood kids, playing on an empty lot, using a baseball and bat that James bought with money he'd earned shining shoes downtown—a ball and bat that James would collect up and head home with if the bigger boys tried to bully them. The two boys shined shoes on the same block of Broad Street at the same time. James, out on the street, was protective of his turf and would fight someone if they tried to take it, while Leon wisely shined shoes inside the barbershop. Years later, after James bought the radio station WRDW, located on the very same corner where he had shined shoes, he would tell visitors, "I used to shine shoes right here in front of this radio station." It always made Leon chuckle, remembering how James would fight someone if they tried to take his corner.

The two were inseparable—except when they went to the Bell Auditorium for the suicide box-offs. Five black boys were blindfolded and placed in a ring with a boxing glove on one hand and their other hand tied behind their backs. They would bash each other over the head until one of them was left standing. Leon refused to do it. His mother would see the bruises on his face and ask questions. But James? James had to make a dollar however he could, even after he'd gotten his face bashed in a few times.

"You ought to quit that, Bra," Leon would mumble afterward.

"Gotta eat, Bra," James would say. Leon understood. He needed money too. But he had a job.

"Sports and the church," he would tell his wife years later, "helped save me." Leon was a track star in school, setting high school records that would hold for decades. And in the early years, he had his piano or organ. He always played Sunday services at Macedonia Baptist, and when their choir traveled to visit other churches, Leon traveled with them. He played events and funerals, a rehearsal here, a practice there. His mom organized the children of the town in a choir. She would parade them in a row from church to church, and he played for that too. Playing the piano and organ helped keep him off the streets during his teen years, whereas James . . . well, James did not have enough money to buy church clothes even if he'd wanted to go to church. His aunt Honey *wanted* him to go, but she was in over her head. She had that big house with all those roomers and relatives. She couldn't force him to go. Plus, Leon told his wife in later years, "She was Willie Glen's mother, not Bro's. Bro didn't know where his mother was."

Bro got hung up trying to make dough by lifting cars to sell their parts, and when James got busted in 1949 for four counts of breaking and entering and sent away for an eight-to-sixteen-year stretch at the boys' reformatory near Toccoa, Georgia, there was nothing Leon could do to help.

But Leon never judged, and they stayed friends. In 1955, when James showed up at Leon's doorstep in Augusta with four country boys from Toccoa who called themselves the Famous Flames, saying,

"Bro, me and my band need a place to stay for a few days," Leon said, "Bring 'em all in here, Bra! Bring 'em all!"

For the next two decades, James Brown would park anyone he needed—band members; friends; even his children, sons Teddy and Terry, and later his "adopted" son, a young minister from New York City named Al Sharpton—at Austin's house, then later at the McBowman's Motor Inn, which Leon ran with his lovely wife, Emma, and then later at Austin's house on Martin Luther King Drive. Leon's home was safe territory, where Brown's problems found a resting place, where band members and Brown's sons were treated as family, housed and fed by Leon and Emma for days, weeks, sometimes months.

The friendship that was born during the grimy poor 1940s evolved into the soup days of the fifties, and then into the laughing wonder and gravy days of the sixties and seventies, when James Brown was at his height. The two Bros watched the civil rights movement unfold in awe. They analyzed Brown's role in it, talking into the wee hours at times like two college students in a dorm room, considering the problems of the world. They traveled together, Leon riding along, sometimes reluctantly, only because Brown insisted. He needed help. He needed an honest man in his entourage. He needed his brother. Both were awestruck at the influence Brown had suddenly developed in the world. The February 1969 *Look* magazine cover featuring Brown with the headline IS HE THE MOST IMPORTANT BLACK MAN IN AMERICA? made them laugh. Bra once confessed to Leon, in a fit of candor that would occasionally slip past the know-it-all bluster that crept into his manner during those years, that he didn't know any more about solving the black man's problem than the Man in the Moon. He wasn't a politician. He was an entertainer. A musician. He had some ideas. The black man needed jobs. But everybody knew that, right? Did the white man ask Fred Astaire or Elvis Presley to speak for *their* people when *they* became stars? "It's all about money, Bra," James said. "The black man needs money." Leon agreed, but allowed that the black man needed education more than money. Brown agreed and confessed he wished he'd at least finished high school.

From 1945 to 1975, the two watched the segregated black community of Augusta, a thriving metropolitan area before World War II, decline into helplessness. Almost every single major black business they had known vanished. What was once their favorite downtown area, the main drag, "the Golden Blocks" of Augusta, located near Ninth and Gwinnett, descended into urban blight before their eyes: businesses, restaurants, hotels, a movie theater disappeared as manufacturing eased away, cotton died, drugs poured in, ambitious blacks fled for the North, and white residents scattered for the suburbs. The once glorious Palmetto Pond in nearby North Augusta, a swimming hole and popular stop on the chitlin circuit where Ella Fitzgerald, Tiny Bradshaw, Cab Calloway, and Jimmie Lunceford once came to perform; the mighty Paramount Motor Motel with more than eighty rooms, owned by Charlie Reid, Sr., a local black enterprising genius; the Penny Savings Bank; the Lenox Theater; the Georgia Colored Funeral Directors and Embalmers Association; the Four Sisters Beauty Shop; the once mighty Pilgrim Health and Life Insurance Company; the Red Star Hotel—where folks waited for hours for Mom and Pop Bryant's magical fried chicken; Crims Service Station; Geffert's Ice Cream Company; McBowman's Motor Inn, owned by Austin's mother-in-law—all gone. Employers like the Silby Mill, the Enterprise Mill, the Plaza Hotel, the Del Mar Casino were also gone. The only big deal that remained in Augusta from their childhood years was the Augusta Nationals, a white man's golf tournament that began in 1933 over on the city's west side and had no relevance to their lives.

"If we don't help ourselves, we ain't gonna make it, Bro," James would say. In the good years, Brown tried everything he could to help. A radio station. Two of them. Three, if you included the one in Baltimore, which was the hometown of his second wife, Deidre. A green-stamps idea, where his face was issued on green stamps used as money-saving coupons; a restaurant; a nightclub. But Brown was not a businessman. They all went bust.

In the early years, the 1950s and '60s, the big dream for young men like those two was to get to the North, where the white man's foot was off your neck. Brown had a ticket out. He was a star. He moved to New York City in 1960. He told Leon, "Come with me, Bra."

Leon refused. He'd married Emma McBowman right out of Fisk University—he'd been chasing after her since she'd graduated from high school. "What would I do in New York?" Austin said. "Emma's here. My home's here." After ten years of floundering in New York— traveling the world and coming home to a city with its own set of racial problems, working with northern white record-company folks whom he never completely trusted, who he felt smiled in his face even as they stabbed him in the back—Brown gave up on the North. He hated New York. "Down home, I know who I'm dealing with," he said tersely. He returned to Augusta.

He came home to Leon. Steady and familiar Leon was the same guy, living in the same house with the same wife, same car. He even played the same piano at the same church, Macedonia Baptist Church, that they both knew as children. He had opened a barbershop by then, and his kindness, his ready ear, his laughter made him popular in town. It was Leon, in fact, who first gave Brown his trademark hairstyle when they were both young. In thirty years of friendship they rarely argued. But when they did, it was bad. And their biggest argument was around the thing that had first united them: music.

As a child playing piano at Macedonia, where his dad and mom were deacon and deaconess, Leon was considered a boy wonder. He could play by ear anything he heard. He was a sought-after musician in Augusta circles because he knew all the great gospel hymns by heart. Brown constantly warned him, "Bra, if you play too many funerals, the next one you play might be your own," but Leon enjoyed giving comfort to the families, some of whom he'd known all his life. He felt he could sing and lay in groove on piano as well as some of Brown's musicians—in fact, better than some. He decided he wanted to leave his barbershop, go on the road, and make a chunk of big money so he could settle back with his wife and not work so hard. He could make a record or two—the record business seemed easy. Big money. Big thrills. Not a lot of work.

He hinted this to James for years and Brown ignored him. Finally, one afternoon when Brown was complaining about one of his musicians, Leon said, "Put me in your band. I play good enough. I gave you your first music lessons."

Brown was flummoxed. He could not easily explain to his friend the headache of running a band. This one wants more money, that one gets drunk, this one can't tie his shoes by himself, the other one forgot his uniform, this one wants an advance, that one wants song-writing credit and hasn't played a note, while this one doesn't want songwriting credit and he played *all the notes*—but if you hit him up with credit, you'd have to pay two guys behind him whom you didn't pay before. And the girls! Not the women he slept with, but the kids he was responsible for. Like little Geneva Kinard, of Cincinnati, who along with her sister Denise Kinard and Roberta DuBois sang background on a lot of his early hits, recorded in Cincinnati at King Records headquarters. These were young talents—but they were literally kids. Geneva was in high school. He was like a father to her. He'd heard her sing in El-Bethel Baptist Church in Cincinnati and had to promise her mom and dad that no one in the band would touch her, and that after gigs he'd send her home by taxi or limo in time for school. And he did! She went on to graduate in 1972 from the University of Cincinnati College–Conservatory of Music as a piano major— one of only five blacks in her class—and later served as pianist with the Cincinnati Ballet and the Middletown, Ohio, orchestra, one of the few blacks in that field. But few of his musicians knew that. Onstage, the musicians were his friends, but offstage they went in different directions. They wanted more, deserved more, and nobody appreciated nothing. They moaned about the fines and the extra rehearsals he imposed; they saw him grab a box of pay money after each show and depart, but none of them knew of the headaches that came with that box of money: dealing with the slick promoters, the record labels, the radio stations, the managers; bribing the DJs—which was illegal even though everyone did it, but if a black guy did it and got busted he was going straight to jail without passing GO; pleasing the promoters, pleasing the fans; dodging the mobsters in various towns who tried to shake you down every time you came to their city—sometimes the same mobster would offer the same threat every time he came, *take my loan or else.* . . . The music itself was a small cog in the mighty machine of entertainment. Leon did not understand that. He just wanted to play. So Brown simply said, "Bra, you got the talent. But you ain't cut out for show business."

"Sure I am!"

"You got a good life, Bra. A good wife. You got a good business. Why you wanna leave that for show business? They'll eat you like a piece of red meat."

"I can take care of myself," Leon said.

"It ain't the music, Bra. It's the money. Money changes people."

"It won't change me," Leon said.

"Money will *make* you change," Brown said. "Your heart may be the same. Your head may be the same. But if people knew you had millions of dollars, you couldn't even stay in your own house."

"I'd put up an electric fence and keep 'em out."

Brown laughed and quit the subject, but Leon barked on about it so much that eventually Brown gave in. He produced several of Leon's records himself in the late sixties and into the seventies. He brought in his own band, the J.B.'s—crack players, some of the best R&B players in the history of that genre—to play the sessions. The records were good. Leon played and sang soulfully, but the records ran into distribution issues and died. Leon, who would give a stranger his last dime, didn't have the heart to be a slickster, paying off DJs and working angles between record companies, bands, the promoters, and all the other things that it takes to be a star. But only after Leon gave up on the idea did Brown confess, "Bra, I don't need you in my band. I need you to be my friend."

Leon never raised the subject again. Besides, he saw for himself the headaches the parade of hangers-on, cousins, second cousins, friends of friends caused his friend. Take Brown's cousin Willie Glen, Aunt Honey's son. Brown had shared a bed as a child with Willie Glen while staying in Aunt Honey's house. In 2000, Willie Glen's son, Richard Glen, robbed Brown's office and then set it on fire, just to hide the robbery—the guy burned the entire office down. It shamed Brown to see his cousin's son get locked up. He loved Willie Glen. And it didn't stop there. In the 1970s, when his daughter Deanna was six and his daughter Yamma was three, Brown gave them writing credits for a couple dozen songs. It was a tax dodge. Twenty-seven years later the two sued him in federal court for $1 million for their cut of royalties. He settled with them for a sum far less, but the suit stung him. It was, Leon saw, always about the money. Everybody needed money: *This* guy borrowed money and never paid it back. *That* guy needed a car, so Brown got him a used car and the guy griped about not getting a new one. As soon as Brown dealt with that guy, another guy popped up with his hand out. And the women? His appetite for them drew the strong and the meek, the good-hearted and the cunning, and all of them chipped away at the man's generosity, leaving him angry and spent. It never ended. Over the years, even the line of people at Leon's barbershop who were trying to get to Brown through him had become a growing headache for Leon. But the door to James Brown—Leon let it be known—that door was closed.

In the earlier years, when Brown first became the King of Soul, these kinds of annoyances were ice cream and cake. Those were the fun years. Brown was young and strong, with girlfriends and cars and his own plane and three radio stations. He and Leon traveled to New York, to the West Coast, to West Africa. But in the later years, the weight of carrying that heavy load began to hammer at Brown. He never slept. He called Leon at all hours. He worried a lot and tried to hide it. His friends kept turning on him, mostly around issues of money. By the late eighties, his great musicians were leaving or gone: his great musical directors Pee Wee Ellis and Fred Wesley had departed; Waymon Reed had joined Art Blakey's Jazz Messengers; Joe Dupars split for the Isley Brothers; Richard "Kush" Griffith, a gifted musician with perfect pitch, had left too—and that was just the trumpet players. The ever loyal sax man Maceo led a revolt. The crucial rhythm players bagged it as well. Drummers Jabo Starks and Clyde Stubblefield. Bassist Sweet Charles Sherrell, with his easygoing disposition and deep talent, Sweet Charles, who played keyboards and bass, sang, and directed the show—who did everything, and whose solid grooves laid out the thundering bass of "Say It Loud—I'm Black and I'm Proud," who helped James keep his band together and pulled him out of bed when he was too tired or too high to go on—Sweet Charles grew tired of him and left. Brown always paid these guys, but who was paying him? He always gave, but who was giving to him? His wives he'd driven off. His cruelty sent his girlfriends packing. There was no one who lived at his level who understood how pained he felt. A man who carries the troubled history of an entire people on his back and a twenty-four-piece band and a record company and three radio stations to boot cannot find peace. Brown was lonely. He remembered every snub, every promoter from the 1950s who'd called him a "black monkey," every girl in high school who'd turned him down because his pants were too short or he wasn't light-skinned enough. The memories kicked back on him at odd moments, twisted him like a pretzel, and, at times, made him unbearable to be around, and that's when he began to reach for the drugs, the PCP, which he smoked secretly. It was so secret that even Leon never saw it. Brown wouldn't let any of his close associates see it. Not the Reverend Sharpton, not Leon, not Charles Bobbit. Leon knew Bra wasn't right, he could see in the way Brown acted that he was taking something, however he took it in.

Leon waited. He learned there was a time to share opinions with James and a time to be cool. Even when James was high, he knew, eventually the James he loved, the James who would laugh and wonder at his own success, who took the whole thing with a wink, would surface.

Brown loved that about Leon, the fact that Bra, whom he sometimes affectionately called Boston because it rhymed with *Austin*, knew the worst parts of him and never judged him, was never put off by his antics, understood and defended him, even to his wife, Emma, who sometimes objected to what she felt could be an uneven friend-ship: "You forget," he'd tell her, "I chose him to be my friend. When I take a friend, I take them through thick and thin." It was something Brown depended on. One of Brown's favorite things in life was to come off the road, drop his bags at his South Beech Island home, hop into his Lincoln, and roll by the modest ranch at 1932 Martin Luther King Boulevard in Augusta, telling the kids who were always gathered around Leon's house, "Go fetch Mr. Leon."

Leon would come to the door and peer through the screen to see Brown in his Lincoln at the curb with his head out the driver's-side window hollering, "Bra! Let's ride!"

They rode together for more than forty years: Brown, Brown's wife of the moment, Leon Austin, and Emma, Austin's wife of forty-two years. Across the state line to South Carolina they'd go, to Brown's "home country"—to Williston and Blackville and Snelling, towns near old Ellenton—to, in Leon's words, "meet Brown's cousins," and gorge at his favorite chicken stand, to wolf down sardines, cheese, and crackers at some godforsaken soul food spot that only Brown knew about. The argument would always be the same. "Why we gotta eat what you eat?" Leon would ask. "Let's eat something else, Bra. I'll pay."

"Why you gonna burn your little money up? What's the matter with sardines and crackers?"

Leon would always laugh. He knew it was senseless to argue. "How can someone express love or show love if they don't know what it feels like?" he'd tell his wife. This was Brown's way of showing love. You couldn't argue with him. Just like when they were kids playing baseball. If there was a dispute on the ball field, James would take his ball and bat and go elsewhere. It wasn't about sardines and crackers; it was about friendship, about paying a debt, because Leon also owed James Brown as well—and both men knew it. Brown made him ap-preciate what he had: One son. One wife. One home. One car. A nor-mal life, not four wives and thirteen children; not thirty cars and a fifteen-room house that meant nothing to him. Leon owed Brown for helping him appreciate that gift. And in return, Leon let Brown express his love in the small ways Brown knew how. And for that reason, in Brown's later years, when his marital, career, legal, and drug troubles dragged him to earth and he became irascible and almost uncontrollable, it was always Leon who would be summoned to the Beech Island mansion by Charles Bobbit with a phone call and the words, "Mr. Brown's having trouble."

Leon would hang up and rush out to Brown's house to find Brown in bed, lying on his back, his knees propped up on a pillow.

"What's the matter, Bra?"

"I don't wanna work no more, Bra. Don't wanna do no more shows. I'm tired. My knees hurt."

Leon would ask one of the silent, frightened entourage standing about to fetch Brown's hair dryer and comb and hair tools that always lay around the house, because Brown, from the time they were kids, was always funny about his appearance. Then he'd get to work on the hair, wash it, style it, then throw James under the hair dryer, not talking much, knowing how to be silent, because James would want to talk then and did enough talking for both of them, and with the hair dryer blasting, he couldn't hear a thing you said anyway. James didn't want to hear you, really. He just wanted company, not to be alone. He'd shout at Leon, and after he'd shouted himself out, Leon would shout back a few things, both of them airing out, Leon stating the problems of running his barbershop, Brown on the problems of running a multimillion-dollar enterprise that wasn't, Leon knew, so multimillion anymore. They'd talk politics, and women, and cars, and religion. And afterward the two would head to the store for some ice cream—no drinks, no booze, no drugs, just ice cream. Something they couldn't afford as kids. They'd eat enough to start a factory. Any kind they wanted.

Only then, usually on the way home in the car, with the smell of the swampy Savannah River pushing through the windows and Brown's hair done and James feeling good and clean, and both full of ice cream, only then would Leon break in and get to the point.

"Bra, you got to get back to work."

By then James had softened and he'd confess to Leon the real problem. Sometimes it was work. Or money. Or a promoter. Or a lawyer. Or the problem of playing small houses after years of doing big concerts. But mostly, it revolved around love. "Bra, when *you* go home," Brown said, "you got a wife. Somebody to say hello to you who cares for you and will rub your feet."

Leon never interfered with Brown's tumultuous love life. The fact that it never worked out, he told his wife, was not his business. He neither judged nor gave advice. Rather, he always came back to the same business: "I understand, Bra. But you got to work. That's what we do."

And sure enough, the next day, James Brown, even when he was well past sixty and feeling ninety, would get up on creaky knees—even with prostate cancer eating at him, his teeth hurting from numerous operations, a man allergic to penicillin who could be floored by any ailment and could not get the normal respite because he was not a normal man—and he would flail at his life again.

More than any other man on earth, Leon Austin of Augusta, Georgia, knew how far James Brown had come, because it was Leon who, that first day back in 1941 when he met James in class when they were both eight years old, took him home, and told his mother, "Momma, this here's my friend from school, James Brown."

Mrs. Austin took one look at the two boys, her son and his little friend—snot in his nose, hair nappy, unkempt, ragged clothes—and said, "I can't stand y'all." She grabbed them both by the collar and carried them to the back of her kitchen, where she filled an iron tub with hot water. She took James's clothes off. She took Leon's clothes off. She threw both boys in the bathtub and scrubbed them down. And when she was finished, she dressed them both in Leon's clothes and said, "Now I can stand y'all."

Chapter 8

To Live Standing

They built a park for one of the world's strongest men in Toccoa, north Georgia, a pretty town on the side of a mountain. Paul Anderson was the 1956 Olympic weightlifting champion. He was born in Toccoa. They have his Olympic team uniform in a museum downtown; it makes you wonder how a guy that small could lift so much. He once set the world record for the heaviest weight ever lifted by a human being—6,270 pounds in the back lift. A sixteen-ton granite marker is located at his birthplace. He's the most famous guy this town has ever produced. Meanwhile, the local library file has about seven references to James Brown, who moved here when he got out of jail and spent his formative years here. Most of the old clippings are about Bobby Byrd, Brown's once-famous sideman.

If a man's dream can shoot into the night sky and glisten with the brilliance of a thousand stars, then die with the sizzle of water poured onto a match, then James Brown's story ends right here. You can find it buried in the shade of a pleasant holly bush on a winding road in the Toccoa cemetery, underneath a tombstone that reads TEDDY LEWIS BROWN, 1954–1973.

Teddy was only nineteen when he died in a car accident in upstate New York. He and two musician friends, Arthur Ricky Roseman, eighteen, and Richard Young, thirty, were riding to Canada. All three were killed when their car crashed against a bridge abutment in Elizabethtown, New York. The inside rumor was that there was some drinking involved, but it's just rumor, and Teddy wasn't driving anyway.

James Brown had big plans for his first two children, sons Terry and Teddy. Terry, the eldest, was the brains, the legal mind. Also, the high school star athlete. Teddy, the younger, was the sparkle. He was a dancer, a singer. The wit.

Such is the level of smoke around James Brown that it's hard to get the real story on Teddy. Everybody you talk to claims they were there, that Teddy had bad relations with his dad, that his dad gave him a sax and said, "Learn to play this," that Teddy said things like, "I'll show you, Daddy! I'm my own man." It's the usual drama, and much of it is nonsense. But all agree on this: Teddy had a gorgeous face, a beautiful smile, and deep talent, perhaps even more talent than his father. And he was all personality. Thirty-five years after Teddy's death, the mention of his name still draws smiles to the faces of the old-timers in Toccoa. "He had unbelievable talent," says Drew Perry, an undertaker and classmate of Teddy's. "Teddy never met a stranger." He was "a real special kid," adds David Neal, a lifetime resident of Toccoa and friend of James Brown. His brother, James Neal, former mayor of Toccoa, told me, "Teddy's funeral was the biggest this town ever saw."

But the mention of Teddy's name does not bring a smile to the lips of the tall, regal woman who sits before the fireplace of her tidy home on Prather Bridge Road. At seventy-two, Velma Brown, James Brown's first wife, is a handsome woman, stylish, tall, with smooth brown skin, a beautiful smile, and the countenance of an African princess.

She's a straight-backed woman with down-home country wisdom and a quick, sharp sensibility that belies a deep thoughtfulness. She rocks in her chair and listens to her son Terry, fifteen months younger than Teddy, talk about his brother in low tones; what her firstborn son Teddy could have been, should have been, might have become. A television is glaring nearby, one of those old ones, big and boxy, with speakers. She ignores it. Her eyes glaze over as she listens. She is in another time, another place.

"Teddy," she says calmly, "was just finding himself. Like young folks do."

She broke down after Teddy Brown died. The wheels came off. She ate nerve medicine for two years, just to see straight. Only God held her up, and for that she was ever grateful. Because she had taught her boys to be strong. To have faith in his word. To seek learning; to stand outside the small town they lived in and look to the larger world—not cruise through life being sons of a superstar. Teddy's trip to Canada, she knew, was not some fly-by-night attempt to drink and go buck wild and show his daddy he could be a man. He could have done that in New York City, where his father had an empty house, since James was mostly on the road. Or he could have gone to Atlanta, just two hours from her house. He could have found all the wildness he wanted there. Teddy went to Canada because he wanted to see the world. He wanted to be free, to think and be clear. He wanted to be Teddy Brown, not James Brown's son. And she approved of that.

"If there's a man in there, you want him to come out," she says. "You don't want your son fooling around playing half man just because he sees everybody else around him is being a half man. You got to work. Educate yourself. Know things. He wasn't gonna get those things here. Not in Toccoa. There ain't but three black families in this whole town, really. We're all related one way or the other. Some around here learned to live standing up. Some learned to live sitting down."

Her branch lived standing.

Velma's father, Arthur "Bug" Warren, was a big man: six foot four inches, well over 250 pounds in his prime, and wide around the shoulders. While he was a polite, kind man, Bug took no guff from nobody. He was born in Birmingham, Alabama, in 1879, just fifteen years after slavery ended. Most of his family were sharecroppers. When work dried up in Alabama, most of Bug's friends announced they were migrating north, to New York and Chicago. But Bug's father told his son, "North or south, it don't make no difference if you're waiting for the white man to get outta your way. Stand where you are. Keep your head up and your back straight so you can see what's going on. Get busy where you are."

Bug made his way to Toccoa, where he'd heard that a colored man could make a good living driving railroad spikes if he had a strong back. Toccoa was all dirt roads and farms in those days, but it was a railroad stop and manufacturing center where they made caskets and furniture. Bug got hired by a white man to join a crew driving railroad crossties, laying track for the Southern Railway that cut through Toccoa. That job was tough. The foreman was rough. You had to be strong—strong on the outside and even stronger on the inside. Some of those black fellas, big fellas from south Georgia and Alabama, they couldn't handle it and they quit. But Bug listened to one of the older drivers, who told him, "Keep your head up and don't bend your back. Bend your knees. You bend your back and you don't have to worry about coming on the job tomorrow. You won't last thirty minutes. Stand straight and swing." Bug listened, kept his back straight, and lasted. He slammed spikes to earth for most of his life until his carpentry eventually earned him a better living. He got married, bought some land, built a six-bedroom house in 1938 with his own hands, and when his boys Son, Robert, Peanut, AP, and Douglass—there were seven kids in all including daughters Margaret and Velma—grew up, he sent them to drive spikes on the railroad just as he had. He taught his boys what he had learned: "Keep your head up. Don't bend your back. Stand tall."

Bug's boys were like their father: they were hardworking, big, strong men. Son was six-five, Peanut was six-two. Doug was six-three, AP was six feet, and Robert, at five-nine, was the runt. They were all quiet, firm country men whose hands gripped hammers tightly and whose dark eyes looked at you dead on. That was a dangerous way to be in the South, where a black man who didn't keep his eyes to the earth and tip his cap and step off the sidewalk anytime a white woman passed could find himself tied to a rope and pulled behind somebody's pickup truck eating dirt till he was done in. That problem nagged at Bug till he died, that one of his boys wouldn't toe that line, because his boys followed their daddy: they weren't prone to tipping their cap to nobody save their mother. But to his relief his boys mostly did okay for themselves. They hammered spikes for the Southern Railway eight to ten hours a day, and every one of Bug's boys got so that when he raised his driver high in the air and brought it down, he could drive those stakes home with just a single stroke. Bug's boys could work that hammer, every foreman knew it, and after a few years most of them hammered themselves right out of the white man's railroad into whatever life they wanted. Bug's eldest boy, Son, became a bounty hunter. Peanut ended up a brick mason and concrete maker. Robert stayed with the railroad for life. Doug and AP became carpenters and never drove another railroad spike again. Bug's boys were good men. His family, the Warrens, were a proper, churchgoing family, pillars in the local Mt. Zion Baptist Church. Bug was proud of the family that God had given him.

But Bug got the shock of his life when he found out that his younger daughter, Velma, was sneaking out of the window of his house on Friday nights with a tiny local runt who stood no more than five foot eight, a kid fresh out of the Alto Reform School at a former National Guard army barracks and training ground, where he'd served more than three years out of an eight-to-sixteen-year term for stealing a car;

a boy who sang good-time music, not church music; who'd done a short stint at the all-colored Whitman Street High School before dropping out to work odd jobs and to occasionally run moonshine to South Carolina. A boy from big-time Augusta with a shady past. A boy they called Music Box.

Fifty years later, Velma, wearing a fine wool sweater and slacks, smiles at the memory of her first love as she sits in her living room in front of the fireplace. "My daddy saw James dance. Saw him sing and perform. He would say, 'Well, James is insane. James needs to work. James needs a job.'" But Velma Warren was strong-minded, just like her father. And when her mind was made up, that was it. She saw the kindness of the young man from Trinity Church, whom she met when he was singing at Mt. Zion Baptist Church one Sunday. The young James Brown promised her he wanted to live proper. "Lots of things in my life ain't as they should be," he said, "but I'm working to make things the way they *could* be. Can't nobody work harder than me." All the time, any job he could get, big or small, he worked. She admired that attitude. James joined her church after they started dating and got together with a local guy from Trinity Church named Bobby Byrd to sing on the side. He was a big-city kid from Augusta among small-town kids, and Toccoa was, for him, a brand-new start.

"James was always neat," Velma says. "Always clean. Always polite. He appreciated your kindness to him. He had a kind heart. What little he had, he took care of. If James had one pair of dungarees, he'd clean and iron those pants and bleach the cuff on them. And if he had two pairs, he'd give you one of them. He ironed his shirts. He was always careful about his appearance."

Few blacks in town wanted part of James Brown in those days. When he arrived from the reformatory, having been helped by a kind white warden who recommended him for a job at a local car dealership, he could not find permanent housing. A black woman named Miss Leeny Wilson finally rented him a room at 235 Sage Street. From there another black couple, a local barber named Nathan Davis and his wife, Dora, living at 144 Emily Street, rented him a room, which is how Brown ended up at Trinity, a Methodist church. "Nathan and Dora Davis took him over to Trinity," Velma says. "That's how he joined that choir." But most of the blacks in Toccoa ostracized him. "They called him Convict," Velma says. "That was his name around here. They couldn't forget that he came out of Alto."

Velma didn't care about that gossip. A sixteen-year stint for stealing a car wasn't unusual in Georgia, where the white man's justice fell hard on African American heads. James was funny. He made her laugh. He had big dreams. He worked hard. He never asked for charity. And he sang like a bird. She fell in love.

Her father was displeased, but Bug saw that Velma was not going to be moved, so one afternoon he gathered the couple before him and announced that young James could visit his daughter only at proper times, on Friday evenings, after work. "I don't want y'all running around to those jukes and good-time houses," he said. The couple, standing before the towering figure of Bug Warren, who carried every inch of his six-foot-four frame in his thick hands and shoulders, readily agreed. James visited on Friday evenings, and they sat in the living room and talked politely into the night while Bug repaired to his back porch to enjoy a sip or three of white lightning, which never kept him from making it to church on Sunday mornings. They would wait for the joy juice to do its work, and once Bug crawled to bed knocked out, they would climb out the window and dash off to the very spots that Bug had ranted about. "Those were some crazy times," Velma says, laughing.

Off they went to the S+M Grill, Berry Trimier's place, Bill's Rendezvous, and the local black juke joints where James and his band of Bobby Byrd, Sylvester Keels, Doyle Oglesby, Fred Pulliam, Nash Knox, and Nafloyd Scott and his brother Baby Roy Scott would sing. Velma watched James with one eye and watched the door with the other, hoping Bug's big frame wouldn't darken the doorway. That was the nightmare, that her father would awaken, stumble into the living room, find them gone, then seek them out. The thought of Bug Warren, hot, walking into the S+M Grill, his fists balled tight, gave James and Velma the shakes. James was scared stiff of Bug, and when he finally said to Velma, "Will you marry me, Velma?" she happily agreed. That would be one problem scratched off the list. Bug could not be mad if she was the man's wife.

They married on June 27, 1953, in Mt. Zion, and rented a house on Savannah Lane. Velma got a job at a local furniture factory. Mr. Lawson, of Lawson Motor Company, had taken James on at the urging of the warden, and partly because the booming factories in Toccoa—which were not keen on hiring a young convict out of Alto—had claimed most of the labor pool. Lawson was a kind man who'd taken a chance on Brown, but he didn't pay enough. James wanted more, and after a while he got a job shoveling coal as the janitor for the all-white Toccoa Elementary School.

It would have been a smoother marriage had James's band not become popular so quickly over the next three years. In a small town where there is little for young people to do, the band James sang with, who called themselves the Famous Flames, played high school dances, juke joints, clubhouses, the white high school football games, and school cafeterias, then ventured to Macon, Georgia, knocking the walls off the clubs there, competing with Little Richard, Otis Redding, Clyde McPhatter and the Drifters, the Five Royales, Hank Ballard and the Midnighters. Five country boys from a no-place town would mount the stage of those small joints and howl at the moon, guitarist Nafloyd Scott playing behind his back, pianist Bobby Byrd hammering the keys like his life depended on it, and the lead guy, James Brown, dancing on the tables, leaping off the piano, daring anybody to outdo him. During those years, Brown held down a day job, supporting a home on Savannah Lane and later on Spring Street with Velma and Teddy and Terry. Even then, he couldn't stop the music from busting out: he sang in the house, on the street, on the job. Brenda Kelly, the retired principal of Stephens County High School, attended Toccoa Elementary School as a kid and remembers the sight of the school custodian, young James Brown, practicing piano in the school basement after slinging coal all morning. "I guess it was 1955 or so. I was in maybe the sixth grade. There was a room down in the basement, down a set of stairs that led under the cafeteria. It held the shop class and the custodian's room. Us kids weren't allowed to go down there, but you know how kids are. There was a piano down there in the hallway. Me and my friend Liz Hoffer would sneak down there at lunch to hear the janitor play the piano. He sounded wonderful. We were his only audience."

But Brown's audience was growing bigger. His first hit, "Please, Please, Please," broke a year later, in 1956. The Famous Flames' road gigs demanded they travel farther and farther out: Atlanta; Jacksonville, Florida; Houston. James's onstage antics drew crowds. His road trips became more frequent. He was gone from his wife for longer periods. And he began to change.

Velma saw it happening. "James had a strong mind. He could get stuff together. He could tell people what to do. He'd be sitting in a room with the band, he'd light a cigarette, and then suddenly the whole room would light a cigarette. I said, 'What's wrong with these people?' I couldn't see that."

She saw the way the women chased him, saw the accolades pouring in, saw James drift away. He quit the janitor's job. He was on the road all the time. Gone to Macon. Gone to Atlanta. She didn't like it, but times were difficult. "We were very young people," she says, "and I had no intentions of standing in his way. Those were hard years, and this town was a prison for him. This was his chance to make something of himself. When I heard in the later years what went on between him and those other women he was seeing, that was between him and them. It didn't have anything to do with me. Because he never disrespected me. And I never disrespected him."

She rocks slowly, thinking back. It's a hard memory. "He was a good father," she says. "He was never neglectful. Not towards me or his boys."

When Brown bought the house in Queens, in 1964, he and Velma had already separated. Velma stayed behind in Toccoa. "I told him, 'You do what you want. I don't need a thing from you. I have my own job.'" She didn't ask James for a dime, but said, "We have two children and I have to raise them." Without protest, James paid $150,000 for land and a house near Prather Bridge Road—he had the house built brand-new from the ground up—and handed the title to Velma. She never pressed him for a dime further—never needed to. *He* would ask, and only then, if he'd ask, she'd say, "Well, the boys need this. . . ."

She worked at the furniture plant for thirty years, starting out at a salary of $1.10 an hour, and sent her boys to be with their father in New York City during the summers. "If I had trouble with them, I called their father. And he would respond. If they did wrong here, and I couldn't manage 'em in some kind of way, I'd hand them over to him. Now, I wasn't gonna have one of his women friends fooling with my boys. I wouldn't have that. But they loved their father. And he loved them. And I never kept them from him.

"I do believe James appreciated that. He knows how I am. We were young together. You know just about every funeral in my family over the years, James came? Just about every one. He would come off the road and come here from however far off he was. He'd come from far-off distant places, to show his respect. He was good that way."

And she was good in her way too. More than once over the years, while James was alive, she'd answer a knock at her door and find a white lawyer in a suit saying, "I can get you millions from your ex-husband." She closed the door in their faces. "When you fight wrong," she says, "you lose." For years she read various accounts of James's life in Toccoa, how so many people seem to remember so much about him, building air castles about the good old times when James Brown asked them for a lift, or asked them for money, or wanted to date their sister, or played baseball with them when he was broke, or stayed in their homes. The fiction, some of it stamped pretty deeply into the James Brown myth, has James Brown staying in the basement of sideman Bobby Byrd's house, care of Byrd's grandmother, who somehow "signed him out" of the reformatory and put him up in her house until he broke big. But the actual dates display the fiction: Brown was released from the reformatory in 1951. His first record, "Please,

Please, Please," was released in 1956. That would have been a stay of
about five years living in Byrd's basement, during which, at least part
of that time, the deeply talented Byrd was attending college at North
Carolina A&T.

"Truth is, nobody gave James much here," Velma says. "He earned
his way. He didn't go round here asking for nothing. We had our own
house. We worked. We took care of ourselves. James didn't go around
asking for anything, because no husband of mine would do that anyway," she says simply.

Nobody in Toccoa had any idea what he would become, she says.
"If you asked some of the folks around here, they'll tell you that back
then he was the best thing since sliced bread and peanut butter. But
they were not that nice to him. He was always 'that one that just got
out of Alto.'"

She stares into the fire. "They never forget that. He could never get
past that no matter what he did. After he got big, that's the first thing
that come up in the papers, how he come up out of Alto and didn't
have nothing; how they all had to help him and give him this and that.
He never forgot that," she says. "I haven't either."

The two legally divorced in 1969, but for the rest of his life, Brown
would slip away from his life in Augusta—the wives, the entourage,
the bills, the lawyers, the madness—jump into his Lincoln, and drive
the two and a half hours to Toccoa to sit on Velma's living room
couch and spend hours talking to the woman he described in his autobiography as "my close friend." The house he built for her he often
referred to as "our house." Their boys Terry and Teddy—and Velma's
son Larry, from a later outside union, whom Brown treated as his own
and included in his will—Brown referred to as "our boys." Their
grandson William Forlando he referred to as "our Flip." Brown adored
the kid. He gave William the nickname "Flip" because the kid was
funny and reminded him of the popular black comedian Flip Wilson.
He checked the kid's homework, paid his college tuition, and, along
with Velma, was bursting with pride when Flip hit his college books
hard. The couple shared a special bond—and a huge heartbreak, one

that would mark each of their lives for as long as they lived, for they each left a great chunk of their souls on a lonely highway in upstate New York during the wee hours of the morning when Teddy moved on to heaven.

They weren't the only ones whose lives were upended. Teddy's younger brother Terry had been accepted to the prestigious Morehouse College in Atlanta, alma mater to Dr. Martin Luther King and many others. He was about to leave for college when Teddy was killed. Teddy had invited his brother on the road trip, saying they should spend time together before Terry went off to college. Terry had refused. "Momma and Daddy want me to stay home and work because I'm getting a new car to drive to college," he told his brother. After the accident, Terry tanked. He turned down his acceptance to Morehouse, attended North Georgia College and State University on a basketball scholarship, and quit after two years. A long period of aimless wandering would follow in his life, in which he took on endless manual jobs and worked for his dad's radio station, quitting after arguments with his dad, who leaned on him harder after Teddy died, and falling into drink, until finally righting himself to help his father in Brown's later years. Velma's nervous breakdown did not help matters. Teddy's death changed their world.

And it changed no one more deeply than James Brown himself.

Teddy's death came at a time when Brown was at the height of his career. He had assembled one of the greatest groups of R&B musicians of all time, superseding, it can easily be argued, even the majestic Motown machine factory out of Detroit. James Brown and his band kicked out one hit after another: "Soul Power," "Say It Loud—I'm Black and I'm Proud," "Sex Machine," "I Feel Good." He had become a musical force of nature, black America's biggest and most unique star. His live performances were real revues, loaded with gags, jokes, free giveaways, and warm-up acts who on their own drew big audiences, often backed by his band, a pounding, tight, chink-a-chink soul music outfit that would change the landscape of American music forever. Moreover, his social message of staying in school and standing on your own was like gold to black America during the civil rights era. Everywhere he went, Brown pleaded with young people to stay in school. He showed enormous generosity to children. He gave out free tickets or charged kids ninety-nine cents to attend his concerts. He gave out scholarships and rarely declined an autograph request. Thirty years after he played the Apollo, there are still folks who recall the night he gave out ten-speed bicycles to raffle winners, or how he stopped his show to congratulate a college graduate someone had introduced him to, or the way he stood outside the theater to chat with children who were waiting in line with their parents to see him, a line that inevitably ran around the corner. Brown's bright love for children burned in his heart for his own two sons more than any others in those years. The loss of Teddy was unfathomable to him.

He covered the pain, of course, with the true mantra of southern pride that he preached to his remaining son Terry. *Keep it tight, Terry. Keep it proper. You gotta work. Smile. Show your best face.* That was his mantra to Rev. Al Sharpton as well: *Never let them see you sweat. Come important. Leave important.* Too many folks had already seen his suffering and humiliation when he was a boy living in rags, walking around with a snotty nose, shining shoes and dancing for quarters. He would not let them see him cowering or crying as an adult. Letting folks see you hurt was a form of weakness, a form of dying, in a way.

And Teddy's death was just that. It was the death of something bigger, the death of a dream, the closeout on a kind of immortality that would forever elude Brown. And after it happened, as much as he tried, for the first and only time in his life, James Brown, father of proper, could not keep up the front.

James Neal was the director for Teddy Brown's funeral in Toccoa. "I'm seventy-nine years old and been in the funeral business fifty-five years," he told me. "I've never seen anything like that funeral. Oh, God, the church and streets and everything down to the corner, packed with people. Maybe two thousand people trying to get into Mt. Zion. Every funeral director in my district and some in Atlanta called me, saying, 'Hey, Neal, we're going to bring a car. You all might need an extra limo. We're going to bring it.' They just wanted to be there.

"James spent twelve thousand dollars on Teddy's casket. It was solid bronze. With the clear glass bubble on the top, so no one could touch the body. Well, we could open it if we had wanted to, but once we had turned all of the turns on there, it's about twenty-five or thirty of them, you don't want to take it loose no more. But it was beautiful.

"I will tell you something that you don't know: we had to go to the Sheraton and pick up that entourage because Mr. Brown brought two buses from Augusta, tons of folks. And we had to lead that motorcade down Prather Bridge Road and make the circle and come back up. God almighty. So many people. So many cars. A doctor from Atlanta called me and said, 'I'm Mr. Brown's personal physician and I need to sit close to him.'

"I said, 'Doctor, I'd like to put you close to him, but I can't get another person in that church. It's full.'

"He said, 'Well, can you get a chair and put it there?'

"I said, 'I'll try.'

"So I found a folding chair and brought it down and put it in the second row and let that doctor sit there. Now that doc was telling me a lie. I knew him when I was in school in Atlanta. He was a brother to a funeral director friend of mine in Washington. He just wanted to be in on it.

"I remember the flowers that Aretha Franklin sent. She sent something that would touch the ceiling of this building in here. A huge set of roses. But they hadn't come out yet. And when I first saw the bouquet, I said, *Those are the ugliest flowers I've ever seen in my life.* But they bloomed the day of the funeral. That was the prettiest set of flowers I had ever seen. God almighty, every time I see her on television or hear her music I think about that flower set she sent. People sent so many flowers that we stopped carrying them to the church. We started carrying them to the cemetery so we could line them on the cemetery road. They lined clear to the gate. As you go in, there were flowers all the way around.

"Now Mr. Bobbit, James's manager, he called me on the morning of the funeral. He said, 'Mr. Neal, Mr. Brown wants to be in the first car in the funeral procession.'

"I said, 'That's fine. If he's in the first car he's going to be with his first wife, 'cause ain't nobody going ahead of Velma.'

"Mr. Bobbit said, 'Hold the phone.'

"I didn't hear what they were saying. But Mr. Bobbit came back on the line and said, 'Okay. He'll do the second car.'"

At the church, when Brown's limousine pulled up, Brown refused to get out of the car. Bobbit had to lift him out. When Brown reached the stairs of Mt. Zion Baptist Church, the church where he'd married, where his two eldest sons were baptized, where he'd started his second life after the Alto Reform School, he collapsed. "Please! Don't make me go in there," he pleaded. "Don't make me go in there."

But make him go in there they did.

James Brown could not stand up to walk into his son's funeral. It was too much for him. But Velma Brown, Bug Warren's daughter, needed no assistance in getting out of her car when she arrived. She got out of the car, wiped the tears from her face, walked up the stairs and into the church, and said goodbye to her son as she had lived, as Bug Warren's daughter would, leaning on the Lord's everlasting arm, standing tall.

Chapter 9

The Last Flame

A blind man sits before me in a tired, empty restaurant in downtown Toccoa. He's holding a menu in one hand and a photo of himself and several other young men in the other. He holds the photo up higher so I can see it, though he cannot. *Here,* he seems to be saying, *here I am. Look at me.*

I gently take the photo from his hand and look at it. That's him, all right, standing there with four others.

These are the Famous Flames, the original guys. The roots. The ones who sipped a little moonshine with James Brown. Who went to church with him. Who played baseball against him when he played on the Alto reformatory baseball team that competed against the local all-black Whitman Street High School in the late 1940s. These were his classmates during his brief stay at Whitman after he got out of the juvenile prison. In those days they were hungry, willing to do anything to get a gig, working for the white man by day, playing dances at night, and hustling occasional moonshine in the wee hours across the Prather Bridge from South Carolina, which was burned down five times in forty years. Something about them South Carolinians made Georgians mad, or was it the other way around? They didn't care. They had gigs to do. Jobs to make in the morning. James wasn't a star in those days. He was just like them, a good guy with a dream, trying to make good in a world where the wall to success was as high as the Kelly Barnes Dam up over the mountain, a dam that would one day in 1977 burst open and flood the nearby Toccoa Falls College and drown thirty-nine people in their beds as they slept. God controls everything in the world, including the fate of the Famous Flames. Including the fate of Nafloyd Scott.

I hold the photo higher up to the light: there's Sylvester Keels, Nash Knox, Fred Pulliam, James Brown, Bobby Byrd, and his younger brother Baby Roy Scott. Everyone in that photo is dead—except for him. Nafloyd Scott is the only one in that photo holding an instrument, a guitar.

Like everything involving James Brown, there are several versions of who shot John, as the old black folks say. In other words, the Famous Flames existed in another form, with another name, before Brown joined, but how they started as the Famous Flames, who said what, wrote what, and who did thus and so to help make James Brown great: everyone has a version. Even their membership is a matter of dispute. If the Rock and Roll Hall of Fame—a place that is a cross between a theme park and a *Rolling Stone* magazine ad—is any reference, the last living Flame, Bobby Bennett, died in January 2013. Apparently, in his last years, Bennett, like a lot of folks who worked with Brown, let anyone who came near him with a pencil and pad or video camera know that he once played with James Brown, that they were a group. In fact, he would intimate that he was once nearly on par with James Brown, that Brown was, in a sense, the same as he was, that they were all Famous Flames together, like privates in the army, all for one and one for all, as if Brown were just a soldier, without vision, and who knows, but for a twist of fate, the luck of the draw, a flick of the cards, a gust of wind, a kick of the heels, why, another black guy in the Flames could have been Mr. Dynamite. . . .

It doesn't help matters that black history being what it is, the various versions of the Flames' origins have been fumbled about like a hot potato and dumped into the usual bin of lost black history. The various background groups were known as the Flames, the Famous Flames, the James Brown Revue, and the J.B.'s. The dancers that hooted behind him in the late eighties and nineties were a mishmash of spectacular singers from the sixties to the eighties and cheerleader-like dancers in the nineties, especially in the late nineties. Some of the members ended up leaving after a few weeks. Some stayed for years. Some, like the gifted female soul stylists Vicki Anderson, Marva Whitney, Beatrice Ford, Lyn Collins, Tammi Terrell, and Martha High—all of whom sang with Brown for long stretches or did records under him—are among the greatest soul singers America has ever seen and will ever see.

All were important, but none as important, or as crucial to James Brown's stardom, as the guys in this photo that Nafloyd Scott is holding. They were crucial to Nafloyd Scott as well.

He sits here dressed in khakis and a short jacket and sunglasses, with a black stocking cap covering his head and a handkerchief wrapped around the stocking cap. Glaucoma took his right eye eight years ago. A guy with a brick took the other.

He began with the Flames roughly in 1953 and lasted until 1957. "There's a lot that I forgot about those times," Nafloyd says. "But one thing is we craved music. We loved music. And we always gave 'em a show. No matter where we went, we always did that."

The picture sits on the table now, tucked between the ketchup, mustard, and napkin holder as Scott sits pondering the past. He's a soft-spoken, tall, rangy-looking man. His face is as smooth looking as a baby's skin. His hands are long, his fingers supple looking. Whiskey ruined his health—it ruined a lot of fellas' health in those years, he's the first to confess it. And were it not for his daughter and her husband, there's no telling where he'd be. But Nafloyd Scott always had deep talent. He could play that guitar. "My daddy always had a guitar. I'd use his guitar when I was coming up."

If one looks at Scott's early work, one could argue that he was one of the most underrated guitarists that north Georgia has ever produced. He was the original guitarist on "Please, Please, Please," the composer of the blues song "Chonnie-On-Chon," and he was the only pure instrumentalist to stay on with Brown after the group fell apart, touring with Brown as his de facto music director, teaching the songs to pickup musicians up until 1957. Even today, Scott's work on the early Flames records sounds refreshing and unique. "I was happy to do it," he says of his early recordings. "But a lot of guys wondered how I could play stuff after hearing it just one go-through. I always picked up songs fast."

If the world were just and fair, Nafloyd wouldn't be sitting in this worn-down joint eating lunch care of me and my publisher. He wouldn't have to. I wouldn't even have access to him. I'd be negotiating with his publicist, because he'd be a star. That's the raw truth of it. But that's not in his cards. Guitar is an odd instrument in the R&B genre. It's crucial to the creation of the music, but it doesn't necessarily create stars. I can think of half a dozen guitarists whose signature licks and plucks created the hooks and choruses of major pop hits that will last forever, but the players themselves are relatively unknown. Jef Lee Johnson of Philly comes to mind, the greatest guitarist I ever personally worked with. David Williams, who created the unmistakable signature groove licks in Michael Jackson's megahits "Beat It" and "Billie Jean," certainly deserves acclaim, as does Hiram Bullock. All died too young. Johnson was fifty-four, Williams was fifty-eight, and Bullock was fifty-two. And any list of great R&B guitarists will certainly include Brown's great guitar men, the ones that came after Nafloyd: Hearlon "Cheese" Martin, Alphonso "Country" Kellum, and the incomparable legend Jimmy Nolen, who basically created the category of guitar "chicken-scratch" picking. A lot of guitarists who did stints with Brown and are frequently quoted as "James Brown's guitar player" were playing Jimmy Nolen's music. They were good players. But Nolen was a master creator who cut turf.

As did Nafloyd. In the late fifties, rhythm guitar was still evolving into its own sound. Nafloyd Scott's playing is one of those key cogs that are the bridge from straight blues and country to R&B. Clean, precise, unique, and highly rhythmic.

I ask Scott about it, but like many musicians, he can't tell you what he did. "I played what I heard," he said. "I was women-crazy in those days."

He turns his head to hear the waitress's footsteps as she approaches. There's nobody inside this restaurant but our tiny table. Scott tilts his head the other way as her shoes click, as if hearing the distant clattering of history's bones.

"What you having?" he asks.

I want to say, *"The truth will do. Tell me how you've been screwed. Tell me how you created this great music and how the business has wrung you dry and taken every bit of your soul. Tell me it's somebody else's fault."* But instead I say, "Just tea. What about you?"

"Roast beef sandwich. And a Coke."

He holds his hand out for his picture after the waitress departs with the order, his hand reaching for air. I place it back in his hand. He smiles, a shy smile. He seems happy. Someone has come to see him, a voice from the dark with a New York accent, who picked him up at his house and asks him to blab about the evils of the past. I try again, and now I speak it. *"Tell me about the past,"* I say. *"Tell me how you've been screwed."*

But Nafloyd Scott has no more interest in pissing on the past than he has in the roast beef sandwich that eventually lands in front of him. He barely touches it. His mind is far from this diner, back in a Toccoa that was much different when he was young, a world of dirt roads and farms. We were high school kids, he says. We just loved to play. We lived for music, rehearsed, stayed up late to listen to *Randy Records*. The show played R&B out of a Nashville radio station. They only played R&B after eleven P.M.—that was a great thing, he says. He recalled when big black acts made rare stops in Toccoa: Rosetta Tharpe, Cab Calloway, Jimmie Lunceford, Louis Jordan. They loved the country singers, too, Tennessee Ernie Ford and Roy Acuff—just about any music, we liked, he says. "Most of the bands we heard on the radio, we never saw them play. To see them would have been a dream." To *be* them . . . well, that was beyond dreaming. That was the moon and the stars.

He remembers the jukes and the waitresses, the other musicians. "Cal Green played guitar for Midnighters. He liked the way I played. I liked the way he played." He nods, recalling the shouts of joy, the long rides in the '57 Ford, the fights, the crowds, the women, the whiskey. He smiles shyly.

. . . The whiskey.

"I'm doing fine," he says. "I feel pretty good. I'm a diabetic, but I can get my teeth pulled for free. I can go tomorrow and do that because my insurance will pay for it."

I ask him to tell me about the whiskey.

He thinks a moment, then tells a story. "I met a girl in one of those towns, when we were touring. Me and her, we went to a hotel. The next morning I got up and left out with the band. Left early in the morning while she was still asleep. Stuck her with the hotel bill. Never saw her again.

"I shouldn't a done that."

He doesn't say more, but I get it. More than fifty years later, he still remembers that sin. That's what the whiskey'll do to you.

"How we got started was in school, really from the chapel. Whitman Street school," Nafloyd says. "We played for chapel programs on Fridays." Whitman Street was the all-black school in Toccoa's segregated school system.

"James Brown went there?" I ask.

"Just for a short period. Maybe two or three months. See, James would never tell his real age, and I don't think he ever showed anybody his birth certificate. James always told me he was born in 'thirty-four. I was born in 'thirty-five. He always said he wasn't but a year older than me. He was born May the seventh, but it wasn't in 'thirty-four. It was about 'thirty or 'thirty-one, because James really was four years older than me. He wanted to pretend he wasn't but one year older than me. He never did tell the truth about how old he was. He always wanted to be the youngest out there and doing the most."

"Did he do the most?"

"He sure did. He did do the most."

The waitress returns with drinks. His hand places the picture down and he carefully reaches over to grope for his Coca-Cola with his long, slender fingers. Guitar fingers.

He produces a second picture now, this one with just James Brown and another guy holding a saxophone.

"Where's this picture from?"

"Nineteen fifty-four," he says. "It was taken down at Berry Trimier's place, way down on Barlow Street."

"What's it about?"

"I don't remember exactly," he says.

"Did y'all have a sax player?"

"No, we picked 'em up later on the road sometimes. In the beginning we couldn't afford a bass. So what James did, he got a foot tub, and turned it bottom side up, and got a slab of wood. And nailed it to the side of this tub and run the strings up from the top of that down to the tub."

He places his elbows on the table and holds his hands in the air, his slender fingers folding, his head nodding slowly, eyes hidden behind his glasses.

"Who played it?"

"James played it. Just a little something to practice on, you know. And then my brother got hold of some bass strings. He put them on his guitar and played bass on that."

"What about you?"

"My daddy always had a guitar. I'd use his guitar, and when we played these dances, we would take the money we made and put it on a set of drums or guitar or whatever we needed. And after we'd get them we divided up whatever money was left. James always said, 'We can't make our sound like Hank Ballard and the Midnighters, or Clyde McPhatter and those other groups. We have to create our own style.' Well, you know James did most of the arranging anyway."

"Did you mind?"

"We didn't mind at all."

His feels his sandwich with his fingers, lifts it, pauses to bite it, and chews slowly, his face stony, impassive behind those dark glasses. You can't even see the outline of his eyes. But his words sound heartfelt. Looking at him, I'm feeling old myself. How many times have I seen this? A black musician who never got paid. Take his head off his body and screw on another head and you'll see half my friends.

Call me naïve, but how is it that one of the richest nations in the world does so little to aid the artists whose sacrifices created one of our greatest cultural and economic exports? Corporate contributions and government taxes help provide pensions for retired classical musicians in many major cities, musicians who play the music of composers who have been certifiably dead for centuries. They get paid—not enough, certainly, but what's the difference between a guy who plays music that came from the back roads of Vienna, in 1755, and a guy who plays music that came from the back roads of Toccoa, Georgia, in 1955? The music comes from the same place: pain, suffering, joy, life. Half a click from where Nafloyd sits is the old military base where the 506th Infantry Regiment trained. That military base became the boys' prison that held James Brown, and an entire HBO series, *Band of Brothers*, was based around the experiences of those soldiers. There's a big museum nearby filled with material from the show. Wouldn't it be nice if we glorified our greatest export outside of war in the same way?

It's a story so big, and an injustice so wide, that most musicians don't fool with it, Nafloyd among them. He only remembers the good. "We would take the money that we made and buy uniforms," he says. "I remember the first red suits. We had them made in Dallas, Texas. We had a tour through Texas and Louisiana. Each city we played was pretty far apart, sometimes three hundred, four hundred miles. We'd play one night, maybe stay overnight or half a day, then ride overnight till the next morning and get us a hotel room or rooming house and sleep a few hours."

He picks up his sandwich, takes a bite, and chews slowly, remembering.

"There was a sign on the road to Baldwin, Louisiana. It said, RUN, NIGGER, IF YOU CAN READ THIS. IF YOU CAN'T READ IT, RUN ANYWAY."

He laughs.

"But I still, all my life, I always said I didn't want to live in no big city."

The memories of 1955 roll off his lips as easily as the whiskey once poured down them, because he confesses that whiskey is what threw him off. That and the women. His fingers dance around the edge of the plate as he talks, thoughtfully spinning backward, confessing to the time when he could roll with it for forty-eight hours, working on three hours of sleep, whiskey or no whiskey, when managers like Clint Brantley and artists like Little Richard and record companies like Federal and King appeared like angels with money, help, commands. Go here or there. Do this gig. Do that one. Play here. Play over there. And there was always the money—thirty-five dollars a night, more than any of them could make slinging furniture or washing cars back in Toccoa. But the road was hard. They worked their way all the way to California twice, maybe more than that, he thinks, and to more places than he can remember: Macon, Pensacola, Houston, Dallas, Fort Worth, Chicago, Detroit, New York. They burned out a '56 wood-paneled Ford station wagon like it was a rolling pin. Then they burned out another car. "One-nighters are a killer," he says.

I know the feeling. I did tours of one-nighters in my life, once in the States and once in Europe. Never again. You forget how big this world is till you drive it. And I did it in a tour bus, with ten musicians and two drivers. After a week of bouncing from one town to the next, you're exhausted. After six weeks you're ready to lose your mind. Nafloyd did it for the better part of two years, first in 1954, then from 1955 through 1957, in that Ford station wagon, without air-conditioning, in the Deep South, where they were limited in where they could stay, or eat, or go to the bathroom. They'd be burning in the summer, freezing in the winter, always searching for something to eat. They'd experience the rise of playing for the howling audiences, the fall of being the last to leave the club, trying to get your money from some slick hustler, then staring at the grim white line of the highway in the wee hours, half awake, watching the driver—often Nate Knox, brother of band member Nash Knox—fight off sleep, knowing your turn to drive is coming and you're sleepy too.

Nafloyd burned through several guitars trying to keep up: an old Sears model from his dad, then a Gibson, then a Vox. The guitars couldn't hold up to the onstage antics and being tossed from city to city, car to car. He played behind his back. He played between his legs. He tossed the instrument around. The strings busted. The pickups broke. The necks bent. The bridges gave out. As the one-nighters got harder, Nafloyd says, Brown seemed to get stronger. He was impassioned, a man on a mission. And as Brown grew more intent on pushing the band and playing more dates, some of the Flames began to falter, then fall away. As they burned from one city to another, the distances between gigs seemed to grow greater, the long drives grew harder. Arguments broke out. Some guys began to miss their families. Some began to miss dates. The Flames had to find local musicians. It fell to Nafloyd to teach the pickup musicians the songs for the one-nighters. He knew all the keys and all the grooves. "We favored G major and C minor," he says. The fellow guitarists would ask, "How can you play like that and not read no music?" "I just played what I heard," he says again. He taught them the music, and when the teaching was done and the gig was a wrap, the Flames moved on to the next town.

"When did the Flames become James Brown and the Famous Flames?" I ask him.

"In the beginning it was nothing but the Flames," he says. "I never will forget: one day we came from the Douglass Hotel in Macon up to the main house where we would all meet up. And the manager's there, and all of us are there. He said, 'How do you like these placards I made?'

"We were all together and James was standing by himself, you know. And we look at the placard and it says 'James Brown and the Famous Flames.' James looked at it. We looked straight to him with his head down. Didn't nobody like it in the beginning, but we had to do it."

"So the manager made that choice?" I said.

"I think so. But he explained it to us saying people were still coming to see the Famous Flames, but they'd be coming to see two shows. They'd be getting two for one. They'd be getting James Brown *and* the Famous Flames. So everybody finally got over that. James was due most of the credit anyway. He put on a show. We did a lot of shows with Little Richard. Little Richard didn't do nothing but stand up and play that piano and sing. But we put on a show. I played my guitar all over. I changed my strap on the shoulder. Under the leg, played like that. Throw it behind my back, play like that. Throw it behind my head, play like that. People would go crazy. And James—"

He smiled at the memory.

"You know those upright pianos? Where you've got your soundboard on top up there? James would dance and get up on top of that piano and come off that piano in a sweat. And people would go crazy for him." He chuckled. "James was something."

Scott left the band in 1957, not because James Brown was stealing the show or mistreating him. He simply wanted to come home.

Thirty-five dollars a day was good money, but after more than two years, he'd had enough of the road.

He came home and watched life shove past him with the speed of a passing car. These days he lives with his daughter in Toccoa in a neat, simple house with lots of religious artifacts. With the exception of a brief stint in Pensacola, Florida, he's been in Toccoa all his life.

"What's your favorite song?" I ask.

"Well, James wrote most of them. But my favorite, the beat I like, I think, is 'Chonnie-On-Chon.' It's got my name on it. I never hear no royalties out of it though, so I guess it never did make no hit. I remember one time after I had quit the band, I was talking to James in Pensacola. James told me if I could find any one of the old records with my name on it, he could get me somewhere around $25,000. But I never found one with my name on it."

"Did you see him after you left the band?" I ask.

"Sure. Saw him through the years many a day. Anytime he'd come through to Toccoa he'd always come see me. Me and Nash Knox. He'd send his son Terry to fetch us. Or he'd come see us by hisself. One time I was at my house on Whitman Street. That's when he was driving that white Cadillac. He drove up there and so many people came out, he said, 'Meet me down at Velma's house. They ain't gonna turn me loose.'

"So I went on down there to Prather Bridge Road and met him at Velma's. They wouldn't turn him loose up there on Whitman Street. See, James was too good to some folks.

"He always gave a little something when he came by here. He didn't want to give it in front of the people because they couldn't stop asking him for stuff. He was always generous with me. Even when I moved to Pensacola. He was down there playing, and after the show I went backstage to see him. I told them [the security guards] who I was and he said, 'Git him back here.' He was always glad to see me."

The sandwich sits with two bites gone, barely eaten. It's the dead hour between lunch and dinner, and this place was already dead when we walked in. Nafloyd seems tired. "Is that enough?" he asks. "I'll take the sandwich home. Wanna get back home before that sugar gets down on me."

We chat a bit more as we prepare to leave. "I feel like you're just trying to say good things about James Brown," I say. "You don't have to."

Nafloyd raises his head and stares off. His shades are a mask; his expression is a blank. He smiles a small, sad smile. "James don't need my protection," he says.

The sandwich arrives in a bag and the waitress hands it to me. I slip it into Nafloyd's hand, the one without the pictures in it. He crinkles it in his slim fingers and says, "You gonna run me home?"

"Yeah, man."

He stands facing the empty street of the town that no longer knows him. There's the museum nearby filled with memorabilia from the HBO series about war, in a town that has a spring fest and a summer fest, and a train museum, and every other kind of celebration of the past good life, but little celebration for the local black musicians whose lives and music are folded into the annals of world cultural history. We move toward the door, him holding my elbow with one hand and his roast beef sandwich with the other. Outside, the fresh air hits him and he stops. Something occurs to him.

"One time James come right out here on Seventeenth and Quincy. He came and got me and took me in the bathroom and gave me fifteen one-hundred-dollar bills. He said, 'Put it in your pocket.' One thousand and five hundred dollars. And guess what he said. He said, 'Nafloyd, you better quit drinking that whiskey.' He smelled it on my breath."

He laughs, a light easy laugh, and we move toward the car.

Three years later, on August 15, 2015, he would be dead at age eighty, broke, his family getting financial help to bury him from a friend and James Brown's grandson William. And thus the last Flame, the last original Flame, is gone.

Chapter 10

The Rev

The Lincoln Town Cars and black SUVs are lined up from the corner of Fifty-Third Street and Fifth Avenue all the way to Sixth Avenue. The Grand Havana Room cigar club is upstairs in this shiny building and I can't find parking. Trouble is, I'm riding my bike and there's no place to lock it up. The black, double-parked cars on the street don't have that problem. They have waiting drivers. I guess they don't have many bike riders pedaling up to the Havana cigar club who need to lock up their bikes, and why should they? This is a smoker's joint. A private outfit. No hipsters. No cyclists. Women? Not very many that I saw, anyway. This is a tobacco lover's club, where the big boys come to eat, toke, and chew Havana cigars. This is where Rev. Al Sharpton comes to eat.

I watch from my bike as he cuts across the windy street like a ghost, slipping past the double-parked SUVs with the ease of a cat burglar and into the building. I find a good spot and quickly lock my bike up and sprint to catch him, which takes some speed. This is our second meeting, and he nods as he sees me coming, slowing only for a second as I slip into the elevator with him. I'm winded, but he's breathing easy. He moves like a wisp of smoke, quick and slim, 162 pounds lighter than he was in years past, looking smooth and fit in a long black wool-mohair coat, suit and tie beneath it. He punches the elevator button and looks up to watch the monitor . . . 1 . . . 2 . . . 3. . . . He bears no pad, pencil, or notebook, even though, technically, he's a reporter. He's just come from doing his talk show on MSNBC on this chilly February night. Two passengers in the elevator eye him. One of them blurts out, "Hey, Rev."

"Evening," he says. The greeting is friendly and warm.

The elevator arrives and he enters the smoky club. The coat-check lady knows him. The guys at the bar wave. Another fellow across the room waves a greeting. He eases into the room, nodding here and there, and takes a seat on a comfortable couch with a coffee table, just as he does most evenings after his telecast, to chow down on veggies, chomp on a cigar, and talk on his cellphone with the power brokers of the world.

Just as the Rev sits, his cellphone rings.

"Hey . . ."

As he talks, the other folks in the club, mostly white men, eye him out of the corners of their eyes. A couple of white guys in suits drift by, lollygagging to take a closer look, smiling, as if to say, *Is that Reverend Sharpton?* Twenty-five years ago, these same guys would have backed off him like he was a two-headed Godzilla. In the old days, when he wore jogger suits, sneakers, and gold medallions, back when he tossed New York City on its ear by pulling back the thick quilt of northern liberalism to reveal the institutionalized racism underneath, he was despised. One of the jokes floating around New York back then went like this: *You're in a room with Hitler, Saddam Hussein, and Al Sharpton. You only have two bullets. Who do you shoot? Al Sharpton. Twice.*

This is the guy who took a knife in the chest while marching in Bensonhurst, Brooklyn, to protest the 1989 murder of Yusef Hawkins, a young African American killed by a group of white men; this is the guy who ran for the Democratic nomination for the U.S. presidential election in 1994; who defended a teenager named Tawana Brawley through an infamous lie, in which she claimed she was gang-raped by a group of white men. This is the guy who served time in federal prison for protesting naval bombing experiments on Vieques, Puerto Rico; who stood alone with Michael Jackson against what he considered trumped-up child-molestation charges when no one else in Hollywood would. Sharpton has been sued, stabbed, slimed on, marched on, spat at, hustled, and hated, but he's still here, an easy, grooving 138 pounds of slim, a far cry from the nearly three-hundred-pound fireplug in the James Brown hairdo that once bedeviled the New York media. The same city officials who twenty years ago would reach for the phone to call the cops when Sharpton showed up drop to their knees when he appears these days, hoping to God that whoever created the great sin that brought him to town in the first place will either plop down dead or fall off a bridge someplace. Sharpton wields that kind of influence. He is one of the most powerful black men in America.

And a creation, in part, of one James Brown.

He will tell me that himself tonight, and on subsequent nights, over the course of three hours and a few cigars. That and more. The years they traveled, when Brown was broke, his business collapsing, his private jets confiscated, his radio stations gone, the IRS breathing down his throat, the insufferable weekly drives Sharpton undertook from New York City to South Carolina to see Brown when he was in prison. He was a living witness to Brown's indomitable will, which kept the old man afloat when everyone else considered him finished, polished off by the advent of disco. But before the Rev talks, he must eat. He's hungry. He looks tired. He should have been here eating an hour ago, but he had to do an appearance at CNN after his own MSNBC show was done. "I owed somebody over there a favor," he says.

He orders as he's talking on the cell, and the waitress disappears.

She returns instantly with food, all lightly cooked veggies. No more chicken for this preacher.

The Rev hangs up his phone. He pulls the plate closer. He picks up his fork. It's time to eat.

Just then, a young white man in a suit appears, hovering over him with a pen and a piece of paper. "Hey, Rev? Can I get an autograph?"

You can see he'd like to eat. The man is hungry. But before he became Rev. Al Sharpton, the civil rights hell-raiser, or Rev. Sharpton of MSNBC, he was just plain Rev, a teenage preacher sitting at the feet of the Godfather, listening to the lessons the old man taught him in those hard, lean years. It's a voice that still rings in his head: *You fought all your life to be known, and you're mad at the people knowing you? You don't have time to sign an autograph? You don't have time to talk to people? Who made you?*

The Rev puts his fork down, reaches for the pen, signs the autograph, then chats with the guy for several minutes as his food gets cold, listening patiently as the guy tells some corny story about nothing. Finally the guy leaves, happy.

The Rev turns to his food, his expression blank. The warm veggies are cold. The tea is too. He reaches for his fork and tosses some veggies into his mouth. "Everything I am today," he says, "a lot of it, is because of James Brown. The most important lessons I learned, I learned from him. He was like my father. He was the father I never had."

Spin back the clock to New York City in the 1960s, before a delightful Jewish mayor named Ed Koch walked the streets joking and asking, "How'm I doin'?" When Staten Island was still called Richmond and the South Bronx was newly decimated, destroyed by urban planner Robert Moses's Cross Bronx Expressway, which ran through its heart like a butcher knife, sending working-class families fleeing to the suburbs. Back then, Queens was suburban bliss, for black families anyway, most of whom had backpedaled there from Brooklyn and Harlem.

Even Manhattan was different tundra, much of it rough land. The Upper West Side was a place where you could get your head bonked in. Times Square was a run-for-your-life situation, with whorehouses and X-rated strip and video joints; and over in Hell's Kitchen, Irish and Italian mobsters were hard at work killing each other—rumor has it that the gangsters cut up corpses at the bar downstairs from the beaten flat at Forty-Third and Tenth where I write these words. New York was a fifteen-cent subway ride to a world spookier than voodoo. It got worse in the seventies. Drive out of the Lincoln Tunnel in those years and a squeegee guy with a face that looked like a combination wire hanger and mop would suddenly appear, covering your windshield with glop and spit, daring you to pull off without dropping a quarter in his hand, which looked like you could get tuberculosis from just looking at it. New York was funky. That was Alfred Sharpton's New York. It was mine as well. We're close to the same age.

Sharpton grew up in Brooklyn, got a taste of middle-class life in Hollis, Queens, for a short spurt, then later was swooped back into the urban jungle of Brooklyn after his father abandoned his mother. He was a boy preacher at Washington Temple Church of God in Christ, one of the oldest and largest in Brooklyn, a child phenomenon who gave his first sermon at the age of four, steeped deep in the soup of black religion. He toured with gospel great Mahalia Jackson at age eleven and was tutored by Adam Clayton Powell, Jr., as a kid. In the sixties, when he was a teenager, he was swept up by the civil rights movement, but he was an outsider. Most of his teen friends were black nationalists or Panthers, but Bible preaching and the gospel did not sit well with the little red Mao books that soul brothers were carting around Brooklyn in those revolutionary days, particularly his conservative bent of Pentecostal holiness. Sports? Football? Basketball? He avoided those. His gift was his tongue.

He joined Rev. Jesse Jackson's Operation Breadbasket at age thirteen, then joined Operation PUSH (People United to Save Humanity), but the ultrareligious Pentecostals trusted neither Martin Luther King nor the black radicals like Malcolm X—in those days New York

City was Malcolm X's town—nor the white kids who wore SDS buttons and were screaming against the Vietnam War. Sharpton admired both King and Malcolm X; he shared common ground with all of the radical movements, yet fit with none of them. How do you follow God in a world that is gray? What do you do when black power turns out to be a cobweb of continual adjustment, where the Baptists like King and Jesse Jackson looked down their noses at the Pentecostals like him—even as they needed a young voice like his? He saw no space for himself, so he created his own.

Guess who was the guy who showed him how to do it?

"I met Mr. Brown when I was seventeen," Sharpton tells me. The previous year, he says, PUSH fell apart, and so in 1971 he started his National Youth Movement, a voter-registration outfit. Brown's oldest son, Teddy, joined that movement, and the two were friends for about a year until Teddy's sudden death. At that time, a local New York DJ named Hank Spann introduced Sharpton to Brown during an event at the old RKO Albee Theatre in downtown Brooklyn, to honor Teddy and get black youth to register to vote.

Even now, forty years later, Sharpton, a master of the sound bite, a man who rarely shows his true face, who will keel over before he shows hurt in public, mists a bit sentimental as he pushes back into the memories of his first actual conversation with Brown. They met at a Newark theater to discuss the upcoming voter-registration concert, before a scheduled Brown performance. Just before the curtain rose, Sharpton was ushered into a backstage dressing room. Standing there, combing his hair in front of a mirror, was the Godfather himself. I asked Sharpton, "Were you floored?"

"Are you kidding? The only recreation I ever did with my mother and father was we'd go see Jackie Wilson and James Brown every year at the Apollo. When I met Adam Clayton Powell, I felt I had met the man close to God. When I met James Brown, I thought I had met God. It was like that. I was swept up."

Brown was very abrupt and businesslike. "He looked at me full, said, 'What do you want to be, son?'"

"I said, 'Excuse me?'

"'What do you want to be?'

"'Well, I'm in civil rights.'

"'I'm gonna show you how you get the whole hog.'

"'Excuse me?'

"'Gonna show you how to get the whole hog. But you gotta think big like me. I'm going to make you bigger than big. You got to do exactly what I say. Can you do that?'"

Half of it Sharpton didn't understand. It would take him a year before he could translate the South Carolina twang and rat-tat-tat of Brown's garbled, fast-and-furious delivery, terms that sounded half crocked and some made-up. But he heard the magic words: *I'm going to make you bigger than big.* Sharpton agreed to do exactly as Brown said.

Brown gave him instructions on how to promote the upcoming voter-registration show. Sharpton, still a teenager, walked out of the room thinking, *I've never promoted anything in my whole life.* A show was not church. A show was not a sermon. A show involved tickets, and money, and businessmen—promoters—who wanted their money back if things didn't work out. And fights, maybe. And cops sometimes. This wasn't some change-the-world rap session with brothers who wore MAO buttons, or some heart-to-heart conversation with his white classmates who marched around hollering about Vietnam. It wasn't anything like preaching under the protective arm of the minister of his home church, who treated him with love and kindness. This was real money. Real business. And if you screwed up, well . . .

He decided he wouldn't screw up. The kid got busy. He spent the next few weeks posting signs, seeking out promoters, calling on radio disc jockeys and volunteers, hustling up customers for a James Brown concert in Brooklyn to register blacks to vote. He called on friends, neighbors, friends of friends, hustlers, scoundrels, militants, church parishioners, and teenagers like himself who were wild about James Brown. He hauled posters and tape and staple guns around on the subway, and on the bus—for he would never learn to drive himself—

hanging up posters in East New York and Bed-Stuy, Jamaica, St. Albans, Hollis, and Harlem, declaring far and wide: *James Brown is coming to Brooklyn! Come see him. Come register to vote.*

A few months later, Brown came back to play the event. Sharpton, not knowing how ticket sales were going, walked into the RKO Albee and saw a full house. He was summoned backstage again and ushered into the RKO dressing room to wait for Brown. When Brown walked in, he didn't look at Sharpton. Instead, he looked at his manager, Charles Bobbit.

"How'd he do, Mr. Bobbit?"

"Mr. Brown, the kid did all right."

"What do you mean, Mr. Bobbit?"

"He sold out both shows."

Brown turned to Sharpton. "You did everything I told you?"

"Yes sir, Mr. Brown."

Brown nodded, clearly pleased. Without another word, he turned on his heel, marched out onto the stage, and his band hit. Sharpton watched from backstage as Brown wowed the audience in his first show. Between shows, he was summoned to Brown's dressing room again and found his idol sitting with his hair in curlers under a hair dryer. Brown shouted out at him from under the dryer, unable to hear Sharpton's responses. Now Sharpton could barely make out what he was saying because of the blowing hair dryer, but followed along as best he could.

"Son, you know how I made it?"

"No sir."

"I was an original. There was nothing like me before me. If you're scared to be an original, tell me now. We won't waste no time."

"I was a boy preacher, Mr. Brown."

"What does that mean?"

Sharpton shouted out the answers over the noise of the hair dryer, telling Brown he was born with the Word in his heart, that he could preach before he could read, that he was always different from his

classmates, that he wanted justice for those who didn't have it. "I want
to be like Jesse Jackson—"

Brown cut him off. "No you don't," he said. "You don't wanna be
the next Jesse Jackson. You want to be the first Al Sharpton. It's something special you got, but listen to me. My own kids don't listen to me.
If you listen to me you can do this all over the country. You can register voters, real young people, 'cause those guys out there in civil rights
ain't got no heart. You're a kid from Brooklyn, you got heart. But you
got to be different."

Brown left New York, returned two weeks later, and summoned
Sharpton, telling him, "Pack your bags. We're going to LA."

Sharpton packed his things, climbed aboard Brown's private plane,
and didn't come back to New York for fifteen years. He left New York
City as Alfred Charles Sharpton, a seventeen-year-old boy-wonder
preacher. He returned as Rev. Al Sharpton—the Rev—one of the most
powerful, charismatic, controversial, and unique figures in African
American history. The friendship would last the rest of Brown's life.

There are many great creative alliances that have existed in the American artistic diaspora. Stephen Sondheim and Leonard Bernstein, the
creators of the great Broadway classic *West Side Story,* come to mind.
The Miles Davis Quintet, featuring John Coltrane with Cannonball
Adderley, is another. Miles and Gil Evans. Sinatra and Basie. Conductor Eugene Ormandy and the Philadelphia Orchestra is one of my
personal favorites. But there is nothing in American history like the
collaborative mix of Al Sharpton and James Brown.

It is a collaboration that defies easy explanation, and one that is
easily overlooked by Brown's historians, most of whom are commercial music writers and not stupid enough, like me, to attempt to explain the amorphous blend of black politics, culture, and music that
helped shape the man. Amiri Baraka in *Blues People,* Guthrie Ramsey
in *Race Music,* Teresa Reed in *The Holy Profane,* and Samuel Floyd in

The Power of Black Music are among those who have done it to greater effect than I ever can. But here is my layman's view:

The entertainment world and politics are more similar than most realize. Every time I go to Los Angeles I am astounded by the similarities between Hollywood and Washington, DC: Money. Power. Influence. Sex. Scandals. Parties. Phoniness. Posturing. Communication as an aphrodisiac. The only difference, it seems, is that in LA the folks are prettier, whereas in DC, they pick your pocket with one hand while saluting the flag with the other. But the basics are the same: business and power. Trying to cram yourself into the tight keyhole of power and fame in either world is hard no matter what your color, and black Americans who manage to squeeze into that tight space are often deadlier than their white counterparts when it comes to slashing those coming up behind them. America likes its black stars one at a time: Barry White or Marvin Gaye, Bill Cosby or Flip Wilson, Sammy Davis or Johnny Mathis, which makes the numbers game a bad one. At his height, in the sixties and seventies, Brown saw himself as a one-man hit machine versus Motown and its powerful cadre of heavy hitters, with each side clamoring to get into white radio, where the giant money was. There were others whom Brown competed against: Jackie Wilson, Joe Tex, Little Willie John, whom he admired, Isaac Hayes, Gamble and Huff, the O'Jays, the Spinners, and Teddy Pendergrass. But the two heavyweights, the Ali vs. Frazier of the record business, were at least for a time Motown versus James Brown. They were the big horses. And both could run hard.

In that crude paradigm, Brown was Joe Frazier, the thundering, dark-skinned heavy hitter out of the North Philly ghetto, and Motown was Muhammad Ali, the light, right, sweet-talking kid from Louisville, Kentucky, who was outrageously interesting and who painted Frazier unfairly as an Uncle Tom. Brown was not fond of Berry Gordy and his Motown crew. He respected Gordy, but deep down he felt resentment toward the light, bright, educated, acceptable-to-white-folk folks that Berry and Motown seemed to represent. The trials and sufferings of the deeply talented Diana Rosses, Smokey

Robinsons, Gladys Knights, Stevie Wonders, the brilliant Motown songwriting teams like Ashford and Simpson, the unsung sidemen like bassist James Jamerson, all of whom paid their dues, did not move him. Brown had climbed to stardom through the Mount Everest of routes, the chitlin circuit, beating off hard-swinging southern competitors like Little Willie John, Joe Tex, the Midnighters, and Little Richard, performers who could pummel your head musically on the bandstand—and some, like Jackie Wilson, who could pummel your head off of it. Brown always felt like a cornpone southerner to his northern black counterparts, who, he believed, had been tricked by the northern white man's cleverly veiled racism. His manager Buddy Dallas, a white southerner, tells the story that in 1988 Brown was staying in the Presidential Suite at the Beverly Hills Hotel in LA while comedian Bill Cosby also happened to be staying there. Cosby, who grew up in the tough neighborhood of North Philadelphia, sent up a plate of collard greens to Brown's room as a joke. Brown was furious. "I'm gonna take these greens to his room and shove them up his ass," Brown said. Dallas had to talk him down.

Brown's prejudice against the likes of someone like Cosby, who was more educated, refined, and somehow a more "light-skinned" or "accepted" Negro, stayed with him his entire life.

Sharpton was a political version of Brown's music, but more versatile. He reflected Martin Luther King's religiosity but favored Malcolm X's directness. Sharpton preached the Word, but unlike the conservative Pentecostals for whom politics was kryptonite, he went at it with the guts of a Brooklyn gangster. Sharpton was young, unafraid, funny, and able to go 360 degrees in ways that Brown could not. With his satin tongue, he could talk to a CEO or play the dozens with Brown's gang of yes-men. Brown surrounded himself with men he trusted—they were mostly men—who were like him: southern, country, tolerant. They were admiring of his idiosyncrasies, willing to eat what he ate, live like he lived, and believe what he believed. Says Brown's son Terry, "He trained you to keep it tight. Don't talk. Do. And watch the money." Many, like Brown, packed .38-caliber pistols in their britches and were not afraid to shoot: Baby James, Henry Stallings, Brown's cousin Willie Glen, and Johnny Terry, who served time in juvenile with Brown and worked as a Famous Flame for a stint. They were generally loyal, hard men. The record business was a rough game, and Brown needed protection. When he showed up at a venue, he usually wanted a certain amount of cash up front. No matter what the problem at the venue was, or who the promoter was, or what the money deal was, if James Brown showed up and the promoter did not have that bag of 50 percent of ticket sales—thirty or forty grand or sometimes more, in cash, Brown's favorite line to the promoter was, "Can you sing _____?" and he'd name a song.

The answer was invariably "No."

"Well, you will be singing it if my money's not here."

During the late seventies, as Sharpton remembers it, the mob had a strong hand in the music business, and when Brown came to New York to play his favorite venue, Harlem's Apollo Theater, certain mobsters, Sharpton remembers, would call Brown and make offers. "They'd say, 'Jimmy'—those types called him 'Jimmy'—'Jimmy, do you need a loan of thirty grand to help you along? We can help you out, keep your show running smooth. Pay us back when you can.'" Brown always refused. When they threatened to beat him down, or release rats into the theater and let them run through the crowd during his Apollo shows, Brown said, "Let 'em," and sent his hit squad, Baby James, Henry Stallings, and other guys who, Brown boasted, would kill a man for a thousand dollars, into the audience with orders to watch the room and deal with all comers. He often felt cornered in the North, a place where some promoters and radio stations, for example, took his payoffs—pretty common in those days—and refused to play his music. At bottom he felt America's North was more racist than the South, a belief tested years later by Sharpton, who pushed New York City to near madness with his protests. Brown's response to northern racism was to carefully select men who were blank slates and shape them into a kind of army that shared his own ideas. Charles Bobbit, Brown's personal manager and a former member of the Nation of Islam, was one of those, as was Brown's younger son Terry. Those two were sharp operators, men not formally educated to the highest order but with minds like bilge pumps, men who could walk into a room and suck the details out of it in seconds, learn who owned what, who did what, who owed whom, then figure out exit strategies and angles to survive. Terry worked for his dad on and off during Brown's great success years, selling radio ads and handling Brown's money and discreet elements, but father-son arguments kept Terry clear at times. Bobbit was a loyal soldier for a good part of four decades. But Brown's greatest child, his greatest invention outside of his music, his greatest contribution to the social fabric of America, may well not be a song, but rather his ability to identify a young man who was hungry, talented, willing to take orders; bold, cunning, quick on his feet; and who could recognize the intricate twists and turns of race in America well enough to take on all comers. Rev. Al Sharpton is the class A, the summa cum laude graduate, of the James Brown school of thought.

"You gotta remember, me growing up in the sixties and seventies, he was more than just a hot artist to me," Sharpton explains. "He was black history. He was so in control of himself. I never met anybody that had that kind of controlling presence. This sounds crazy, but James Brown had such a presence and charisma, you could almost feel him coming in the building. He dominated every room he walked in, and I'm one of the few people who's been in the room with him in the White House with Reagan and Bush, and in his jail cell. It didn't matter. It was his self-confidence. It was his spirit. It was a gift he had. He dominated."

One of the first events that Brown took Sharpton to was a gig at Caesars Palace in Las Vegas on a bill that featured Aretha Franklin, Barry White, and several other top black artists. The two arrived in Vegas at two A.M. in Brown's private jet, only to find that the Presidential Suite was occupied. Brown kicked up a fuss until the hotel moved whoever was in that suite out. Sharpton, who had never seen anything like the Presidential Suite and the first-class treatment that Brown received, was aching to stay on the casino floor and have some fun with the stars, who were eating and fraternizing over the slots and card game, but instead Brown summoned Sharpton to his suite.

Brown asked Sharpton, "You been downstairs?"

"Yeah."

"You see any of the artists when you were downstairs?"

"Yeah, a few are down there gambling and all," Sharpton said, itching to go back down there himself.

"You know what we're gonna do, Reverend?"

"What?"

"What time is the gig tonight?"

"I think you go on about ten."

"Good. We're gonna sit right here. Ain't nobody going to see James Brown till it's time to hit. Everybody else down there, they're being common. Don't be common, Rev. They'll be gambling with people all day. We stay here. Let's call some more disc jockeys."

They worked all day and into the night, "calling disc jockeys," Sharpton recalls. "To make sure they were playing his records. I was miserable."

At eight P.M., Sharpton recalls, "Brown went downstairs and talked to the promoter. The guy said, 'We're honored to have you, Mr. Brown, blah blah—' Mr. Brown cut him off. 'What's the rundown?' he asked. 'Who's first?'

"The guy told Brown that he appeared in the middle of the show.

"'Oh, you can't put me in the middle. You'll put me last. 'Cause when I finish, that's the end of the show.'" The guy agreed.

Brown turned to Sharpton. "Rev, I'm gonna eat 'em alive."

When the music began, Sharpton stood in the wings and watched the other artists perform their shows. "When they introduced James Brown, the band hit, and I'll never forget it," Sharpton says. "He grabbed the mic and threw it, and I'm waiting for him to catch it on his shoulder when he jumps back and grabs it with his hand, and jumps *into* the audience, in between two tables, and does a perfect split. Comes up and pulls the mic down. It was over."

After turning the place on its ear, Brown went through his ritual of having his hair done backstage under the hair dryer, then rose to head back to his suite while the other stars attended an after-party. "It gets worse," Sharpton says. "When we got to his suite—people congratulating him the whole way—he says to Mr. Bobbit, 'Get the plane ready. We're leaving.'"

"Tonight?" Sharpton said. "We just got here."

"Lemme tell you something, Rev. When you kill 'em, Rev, you leave. You kill 'em and leave. You understand that, son? Kill 'em and leave."

They hopped on the private plane and flew to Los Angeles. And they proceeded that way for the next fifteen years.

"Normal life to him didn't exist," says Sharpton. "Jesse [Jackson] and them's status was to get on the A-list. James Brown's status was there wasn't no A-list. *He* was the list. He said, 'Reverend, if I got to compromise to make it, I'm not rising. I'm somebody else rising. I got to be me. I rise on my own terms. That's how I made it the first time. That's how I'll make it back, or I don't have to get back.' And that's what he ingrained in me—success was you making it as you were, not changing who you were to make it."

For a good part of Brown's greatest years, 1971 to 1975, Sharpton rode shotgun with Brown. And then in his career-declining years, from 1975 to 1984 and on, the Rev hung on as well. In the good years, the band traveled by bus while Brown flew in a private plane. The band dreaded flying with Brown, because it was a one-way conversation: he talked, you listened. You ate what he ate. You went where he went. Trombonist and film scorer Fred Wesley, Brown's great musical director and co-composer, laughs aloud when he recalls having to travel in Brown's plane to work on a score or work out ideas with Brown. "Just dreadful," he says. "I'd be crying to get back on the bus." But Sharpton loved traveling with Brown.

"The band would be plotting to get away from him," Sharpton says. "Literally. And I would think something was wrong with them. I wanted to drink all that he was willing to give me."

Sharpton changed his hairstyle to emulate Brown's. "I've had big arguments with people about 'Why did you always defer to him?' Let me tell you something. He was not only a father. People that grow up like I did—a father that was a businessman, then abandoned us, going from middle class, which for the black you were what they call "negro rich," to nothing—you develop, even unknowingly, complexes on 'Why did my father leave me even if he didn't get along with my mother?' I was named after my father, all that. James Brown validated and affirmed my worth, so he could never do no wrong to me. That was part of our relationship. We validated each other. He made me feel self-worth and self-esteem, knowing that a man that enormous wanted me to reflect him—because my own father didn't. And I think for him, I validated what he wanted to be seen as: a big historical person. I believed that about him. So when I said there are four B's in music: Bach, Beethoven, Brahms, and Brown, he knew I really meant it."

Here was a man who could, and did, blow off meeting the Rolling Stones, the Red Hot Chili Peppers, and, if he wasn't in a mood to meet them, dignitaries of all stripes, high and low. According to Sharpton, Brown met President Richard Nixon with his trusty .38 in his coat pocket. When Brown played Zaire in Africa as part of the gala preceding the great Ali–George Foreman fight, with the world watching and the cream of black entertainment in tow, Brown knocked the socks off eighty thousand roaring and screaming fans. He told Sharpton after the performance, "Pack up. We're leaving."

Sharpton didn't want to leave. He wanted to stay with the other entertainers who had come to revel in the pending fight, which was postponed because of an injury Foreman sustained. Besides, President Mobutu of Zaire, a country rich in diamonds, had made it known that he wanted to impart certain gifts to the performers. Brown had no interest.

"But Mr. Brown," Sharpton protested, "we just got here."

"Kill 'em and leave, Rev. Kill 'em and leave."

And kill 'em and leave he did, knocking 'em dead from one city to the next, as the Rev watched, for thirty-five years. What was the point, Brown said, trying to play big. Just *be* big. When disco chased Brown off the radar and his popularity slipped, his great band departed, but Sharpton stayed. He watched Brown fall from superstar playing Madison Square Garden to an oldies act, playing blues clubs for $5,000 per night, working without a record deal, with a new band, the Soul Generals, playing his old hits at high speed, with white background dancers dressed in red, white, and blue pirouetting across the stage like pom-pom girls at a Dallas Cowboys football game. Promoters abandoned him; the IRS cleaned him out. He lost his private plane, his radio stations; the women he had used and in some cases abused terribly began to fight back with lawsuits. His drug problems, which he'd always hidden from the Rev, led him to jail. Yet the Rev stayed, traveling by car two or three times a month from New York to South Carolina to see Brown, drumming up public support to get him out of his jail. Sharpton loved Brown, not only as a father, but as a man who could stand up and take it and not knuckle or beg. When Brown, in the nineties, had no record deal, he sought record-deal financing from promoter Don King. King declined, saying he didn't know the record business, but he offered Brown $10,000 as a gift. Brown refused it. "I ain't asking for charity," he said.

He had lost his juice, really. He'd spent his entire career compartmentalizing everyone: Band members here. Payoff guy there. Women there. White managers here. Black managers there. Black friends here. White friends there. Wives. Girlfriends. It all collapsed around him. And when he looked up one day, most of them were gone. The only ones left were the old-timers: Charles Bobbit, Leon Austin, and, of course, the Rev.

In May 2005, when the city of Augusta constructed a bronze James Brown statue on its downtown Broad Street, Brown invited Sharpton, who by then had become a national figure, to come to speak. After the event, when the two were walking to Brown's car, Brown grabbed Sharpton by the elbow.

"You know what I love about you, Rev?"

"What's that, Mr. Brown?"

"You were the only one who didn't leave me. All the others left. But you stayed. You stayed, Rev."

I remember the Sharpton of those years and beyond. I first laid eyes on him in 1984, when I attended my first-ever LA press conference in Encino, California, when Michael Jackson announced his 1984 Victory Tour. I had never been to LA before, had never seen the glitz and glamour, the cheapness and wildness of the place. The press conference was held in Jackson's driveway, as I recall, and among the cadre of promoters who stood before the press—Chuck Sullivan, then owner of the New England Patriots; Don King; Michael's manager Frank DiLeo—stood the then-infamous Al Sharpton, with his trademark sweat suit and wild hair in the James Brown pompadour. He traveled as part of the six-month tour, but I don't remember much of what he said. I rarely spoke to him during the tour. I was a reporter back then, and I couldn't socialize with sources, especially one as controversial as Sharpton. But I do distinctly remember one thing he said during the course of the Victory Tour, and he said it often: "I'm here because of James Brown." He said, "I'm here to look after Michael Jackson's interests because James Brown sent me." I was pretty naïve in those days, but not naïve enough to say what I really thought, which was, "This guy is full of it."

Turns out what he said was true. He had been sent there by Brown to help Michael out. Long after that tour ended, Sharpton was one of the few in politics or entertainment who stood with Jackson when Michael—as kind a person as I've ever met in the entertainment business—was accused, and later acquitted, of child-molestation charges. Jackson never forgot James Brown's kindness for sending his right-hand man to stand with him in his troubled times. And he would repay the kindness to Brown many years later.

Chapter 11

The Money Man

He steps inside the tattered screen door of Brooker's soul food restaurant in Barnwell, South Carolina, like he owns it. And in a way, he does. He's an old-timer. Miss Iola, working behind the counter, looks up and waves. She runs the joint with her sister, and she called him the night before at home and told him the deal:

"Liver tomorrow," she said. "Come before it gets gone."

That's all he needed to hear. "I come every time," he jokes. "She doesn't have to call twice."

Miss Iola smiles as he approaches the counter. He's a heavyset man, in a collar shirt, with thick glasses. He looks like a lawyer, or an accountant, or a salesman, and he's the only white guy in a room of black folks. Not a safe place to be. That's what a lawyer told him just before he went to prison: "The blacks in prison will kill you." But they didn't kill him. In fact, many of the men respected him. Some even asked for his advice. A couple asked for his autograph, which had never happened to him before. He moved among those black folks like he moves among them in this diner today, with ease and comfort, because he's home. He knows these people. Some are his neighbors. He goes to church with a few. His name is David Cannon. He's James Brown's accountant. James Brown's Money Man.

Cannon takes his tray from the counter and moves to a simple picnic table in the crowded room. The normal buzz of eating goes right on. He places his tray on the table and checks its contents: Collards. Yams. Mac and cheese. A bit of chicken. Sweet lemonade. And, of course, that delicious liver. "Best liver in Barnwell," he says, unfolding his paper napkin.

"When did you come here last?" I ask. I'd met Cannon many times before, but this is the first time I've seen him in public. He has to wear an ankle monitor that prevents him from leaving home at certain hours.

But he's gone. I'm sitting right across the table from him, but he's not listening. His eyes are closed. His head is bowed in prayer.

Cannon prays aloud, thanking God for his food, his health, for his wife, Maggie, and his freedom. And while he's praying, I'm peeking out of one eye and worrying about my own skin. Because I've spent quite a bit of time with this guy, and I like him. He's a straight talker, a Christian, a good old boy, a dues-paying member of the Republican Party, the only guy James Brown trusted with his money—and that says a lot, because Brown trusted practically no one with his chips. But Brown died with millions in assets and left most of his money not to his offspring, or their families, but to poor children. And some of those family members didn't like it. They rallied, smelling big cheese. They needed a flunky. Somebody to blame. There, big as day, sat David Cannon, the perfect villain. A southern white man, a Republican, the guy who handled Mr. Brown's money. Cannon was blindsided. After forty years of building a career as a respected accountant, he found his name and picture plastered across the Internet under headlines full of half-truths—then was committed to jail for a crime that has never been proven in anyone's court.

I stare at him as he fervently prays, eyes closed. And I wonder. This guy's life has been effectively destroyed by the plethora of lawsuits following Brown's death. His wife tried to commit suicide twice. His son was murdered four days before he was sentenced. His ex-wife died the same day in a motor vehicle accident rushing to her son's side. Most of his life savings were spent on legal fees.

Yet the guy is thanking God from the bottom of his heart.

I snap from my reverie and find Cannon staring at me. From the fog of my own head, I hear him say, "How come you're not having liver?"

"I'm not big on liver."

"Then you're missing out," he says, munching heartily. "If you taste this, you won't find a thing to complain about it, I'll guarantee you that."

He eats, lustily, as if it's the last meal he'll ever eat, while I sit there thinking, *Only God can stand a man up this way.*

And I'm grateful to see it.

By 1984, Brown's career was in the tank. Disco had swallowed him. His once-great band—made up of Maceo Parker, Fred Wesley, Pee Wee Ellis, Sweet Charles Sherrell, Jimmy Nolen, Richard "Kush" Griffith, Joe Davis, St. Clair Pinckney, Clyde Stubblefield, and Jabo Starks, among others—was history. Michael Jackson was King of Pop. Every business idea Brown had come up with was going kaplooey or had already gone splat. The great James Brown organization, with offices in New York and Augusta, was gone. His three radio stations were sold by creditors. His soul food restaurant chain, Gold Platter, was kaput. His green-stamps idea had tanked. His plane had been repossessed. A nightclub he'd built with an old friend, Third World, was mysteriously burned to the ground and the arsonists never caught. And most critically, he owed $15 million to the IRS, which had a chokehold on his affairs and had seized his assets. They took his thirty cars and his art. They put his house up for auction. And that was just on the business side. On the personal side, his life was a similar wreck. His union with his live-in girlfriend, the former Adrienne Rodriguez, whom he married in 1985, was a public mess. She'd had him arrested four times. And Brown, who had never been seen even smoking a cigarette in public, had secretly become hooked on PCP, angel dust, a source of great shame to him. His star had vanished. He'd outrun his revolution. He was an oldies act with a terrible reputation.

"Professionally, he was a scourge," says Buddy Dallas, a Thomson, Georgia, attorney whom Brown had approached to help him out of his mess. "He had crashed from prominence. He didn't pay his debts. He didn't even have a home telephone. His bills were unpaid. It was not popular to be close to James Brown." Brown's performance fee, Dallas says, was $7,500 a night. But it cost Brown $9,000 to put performers onstage. "He owed utilities bills. He owed his band. If he owed a guy $500, he'd give them $250 and promise the other $250. That was the James Brown method of paying bills."

Dallas, the son of a Lincolnton, Georgia, sawmill worker, has the keen intelligence and sharp wit of an old country lawyer. Says Dallas, "My daddy would always say, 'Son, you can tell a lie a thousand ways. But there's only one way that you can tell the truth.'" He met Brown at a function, and Brown, who always had an eye for talent and for a man with a sense of humor, played with Dallas's three-year-old daughter while sizing up Dallas. Shortly after that, Brown called Dallas, the two met, and Brown said, "Mr. Dallas, I been checking on you, and I understand you can be trusted. I want you to represent me."

Dallas, a white man, had never worked for a black boss before. He'd grown up in the segregated South, but went through the University of Georgia School of Law in the 1960s dancing to Brown's music and howling to Brown's "Night Train." The two discovered they had much in common. They liked to quote Bible verses. They liked to hunt squirrels. They loved fried chicken. And most important, they were both southerners, country boys who understood the meaning of virtue, honesty, and pride.

Dallas, considering Brown's offer, confessed to Brown, "Mr. Brown, I don't know anything about the entertainment business."

"I'll *teach* you the entertainment business," Brown said. "I need a man I can trust."

Dallas agreed, a decision that would cost him $300,000 in legal fees and years of headaches after Brown died. He came up with a plan to stop Brown's slide. Brown had no cash, but just days after agreeing to represent Brown, on a handshake, Dallas walked into his hometown bank, the Bank of Thomson, Georgia, and borrowed $32,000 in his own name. He bought Brown's house at auction, deeded it back to Brown for a dollar, and then used the rest of the money to put out several financial fires. Brown then sought a tax expert to address his $15 million debt to the IRS. He wanted a man who was completely honest and fastidious, one who had the experience to fight off the IRS. He approached Cannon, who worked as a senior accountant and administrator at a Barnwell, South Carolina, law firm and who had a sterling reputation in a four-decade-long career. Brown sat in Cannon's office, detailed his problem, and asked Cannon to work for him.

Cannon, a careful and deliberate man, listened until Brown was finished, then said, "Mr. Brown, I'm flattered. But I'm about to retire."

"Please don't retire," Brown said. "I need you to clean this up for me."

Like Dallas, Cannon, a native of Columbia, South Carolina, had never worked for a black boss before. Like Dallas, he had grown up in a South where blacks and whites lived as a kind of dysfunctional family, with a familiarity that is hard for outsiders to understand. Cannon's son, for example, was buddies with a black boy named Eric whom he regularly brought over to Cannon's mother's house to play. The black child and Cannon's mother grew close—Eric called her Grandma, and she referred to Eric as her "grandson." She cooked for Eric, looked after him, and admonished him when he did wrong, but one afternoon when her black "grandson" and her white grandson were playing in front of her house, she summoned both boys inside, pulled her white grandson aside, and said, "Don't play with Eric in front of the house. Play in the backyard. I don't want the neighbors to see."

Cannon, when he learned of it, scolded his mother.

His mother was red-faced. "I'm sorry," she said. "I love him, but . . . I just don't want the neighbors to see."

Such is the complexity of race relations in America's South, where race keeps you in a kind of grid in which you never know where to step. Blacks and whites together—but not together. Living as one, but not as one. Living as family, but a dysfunctional family. Cannon recalled that when he was a boy, a hardware-store owner near his grandmother's Turbeville, South Carolina, home had a trained parrot in his store that would chirp, "Here comes a nigger!" every time a black person opened the door and walked in. I laughed when he told me that story, but Cannon sat there grimly. "Even as a child," Cannon said drily, "I never thought that was funny."

James Brown offered him 5 percent of whatever he made, plus extra earnings and percentages of any major deals they put together. It was a gentlemen's agreement. James Brown did not like to pay big salaries. He was afraid of contracts. He worked with Buddy Dallas the same way. "I won't end up owing you money," Brown promised. Cannon sized up Dallas. Dallas was a Georgian—and South Carolinians and Georgians have a historical mutual mistrust—but he saw Dallas as a straight talker and a man of achievement. And like Dallas, Cannon saw that he and Brown had a lot in common. They were honorable men, southerners, who believed in God, respect, a handshake, and hard work. Cannon, near retirement and financially secure, quit his safe job and agreed to join Brown's team.

Cannon's first order of business was to attack the IRS problem. It was a mess, partly because Brown hid his cash everywhere. Moreover, Brown's initial rise to prominence was under King Records founder Syd Nathan and Universal Music promoter Ben Bart. Both were brilliant Jewish pioneers who, by coincidence, died in 1968. Brown effectively became self-managed after their deaths, going through a series of full- and part-time "managers," "promoters," and "road managers." Those are amorphous titles in show business, by the way—they could mean anything. When I was playing tenor in a famous jazz singer's band, a woman who did a short stint with us as a "photographer"—I never saw one picture she took—evolved into "road manager," then later became "manager," paying our salaries. Then she vanished completely—fired or quit, who knows. You don't ask if you want to keep your job. Such was Brown's organization. The few manager types he did trust over the years burned him. Some whom he should have trusted he did not. The upshot was that the boy who had grown up going to sandlot baseball games in Augusta with a ball and bat he'd bought with his shoe-shine money—and who would depart with his ball and bat if there was some disagreement—wouldn't allow anyone to count, collect, or keep his money.

Brown's penchant for hiding cash is legendary among friends and associates. He was of that Depression generation who grew up when the banks closed their doors and left millions of people high and dry. That generation hid their money in mattresses, stuffed it into cookie jars and under floorboards. My mother was that way. She hid quarters and five-dollar bills. Brown, on the other hand, hid thousands of dollars in cash—in vases, safes, buried under trees and in gardens, hidden in the floorboards of a car, under rugs in far-distant hotels that he'd visit every year while touring. For the last twenty years of his life, he walked around with a pocket full of $3,000 in cashier's checks, $3,000 being the number that kept you beneath the IRS's radar. Trumpeter Joe Davis, an ex–band member, recalls Brown telling his band, "If you want to keep your money, bury it in your yard." Brown liked to keep money in every conceivable kind of place, apparently, except for the one place where it would have been safe. "Mr. Brown did not trust banks," Cannon says. "Period. You could not make him." Buddy Dallas concurs.

Brown was just as fussy about money when it came to getting paid on his gigs. I've seen the brown-paper-bag routine myself—where the money passes from the promoter of the gig to the star in a little brown paper sandwich bag. Some bags even have stains on them to make it look like it's loaded with a ham-and-cheese sandwich, except that the thing's got enough cash in it to buy the pig *and* the farm. That was standard procedure for a lot of old entertainers, who had been burned by labels, recording executives, and those DJs who would collect their illegal payoffs to play their records and still wouldn't play them. Some of those stars, including Brown, had gone through the routine of managers buying them a brand-new Thunderbird or the like, instead of royalties or payment, or who would supply them with dope or pay a few dollars for songs or recordings, some of which became classics that would sell forever. John Coltrane and Cannonball Adderley were each paid about $150 per session to record *Kind of Blue,* an immortal jazz classic and one of the bestselling jazz records of all time. Among musicians, the stories abound: there's a legend of one singer being hung by his heels from a tenth-story hotel window for not honoring a contract; there's Sam Cooke's mysterious murder. There's another story I heard from a musician buddy, about a famous female soul singer who came to his city to record a car commercial. Before she sang a note, she made it clear that she didn't want any residuals or royalties. All that fancy figuring, she said, never worked out. She wanted—and got—straight cash, $75,000 in American chips. She sang the sixty-second jingle and out the door she went. Those old stars had been burned so often, they didn't fool around.

The upshot of Brown's money paranoia was that his finances were a disaster. By 1984, he resorted to the 1950s method of doing gigs, collecting the gig money in a suitcase or box—sometimes handing that box to Al Sharpton or Charles Bobbit or, later, another trusted road manager named Albert "Judge" Bradley—and playing ignorant about paying taxes. In 1972, he met Richard Nixon, who was running for president on the Republican ticket. Nixon called him a "national treasure." Brown, who was bombed by the black press and fans for associating with Nixon, ran with that "national treasure" bit when the IRS chased him down. He claimed he didn't have to pay taxes because he was told by the president that he was a "national treasure." Later, as part of an attempt to argue against IRS claims against him, he announced that he was part Indian and claimed, with a seemingly straight face, to be related to Geronimo.

The IRS was not amused, and by the 1980s they came after him with both fists. "He had a show in Texas," Cannon says. "The IRS came and took the money off the date. He couldn't pay the band. They were stuck." That was the financial state of affairs when Cannon was given marching orders to fix Brown's financial life in 1992.

"He didn't even have a tax attorney," Cannon says. "I went to his office to look at his records. They showed me a few files. I said, 'This is all?'

"They said, 'The IRS took eight or ten boxes.'"

Cannon tried to track the boxes down. "The IRS had them all over the place." He flew to Atlanta, called Tennessee. "I never found all of them. I said to the IRS, 'You've got to prove you have his records.'"

"They said, 'No, we don't.'

"I said, 'You've got to show me.'"

They could not produce them. The testy negotiations between Cannon and the IRS took two years. The IRS wanted $15 million and not a penny less. They threatened to toss Brown in the clink. Cannon, with James Brown's shoddy records as ammo, found himself backed into a corner. He had no numbers to work with. The IRS, on the other hand, knew what Brown earned. But Cannon noted that the IRS negotiators seemed worried that Brown would go bankrupt, leaving the government empty-handed or able to collect only the maximum that bankruptcy would allow, which was then $1 million. Privately, Cannon knew that Brown would never declare bankruptcy. Brown had his pride. And Cannon understood that notion of "proper," the southern mentality in which both were raised. Cannon understood that a man like James Brown, who insisted on being called "Mr. Brown" and who addressed everyone, even the lowliest worker, as "Mister" or "Miss," a man who spent three hours after every exhausting gig sitting under a hair dryer so that people wouldn't see him with his hair undone, looking ragged and improper, would never want the world to see him on his knees broke.

Cannon knew that Brown would go to jail before he allowed himself to go bankrupt, but he packed that bullet in his gun anyway, and at the negotiating table, when it appeared that the IRS had him cornered, he discharged it.

"We're filing bankruptcy," he said. It was a bluff.

The bluff worked. The IRS backed down and asked to meet again in a week.

A week later, the IRS agreed to settle the $15 million debt at $1.3 million—with two provisions. The first was that in the future, when dealing with Brown, they would deal with Cannon only, not the plethora of other Brown employees they had seen before. And secondly, "You'll have to do Mrs. Brown's taxes too," they told him.

That nearly killed the thing, because Cannon refused. Cannon and Dallas, the two men who revived James Brown's career, distrusted Brown's third wife, Adrienne, a makeup artist whom Brown had met on the set of a TV music show called *Solid Gold*. Both Cannon and Dallas can fill the room with stories of Adrienne's wild behavior—stealing Brown's money, stuffing his cash into closets and into ceilings, stealing silverware and bread from the Sands Hotel in Las Vegas, reportedly stabbing one of Brown's girlfriends in the rear end with a pair of scissors in a New York hotel suite. They can list her drug problems and expensive plastic surgeries—one of which killed her. She had Brown arrested four times between 1987 and 1995 for assault. Dallas calls her a "kleptomaniac" and "a committed drug addict." But Brown loved Adrienne. He called her "my rat." She was an intelligent, pretty woman of mixed-race heritage, a loyal wife who helped him in his comeback and stayed committed to him when he was imprisoned from 1988 to 1991 after the PCP-filled episode in Augusta that ended in a police chase. She tried to give him some semblance of family, inviting his various children to the house for the holidays to eat and commingle. Living with Brown was not easy. She told Brown's friend Emma Austin, "Emma, I have to get high just to put up with his shit."

But Cannon did not trust Adrienne. He was on the receiving end when Brown would seek a few hours' peace from her by driving his

Lincoln to Cannon's modest Barnwell house to tinker with Cannon's collection of antique swords and lie on Cannon's living room couch and complain about his wife's spending. Cannon listened, powerless. That was a marriage issue, he thought. He knew that Adrienne was helping herself to too much of Brown's cash, which created all kinds of tax and accounting headaches, but "You did not tell Mr. Brown what to do," he says. "You simply did not." And you did not tell Mrs. Brown what to do either. To make matters more complicated, Brown floated Cannon out as a shield against personal leeches. If someone asked Brown for a loan, he'd say, "See Mr. Cannon." Then he would tell Cannon, "Tell 'em no." If someone needed firing, Brown would say, "See Mr. Cannon," and Cannon would do the firing. It created personal enemies within Brown's family, his entourage, and among his old professional acquaintances, who would turn on Cannon viciously after Brown died. It also created a huge personal problem in Cannon's house, because Brown, trusting no one, insisted on stashing a disturbingly high pile of cash in Cannon's safe. Cannon rarely challenged his boss, but in the matter of storing Brown's money, he resisted.

"I told him all the time, 'Mr. Brown, I am not a bank.'

" 'Just hold it for me, Mr. Cannon. Hold it for me.' "

Cannon reluctantly agreed.

"Had I known what was going to happen, I would have never done it," he says. "But who knew he was going to die suddenly?"

Chapter 12

The Earth Beneath His Feet

The first time the villagers heard it was back in 2000. It was early afternoon on a gorgeous spring day in Frome, a town in Great Britain just thirteen miles from Bath. The shops were open. The workers had already gone off to the nearby Whatley and Merehead limestone quarries, and the streets were quiet—the commuters had long since hopped the trains to nearby Bristol and Warminster. Afternoon had settled into its familiar calm. Suddenly, echoing from the town cemetery, came a sound never before heard in the town's twelve-hundred-year history.

It was the sound of a man with a horn.

A lone black man sat on the wall of the cemetery, right in front of Christ Church, playing a tenor saxophone. He was an American, it was rumored, though no one in the town was sure, because no one wanted to disturb him. Whatever he did, whatever he was doing on that horn, by God, it was gorgeous, so they said to one another, *Leave him be.* He'd been seen around town in the shops. He was said to be quiet and mild mannered, but nothing more was known about him. The Frome villagers, ever polite, did not ask. They understand artists in Frome—pronounced *froom,* as in *broom.* They know what it feels like to be different. That understanding goes back four hundred years to the Reformation, when the nonconformist Anglicans of Frome were killed for parting with the Protestants and Catholics and building their churches within a stone's throw of the ancient cemetery where the black man sat. *Don't disturb him,* they said to one another. *Let him play.*

And so he played. He played that day and the next and in the days following, seated on the wall of the graveyard, working the horn, the harmonies, the scales and arpeggios, the songs he knew so well, the songs of his history, dressing the cemetery in the gorgeous melody and drifting beauty of jazz. That cemetery was full of the dead, but the horn man gave their memories bone and substance and sustenance. And when he was done with those in the graveyard, he turned the bell of his horn toward the town square. His thick tenor wail covered the walls of the village and the surrounding hills with melody, the supple notes echoing into the ears of the lorry drivers as they made deliveries on the narrow highway leading to Nunney.

Fifteen years later, Alfred "Pee Wee" Ellis, seventy-two, saxophonist and composer, student of the legendary tenor saxophone great Sonny Rollins, the principal architect of James Brown's sound and one of the most important figures in American musical history, walks down the streets of Frome like just another local guy. It's a cool afternoon in 2012. He and his lovely British wife, Charlotte, are headed to a local ice cream parlor on Frome's famed Cheap Street, a medieval stone avenue split by a tiny stream curved into its middle, a stream that has run along this stone street for at least a thousand years.

As Pee Wee passes the shops, the merchants—manicurists, booksellers, antiques-shop owners, tea sellers—wave through their windows. Some come to their doors to greet him. Every hello is cheerful, every smile is warm. He's the Legend Next Door.

"Morning, Pee Wee!"

"Aye, Pee Wee!"

"Pee Wee!"

"Pee Wee! How goes it?"

Pee Wee moves along the street slowly, his wife at his side. "Going good," he grunts, "Going good."

Suddenly, out of nowhere, the village madman appears. This guy genuinely looks like a madman. Maybe he lives in the Blue House just up the road, the ancient stone building that once housed the poor. Or maybe he sleeps on one of the benches in front of the library, where the townsfolk like to gather to chat and read. Wherever he lives, he looks like his bubble has burst. He holds his head to the side a bit, as if it's screwed too tight onto his neck; his cap is perched on his head like a loose bottle cap. He approaches Pee Wee, who is sporting a neat tweed Irish cap and a short jacket.

"Pee Wee, guess what?"

"What?"

"I got my clarinet back. I'm ready for another lesson."

"Okay. Later on."

The madman is happy. He disappears, and Pee Wee and Charlotte move on. At the ice cream parlor, the shop owner, a young woman, greets him by name. Pee Wee grunts his greeting, sits down, and orders an ice cream called "gin and tonic." I sit with him. I'm amazed at how much of a local he is.

After the shop owner takes my order and wanders off, I turn to him and ask, "Pee Wee, would you ever leave here? Maybe come back to America to live someday?"

Pee Wee, his wonderfully cute face and playful dark eyes moving about the room, scoops up his ice cream and regards it carefully, holding the spoon before his brown face, a face still smooth and cherubic despite his years. He glances outside the window at the lovely shops, the gorgeous old brick walkway, the laughing mothers chatting as they push baby carriages, the passersby who smile and wave at him through the window.

"If I do," he grunts, "I'm walking there on my hands."

There are probably two hundred musicians who went through James Brown's band or played on one of his records over the course of his fifty-one-year career. Of that number, probably ten contributed key components to his sound. None were more important, lesser known, and less credited than trombonist Fred Wesley and the man he learned from, Pee Wee Ellis.

It's a complicated piece of business, to describe the originality of a music that had no previous label until these guys got to it, partly because music is a continuum. Soul music, or rhythm and blues, had pieces of life, plenty of it, before James Brown or any of his musicians got to it. For example, Brown's bassist Bernard Odum, who arguably had as much to do with James Brown's early sound as anyone, started with Brown as a pickup player back in the fifties, when Brown was traveling solo on the chitlin circuit. His looping Fender bass lines on dozens of James Brown's hits, lines that floated above the beat at times and at other times thundered in concert with the kick drum, are a signature element of the James Brown sound. Yet Odum, who started out swinging the blues, is relatively unknown even within music circles. Similarly, Jimmy Nolen, Brown's greatest guitarist, along with Hearlon "Cheese" Martin and Alphonso "Country" Kellum, is a key creator of the melodic, nitpicking guitar licks that are sampled on thousands of records and copied on millions of cheap computer keyboards sold today. He, too, is virtually unknown. The fact is, James Brown's band, the 1965–69 version, fronted by Pee Wee, was, I would argue, the greatest group of rhythm and blues musicians ever assembled.

Music experts can argue this point till they're blue in the face, I suppose, but Motown, for all its dazzle and polish, did not have the grit and fire of the James Brown sound. Motown had a genius—Stevie

Wonder—and the Jackson 5, and other indomitable forces, like Marvin Gaye, Gladys Knight, the Supremes, and extraordinary writing teams like Holland-Dozier-Holland and Ashford and Simpson. And there were others before Motown as well: great bands of the 1950s from Memphis, the underrated, killer soul groups out of Philadelphia International Records in the seventies, and unmatched soul singers like Aretha Franklin and Ruth Brown, the likes of which we will never hear again. But even Aretha, for all her soul and all her tight rhythm sections, could not match the burning fire and individuality of the James Brown sound. They were different sounds. Different musicians. Different cities. Different blacks. But James Brown's uniqueness stood him above them all.

The problem with the categorization of "soul" is that it's a generic term that means nothing and everything. It's like the term "Christian music." It's a label. A sales term. The label leaves out legions of heavy influences and creators whose previous contributions to the form actually made Brown great, including two grandfathers of rock 'n' roll, Lionel Hampton and especially the deeply talented Louis Jordan. Jordan, the 1940s Arkansas-born saxophonist, singer, and composer whose stage antics and theatrical approach Brown later aped and modernized, is one of America's secret musical treasures. Jordan had a tremendous effect on Brown and his contemporaries Little Richard, Little Willie John, and Jackie Wilson. In terms of polish, slickness, musical dexterity, and entertainment value, Jordan and his Tympany Five were virtually unmatched at their height. They laid down a groove in dance and swing shows that drove audiences wild. That band was a well-trained, impeccably dressed musical outfit, delivering swing melody with military precision, playing behind Jordan's laughing wisecracks and show-business guffaws and gags with the efficiency of a groove machine—one that was nearly as tight as Count Basie's band and more fun to dance to than Duke Ellington, who, by contrast, fronted a cadre of knockout soloists playing serious compositions. Jordan's influence on American pop music has never, to my knowledge, been given more than cursory attention. As for vibraphonist and percussionist Lionel Hampton, Quincy Jones, one of the greatest record producers in American musical history, began his career as a teenage trumpeter and arranger with Hampton's band. Q told me that Hampton was the first to introduce electric bass into the rock 'n' roll genre, in the early fifties, via his bassist Monk Montgomery, brother of the great guitarist Wes Montgomery. He insists that Hampton was one of the first real rock 'n' rollers. And while I'm busy hurting people's feelings and riling up music experts, I might as well finish the job by throwing in a nod to legendary Latino musicians like Chano Pozo, Machito, Mario Bauzá, and the great Tito Puente, who the late Jerome Richardson, the tenor player and pioneer jazz flutist, said was a far greater figure in the development of American music than he was ever given credit for. Richardson worked in Lionel Hampton's band back in the forties, and said Hampton's band often played opposite Puente's at New York City dances. "Tito's band," Richardson said simply, "used to give us the mumps." Puente and America's Latino musicians are rarely even mentioned in the discussion of the evolution of soul and jazz, but even the most cursory hearing of their music shows its heavy stamp on that sound—and vice versa.

This question of "who created the music" is, therefore, sticky business, particularly when discussing Brown. It's complicated by the fact that Brown's music, fully evolved, is more easily, in my mind, compared to Count Basie's or Duke Ellington's than to any simple rhythm and blues group, because the "James Brown sound" was an intricacy of shifting parts that moved harmonically, often in counterpoint, back and forth, up and down, patternlike, with each pattern combining to make a whole. An entire industry of samplers, sequencers, and computers, the staple of hip-hop music, is clear evidence of its complexity. That music came from someone—from many someones. Not just one. And not just Brown.

But much of that sound harkens back to the heavyset man who now sits before me in the parlor of his home, with his horn on a stand in the corner facing a music stand that is open to page 34 of Franz

Wohlfahrt's *60 Studies, Op. 45* for the violin, a book of arpeggios and études he practices on the saxophone.

As a fellow saxophonist, I look it over. "Man, this is hard," I say.

"I'm working on something," Pee Wee replies. "I got a concert with Yusef Lateef coming up in Paris. I gotta practice."

Pee Wee Ellis has gotta practice. After forty-five years of being one of the most unique voices in the music world, co-composer of at least twenty-six James Brown songs, including "Say It Loud—I'm Black and I'm Proud," "Mother Popcorn," "Licking Stick," and "The Chicken," he's still practicing. And I haven't picked up my horn in months.

I change the subject. "Let's talk about James Brown," I say.

"Can't we talk about something else?" he asks.

Spin back to late 1964. James Brown was at a musical crossroads. His seminal song "Out of Sight," which took the I-IV-V chord, twelve-bar blues a giant step closer to soul, with its lesser chord movement, had, in part, been dreamed up by saxophonist Nat Jones, Brown's principal arranger and music director. Brown was in his prime then, and a fury to work for: endless rehearsals, cheap salary, constant yelling, heavy demands, fines for small infractions like shoes not shined properly or missing an entry. Jones, Pee Wee remembers, was already showing signs of mental illness. He would later lose his mind completely and fall into such despair that when soul sideman Curtis Pope, who was with Wilson Pickett and the Midnight Movers, saw him at a gig in Florida, Pope was shocked. "I couldn't stand it," he says. "I reached in my pocket and gave him two hundred dollars."

But Jones had only basic music-arranging skills. And when Brown noticed his musical director farming out the chart writing and arrangement duties to the quiet new tenor man he'd just hired from Rochester, New York, he moved Jones aside and tossed the gig into Pee Wee's lap.

"Not an easy thing," Pee Wee says. "Back then, I didn't quite know what the gig was."

"What was it?" I ask.

"It was a hard road."

Pee Wee had already come on a hard road. He was born Alfred Bryant in 1941 in Bradenton, Florida, an "outside child" to Garfield Davoe Rogers, Jr., son of a prominent middle-class minister, who met Pee Wee's mother, Elizabeth, when both were college students at the prestigious black Bethune-Cookman College. Garfield gave all his boys a name with the initials "G.D." save Pee Wee. Young Pee Wee was a shy, skinny, withdrawn child, close to his mother, and at age seven was coming to the awareness of his "outside" status, which in that tight-knit community was no badge of honor. One afternoon he opened his grandma Clyde's bureau drawer and found a saxophone. "I don't know why it was there, or whose it was," he tells me. "I can still smell the mildew." He removed the horn, took it down the street, sat under a tree near a gravel road, put his mouth to it, and found trust.

All his life, up to that moment, Pee Wee had never known trust. No one could explain to him why adults talked about him in hushed tones, or why he, the grandson of one of the town's most respected black ministers, had to walk to school alone, past his grandfather's house, where no one acknowledged him. No one could explain why his quiet, gentle mother had to drop out of her prestigious college to work odd jobs, washing white folks' clothing, scraping by to survive. The world was a place full of hurt. But that afternoon, when he placed his hands around that saxophone, the hurt fell away and there was earth beneath his feet. "I felt like I had something to stand on," he says.

In 1949, when he was eight, his mother wed a kind amateur musician named Ezell Ellis, a U.S. army veteran. Ezell was a resourceful, openhearted man who took Pee Wee as his own, giving the young boy his last name, and moved the family to Lubbock, Texas. Ezell promoted gigs for a living, and Lubbock was a stop on the chitlin circuit. Meanwhile, under the tutelage of a local teacher named Roy Roberts at the all-black Dunbar Junior High, his adopted son Pee Wee became a standout clarinet player. Pee Wee was so gifted that Ezell often fetched him out of bed to play piano at the local juke joint with the bands that came through town. Pee Wee's mother protested, but Ezell calmed her fears. "Pee Wee's got a special thing," he said. "He's got a special talent."

"He gave me something I never had before," Pee Wee says. "He gave me love from a father. I learned a lot from him." Ezell opened a hamburger stand outside their house that constantly lost money. Customers would eat and pay in favors, or kindness, or not at all. Ezell didn't care. He was a happy man with a big heart. He had an ease with people that was infectious. He was never afraid to show love. "Do right by people," he told his son. "Do right by people and the Lord will watch out for you all your days."

But the Lord also moves the earth in ways beyond understanding, and when Pee Wee was fourteen, Ezell's kindness cost him his life.

Working as a promoter, Ezell brought a black band into a white juke joint one night. The band was full-out blasting and a white woman took to the floor with too much to drink. This was west Texas in the 1950s. A drunk white woman on a crowded dance floor was a toxic concoction in the powder keg of race and class that was the American South.

Ezell moved to gently help the reeling lady off the dance floor, and before anyone could intervene to help, a white man leaped out of the kitchen and stabbed Ezell in the stomach with a kitchen knife, then fled.

Ezell staggered outside and collapsed. He was taken to a local white hospital that refused to treat blacks and died in the hospital hallway, waiting to see a doctor. He was a U.S. army veteran. A man with a wife and family. His killer was never caught. And just like that, the earth vanished from beneath Pee Wee's feet again. "Here I am, fifty years later," Pee Wee said, "and I still can't understand it."

Pee Wee's mother grabbed her son and his two sisters and hopped a night train. The four didn't get off the train until they arrived in Rochester, New York, damn near Canada, hundreds of miles north of the Mason-Dixon Line. She enrolled Pee Wee in an integrated high school. His classmates were white kids, kind, generous students, but by then he had retreated back into the solitude and comfort of the only thing outside his family he could trust: the horn.

Two years later, two students from the renowned Eastman School of Music—Ron Carter, twenty, who would go on to become a jazz legend, and trumpeter Waymon Reed, then eighteen, who should have become one—were among a group of musicians jamming on the bandstand at Rochester's Pythodd jazz club, when Pee Wee, then sixteen and skinny as a mop handle, walked in, pulled out his tenor, and burned his way into local history. "Brother, you look awful young to be in here," Waymon said. "I bet you ain't old enough to drive."

"I ain't come here to drive."

The two became good friends—in time Pee Wee would serve as best man at Waymon's wedding to a lovely beauty named Greta, before his second marriage, to jazz queen Sarah Vaughan—but after that summer the two parted ways. Pee Wee drifted to New York, spent a summer studying tenor with the great saxophonist Sonny Rollins, and, after a short stint at the Manhattan School of Music, got a job playing tenor and clarinet with a traveling circus. He hawked his diamond ring in Wisconsin so he could steal away from the circus and buy a ticket to see tenor saxophonist John Coltrane in Chicago, who in those days was the talk of the jazz world. Pee Wee chatted with the jazz giant, one of two tenor giants of that era, his former teacher Sonny Rollins being the other. Coltrane blew his mind so much that Pee Wee hung around Chicago the next day and meandered over to the motel where the saxophone great was staying. He walked up to Coltrane's room and heard Coltrane, a known practice fanatic, inside the room, practicing.

"Trane was a gentle cat," Pee Wee says, "but he let it be known that he didn't like to be disturbed when he was practicing." Pee Wee, dying to talk to Trane, raised his hand to knock, then thought better of it.

But what he heard inspired him, and he absorbed Coltrane's penchant for practice and Sonny Rollins's originality to create his own sound. In his later years, he would become a respected producer and tenor player in jazz, working with greats Oliver Nelson, Dinah Washington, Esther Phillips, Duke Jordan, Sonny Stitt, Frank Foster, King Curtis, Lee Morgan, and legendary producer Creed Taylor. He was beginning to make his mark in jazz in 1965, and had just finished an organ-trio tour with Sonny Payne, Count Basie's fabulous drummer, when he got a call from Waymon Reed, the trumpeter he'd first met years back at the Pythodd club in Rochester. That phone call would set the course of Pee Wee's musical life for the next forty years.

Waymon said, "Hey, Pee Wee. I'm working with James Brown. Want a gig?"

"Yeah, I want a gig," Pee Wee said. Back then, he'd barely heard of James Brown. But he needed the money.

"Come to Washington, DC. I got a job for you."

Pee Wee packed his bags and left for James Brown's world, leaving behind a childhood that never was.

Pee Wee wasn't long on the set before Brown removed the mentally unstable Nat Jones from the music director's chair and placed Pee Wee in it. And Pee Wee almost joined Jones in the nuthouse.

Brown's approach to creating songs is funny to talk about now, decades after the fact. Trombonist Fred Wesley, the other seminal co-creator in the James Brown musical evolution, calls it the "la-de-da" method. That's a funny, inside joke to musicians: *la-de-da*. Lots of singers I've worked with use it. They say, "It goes like this," and sing "la-de-da. . . ." They can't read a lick of music, wouldn't know a bass clef from a bottle of milk, but they know *la-de-da*. That's no great sin, by the way. Wes Montgomery, Dave Brubeck, Buddy Rich, Irving Berlin, and pianist Erroll Garner couldn't read music, and they were all superb musicians. Quincy Jones once told me that Garner, when asked about reading music, said, "Shit. People ain't coming to see me read." Conversely, I know tons of guys who can read fly crap off the wall, but they're not great players. I know of a powerful Broadway contractor, for example, who not only reads music but has handled hundreds of Broadway shows—and plays at the level of a high school student. And while I'm at it, I might as well state the obvious: the guy is white, and despite Herculean efforts by the great composer Stephen Schwartz and Michael Kerker of ASCAP, who have spent more than two decades developing minority composers and lyricists through the ASCAP Musical Theatre Workshop, many Broadway contractors seem allergic to black players. One spectacularly talented African American musician I know—I'll call him Joe—challenged that very contractor on the issue of why he rarely hired black players to play Broadway shows. The contractor claimed that blacks didn't read music, and had intonation issues, and couldn't follow the conductor, and all sorts of jive.

Joe got mad and said, "You forget, man. I've heard *you* play." Joe didn't work a mainstream Broadway show for years after that.

But ultimately it boils down to the music. And someone other than Brown had to help him make it.

In the early days of the Famous Flames in the fifties, Brown sat down on organ or drums with the lesser-skilled Bobby Byrd and Nafloyd Scott and hammered out blues-based hits for King Records. By 1964, the blues wasn't enough. One lesson Brown learned after his 1955 hit "Please, Please, Please" ran its course and he had to push, shove, and scream his way through the chitlin circuit, barely staying one step ahead of the gaping maw that swallowed Cab Calloway, Jimmie Lunceford, Billy Eckstine, and the whole "race records" crew from the thirties and forties, was that your music had to evolve. Lack of evolution gulped down Louis Jordan and Lionel Hampton; later it would eat Kool Herc, Afrika Bambaataa, the Cold Crush Brothers, and the creative pioneers of rap without so much as a burp. The dream-gobbling machine known as the record industry, that self-sustaining combine that gobbles African American culture with merciless efficiency and presents the chaff as African American life—with the whole thing coming to a theater near you thirty years later as a Broadway show called *Porgy and Bess, Five Guys Named Moe,* or *Dreamgirls*—

demands change. Brown watched the artists who could not evolve fall away, dying on the vine or spending their declining years as oldies acts, forced to run the film of their revolution backward in supper clubs to audiences who were moving on, or aging out.

He didn't want that. Besides, he was hearing something different after his 1964 hit "Out of Sight." He was hearing a downbeat. The downbeat—laying fat snare to the two and four of every bar—had expanded in Brown's mind to a big hit on the one-beat of every other bar. He heard a new groove. And he needed the best players he could find to translate that groove, his "la-de-da" grunts and commands, into hits.

It was not easy. For one thing, a band—any band—is hard to handle. And the 1964–65 version of the James Brown band that Pee Wee joined was not just any band. The players who would eventually fill out Brown's outfit from roughly 1964 to 1969 would set the tone of American popular music for decades to come. The band was big, made up of male players and female singers, most from the South. Some were country boys, like drummer Clyde Stubblefield, of Chattanooga, Tennessee, who grew up outside a railroad yard and emulated the "chug-a-chug" of the Southern Railway train that he heard passing his mother's kitchen window every day when he was a boy. Others were all-stars in their cities, like trumpeter Richard "Kush" Griffith, from Louisville, Kentucky, who had perfect pitch and had played in his local symphonic youth orchestra. Violinist Richard Jones of Philadelphia was a jazz pioneer and one of the first blacks to attend what would later become the University of the Arts. Trumpeter Waymon Reed would leave Brown to join Art Blakey's Jazz Messengers and later Count Basie. Bassist Bernard Odum was later replaced by bassist/pianist/vocalist Sweet Charles Sherrell, a music whiz from Nashville, and later the deep-grooving Fred Thompson of Brooklyn. Odum also brought to the band two fantastic young musicians from his Mobile, Alabama, home: drummer Jabo Starks and trombonist Fred Wesley, who would later take over Pee Wee's job. Saxophonist Maceo Parker of Kinston, North Carolina, who contributed mightily to Brown's sound as a soloist, later became a unique R&B star in his own right. Augusta-born reed man St. Clair Pinckney, with his trademark shock of white hair, was an underrated performer who, according to the inside joke, had been in the band longer than James Brown had. Jimmy Nolen, Hearlon "Cheese" Martin, and Alphonso "Country" Kellum's guitar picking—Kellum also played bass—created what they called "that washing machine thing," which would set the tone for pop guitarists for the next few decades.

The records say it all. These men had grown up under segregation listening to the blues, jazz, and country. Some were hard men like Odum, a light-skinned, rough fellow who grew up in the tough "Down the Bay" section of Mobile and was known to carry a knife that he was not afraid to use. Drummer Stubblefield, though shy and quiet, was stubborn as a mule if you hit his button. Ditto about his more outgoing fellow drummer Jabo, who refused to accept fines when Brown levied them. These musicians were young, talented, and at times wild and unruly. Several were drinkers. A few smoked pot. Some read music with ease, while others couldn't read music at all. Individually, with the exception of Ellis, Wesley, and Reed, they were not pure jazz soloists. But as a band, they were an unstoppable force. And the one who shaped them, and often stood between them and the taskmaster, was Pee Wee.

Says trumpeter Joe Davis: "Pee Wee was the one who put the sound together, in terms of locking it in, translating what James wanted. That was Pee Wee." The arrangements? "Mostly Pee Wee," he says. Adds violinist Richard Jones, an exceptionally skilled reader and technician, "Pee Wee was the opposite of Mr. Brown. His gift was that he made even the guys who couldn't read music musical. He guided them to their strengths. He was very patient."

The result of Pee Wee's work is most evident in "Say It Loud—I'm Black and I'm Proud," which Pee Wee wrote on the spot at three in the morning in a Los Angeles studio and recorded with thirty kids that Charles Bobbit had miraculously dug up from Los Angeles somewhere to sing the chorus. That song is drooping with jazz—the movement from the I chord to the IV chord, tightly voiced horns on a sharp nine chord, very unusual in pop music, even then, band hits accented by the snare of Clyde Stubblefield. Even today there is nothing like it. Pee Wee's other works, "Mother Popcorn," "Licking Stick," and the instrumental "Chicken," are long-standing favorites. "Chicken" is a jazz classic, generally assumed to have been written by the fretless-bass genius Jaco Pastorius. Another Ellis hit, "Cold Sweat," is drawn straight from Miles Davis's "So What."

"Miles affected everybody," Ellis says. "He grew till the end of his life." Even a novice can listen to Miles's lead horn line on "So What" and the horn hits on "Cold Sweat" and hear it: they're in the same key, but the difference is the groove. "So What" swings. "Cold Sweat" grooves.

Let me take a moment to mention groove here. And funk. When I was coming up, a lot of serious jazz players couldn't stand funk. Their reasoning: it was technically simple. Unlike jazz, there was no harmonic or technical challenge, no furious chord changes that required mathematical efficiency in your head to figure out where the thing was going and how to make your knowledge of theory and harmony fit. Jazz requires a blend of split-second timing, skill, and training. It's like playing basketball. You need a lot of skills to play basketball: running, jumping, shooting, defense, conditioning. On the pro level, you have to put all these things to use and shoot the ball with a guy your size or bigger sticking a finger in your eye with one hand, pulling your shorts down with the other, and calling your mother names. Jazz soloing is akin to that. Funk soloing, on the other hand, is more akin to playing baseball. Baseball requires athletic talent but specific learned skills that have to be exercised flawlessly. Hitting a curveball can only be learned through years of practice. No matter how gifted you are athletically, you cannot step up to home plate and hit an eighty-mile-per-hour major-league curve or splitter without learning how to do it. And you cannot swing at every pitch. You only get three strikes. So you have to recognize the pitch in a split second, decide where it's going to break, adjust to it, and know when to swing. And you must do this flawlessly. Enough to stay on the team, anyway.

That's why funk is as challenging as jazz. You must know *when* to enter the groove, and *what* to play. Funk—any good music, really— requires space. Knowledge of when to throw in your small contribution and when to lay out. Musical silence is one reason trumpeter Miles Davis was such an extraordinary musician. He epitomized the use of space. There are gorgeous silences in Miles's music. Many jazz players, especially horn players, can't adapt to the demands of space that funk requires. They find funk frustrating and blow right past it. That's why Brown's longtime saxophone soloist Maceo Parker is so revered. There are dozens of horn players more skilled than Maceo. They have more chops. They play better, faster, more. But Maceo, like Miles Davis, knew when to play and when not to play. He knew how to groove. He played with simplicity, which is difficult. He played so rhythmically that he basically played drums on the sax. That's the difference between him and most of today's young players who try to ape his sound. Those who try to cop his sound are schooled on patterns, learned licks, various approaches to specific chord changes, things they learned out of books—things that were new when Charlie Parker played them in 1941, but sound old now. To play funk, you have to be less methodical, feel it, lay out, use space, understand that your moment might come on, say, beat three of bar seven. And put your thing there. Consistently. Every time. Consistency is often a key to great music. Consistency on the inside can make the outer part beautiful, if that's what the composer wants. If you pull the second violin part out of a Beethoven or Brahms concerto, it will still sound beautiful. Pull out the guitar part of a James Brown song, it might not sound beautiful. But though the language is different, rhythmically and aesthetically it will make sense to the human ear.

It's like driving a race car. Anyone can drive the straightaway, but who can drive the curves? That's what made Pee Wee Ellis, and later Fred Wesley, stand out among the great musicians that worked under

Brown. They were co-originators. Brown wrote the lyrics, handed them the recipe, and they were the cooks; they translated Brown's grunts into musical language, which in turn set up his onstage dances, creating a backdrop of musicality that was original and, to this day, infinitely interesting.

"Pee Wee was studied," says Fred Wesley. "He had mastered a lot of things. A lot of what I learned about music, I learned from him."

But the demands of those four years working with Brown ground Pee Wee down. Brown was insecure around studied musicians—he certainly wasn't alone in that—but in that regard, his musicians complain he could be simply unbearable. Pee Wee doesn't like to talk about those years. You can bend him this way and that, joke with him until he gets loose as a ball of cotton candy, and still he will not tell it. Sitting in his parlor, in his room full of instruments and awards and drums, you ask him about those years again and again and watch his friendly smile and happy grunts descend into silence. He backs into that silent corner and stays there. There's pain in that corner. He doesn't have to tell the stories. I've heard them. The fines, the cruelty, rehearsing for hours after a gig for a tiny mistake made by one person. *My band. My show. My gig.* I know that feeling, when you work for a lousy musical boss. You sift through your own memories and feel the painful push against your gut, thinking of the humiliation, the lack of dough, the we're-all-in-this-together bit the star sells you until it's time to get paid. Then, as you look at that twenty-dollar bill in your hand, you realize there's no democracy. It's a horrible feeling when the whole gig, the life-as-a-musician thing, backs up in your throat, like cheap whiskey that you can smell on your breath from one room to the next. A musician knows that smell. It's the smell of *the game.* Show business. You practice all your life, for days, months, years, waiting for the Big Gig, your moment in the sun, and suddenly the gig of a lifetime comes along and it ain't what they said it would be. You find that the gig is just a soap commercial, or the guy holding the strings is a graceless, selfish, narcissistic, self-hating jerk who plays humble and smiles for the audience while holding his foot on your neck at the same time, knowing you can't complain since you need the dough, running his hand through your pocket to make sure you're broke while sleeping with your girlfriend, and you wake up to the whole thing feeling like a worm living inside a peach who pops his head out one day and sees a bunch of white chompers and suddenly realizes what the whole deal is.

Brown's behavior toward his musicians is one of his saddest legacies. In two years of gathering the data, I found that the answers were pretty much the same: "He didn't pay enough." "He was mean." "Outright cruel." He fined musicians for small infractions onstage—missing a cue, shoes not shined, missing a tie. He was divisive. He slept with his female singers. He was a master of manipulation. He tried to get his musicians to buy big houses and cars, only to fire them and watch them suffer under heavy debt, then hire them back at a lower salary. He ran senseless, endless, punishing rehearsals for hours, sometimes right after the gig, sometimes till daylight, for no reason other than to show who was boss. The band traveled by bus. Brown traveled by private plane. He demanded instant acquiescence. His temper was frightening and seemingly anything could touch it off. He slapped this guy. He pulled a gun on that guy. He made this one buy a Cadillac from him. Fred Wesley, in his clairvoyant autobiography *Hit Me, Fred,* describes how Brown once went around the room at a rehearsal and forced each of the band members to say the order of songs in his sets at fast speed, timing each of them, which was a problem, because musicians remember their part or the chord changes, but they don't necessarily recall the title to every song, let alone the song order of a show. He kept spies on his buses, bodyguards or hairdressers or plebe-entourage members, who ratted out any musician who spoke poorly of him. In short, Brown dehumanized them. Most of them, while respecting his musicality and utter showmanship, disliked him intensely.

But that card flips the other way too. In a band, democracy does not work. Somebody has to be the boss, collect the money, deal with the promoters, the agency, the record company; someone has to order the sets, dream up the thing. Musicians are hard to work with. This one drinks. That one hates the other one. This one needs more money. That one can't cut the part but is a nice guy. This one is a hell of a player but a troublemaker. Quincy Jones told me he nearly went mad the first time he ran his first big band around Europe in 1960. Taking care of so many people is a big job. And Brown did not know how to be a friend. He needed his men, but he did not need them. He vacillated between being one of the boys onstage and the boss man off of it. But when faced with a choice, he had to be the boss. Only in his later years did he realize what he'd had in his great bands of the sixties and seventies. The last of his great musicians that remained, bassist Sweet Charles Sherrell, sax man Maceo Parker, and St. Clair Pinckney, often had to help him keep his show together in those later years—Sherrell recalls rousing Brown out of a PCP-induced slumber by pouring milk down his throat to get him out of his hotel room and onstage. By then most of his great singers and musicians had been replaced by younger musicians who did the old hits at ridiculously fast tempos, with showgirls shaking and baking behind Brown in cheerleader get-ups. By then his two greatest bandleaders, Pee Wee and Wesley, had long since departed. Pee Wee walked off the gig in 1969.

"He deserves credit," Ellis says quietly. "I learned a lot. But it ran its course. He felt he was a king. You have to raise an army for the king."

He peers out of his parlor window, and I watch him. I'm dying to ask the question, the answer to which I already know.

What happens to the king when the king's men leave?

I start to ask it, but then what's the point? In another year this guy will receive an honorary doctorate in literature from Bath Spa University. Dr. Alfred Ellis. He's a legend, more recognizable in Europe than he is at home. And I'm sitting with him. So instead I say, "You wanna eat? I'm buying."

His face crinkles into a smile. The old jazzman reaches for his cap. "My man . . ."

Chapter 13

More Money

As early as 1987, James Brown began to think about his death. He would formalize his will and trust thirteen years later, but by then his life had unraveled. His second marriage, to Deidre (Dee Dee) Jenkins, had ended in divorce. His father, whom he'd held dear, had died. His third wife, Adrienne, was lifted into God's kingdom tragically two years later, after liposuction surgery in California, a crushing blow for Brown. His fourth marriage, a December 2001 union to Tomi Rae Hynie, a backup singer he met in Las Vegas, would unravel into a marital disaster that would spill into court for years after his 2006 death. He was sixty-eight when they married. She was thirty-two. She bore a son, James, Jr., that same year. But Hynie had not divorced her previous husband, a Pakistani national named Javed Ahmed, before she married Brown, which broke Brown's heart when he discovered it, according to Emma Austin. (Hynie's marriage to Ahmed was annulled three years *after* her marriage to Brown.) Brown's children—six claimed, one adopted, and at least four others unclaimed—were a mishmash of grace, tragedy, or greed, depending on whom you ask. They had to make appointments to see him. Brown, by 1998, had become an increasingly isolated old man.

He was still a force, though, irascible, unbearable, opinionated, impulsive, and even successful, having made a remarkable comeback after leaving jail in 1991 with a Kennedy Center Honor, an HBO concert, a couple of movie cameos, and a new management team of Buddy Dallas and David Cannon, who brought him back to solvency. But the glory days were gone. The record business had a new king, rap music, and Brown's body was breaking down. The years of dancing had created chronic pain in his knees and toes. He fought off pancreatic cancer. His teeth constantly bothered him. They were implants, those of a man with tight teeth who had lived a life full of loose ends and deep disappointments. Even the city Brown loved, Augusta, had deteriorated to urban blight, with white flight, drugs, the emergence of violent hip-hop, and the usual array of complicated difficulties that helped destroy black families. Brown, though generous to the poor himself, was no fan of welfare. He disliked anything that took away a man or woman's incentive to work. Cannon recalls Brown visiting a New York City men's shelter, where his appearance caused so many men to crowd him that he had to stand on a stepladder to address them. He looked around the room full of men, many of them seemingly able-bodied, and said, "Y'all ought to be ashamed of yourselves. You ought to be out working instead of being here."

"There ain't no jobs out here," a man said. "We're poor."

"I'll tell you what," Brown retorted. "You take my clothes and I'll put on your clothes. Come tonight, I'll have me some kind of job. I won't be the boss. I won't be wearing the boss's uniform. But I'll have me something."

The world had become complicated, and there he stood atop it once again after years of being down, a mass of contradictions himself, a man with miles of scorched earth behind him. He'd spent most of his entertainment life preaching the gospel of education and hard work, and now he was seen as a kind of clown. James Brown the vict. James Brown the troublemaker. James Brown, who fell down his face like so many of them eventually do. He knew it. And it hurt him. He sought to make amends. Brown decided to give back.

In 2000, he spent $20,000 in legal fees to have an airtight will and estate drawn up. The will left his personal effects to his children, plus a $2 million education fund to send his grandchildren to college should they decide to attend. The rest of it, the bulk of his estate—songs, likeness, music publishing—he left in a trust fund that he named the I Feel Good Trust, said by Cannon to be worth conservatively at least $100 million when he died. The trust was set up to help educate poor children—white and black—in South Carolina and Georgia. Brown was specific about that—the main criterion: need. Not black over white or vice versa. With regard to race, he said, "There's enough of that." The trust was to be run by the same two business partners that had brought him back to prominence, David Cannon and Buddy Dallas, and a trusted African American road manager and local magistrate named Albert "Judge" Bradley.

At least $100 million left behind to educate poor children of all races in South Carolina and Georgia. And nine years after he died, not a dime of Brown's money would go to educate a single impoverished kid in either state. Why?

The short answer is greed.

The long answer is boring, which is how lawyers like it. That's how modern-day gangsters work. They don't pull out a gun and stick it in your face. They paper you to death. They bore the public, hoping you'll turn the page, change the channel, surf the Internet, watch the football game, mutter about how shameful the whole bit is, say the hell with it, and move on.

And that's exactly, more or less, what happened.

It's a complicated business, describing the legal morass of South Carolina, a state that feels fifty years behind the rest of America in the matter of race and class. This is a state where nearly 30 percent of children live below the poverty line, where you see poor blacks in Barnwell County shuffling up and down the roads in white T-shirts, farmer's pants, and old shoes, looking like slaves of old, some having never left the state in their entire lives, and where internal state politics are rife with political cutthroats who at the smell of red meat will knock one another over the head hard enough to send the most grizzled political veteran blabbering to therapy. The horrific massacre of nine African American parishioners at Emanuel African Methodist Episcopal Church in Charleston by an avowed racist peels back only a small window to the tumultuous boil that exists beneath the outward calm of that state's swirling racio-political world. If all politics is personal, it's nuclear-strength personal in South Carolina, where four state legislators, known as the Barnwell Ring, basically ran the whole state for nearly thirty years, where the Speaker of the House in 2014 went down in ethical flames only after the most embarrassing public disclosures of his oversight, and where the current network of male bully-boys and legal bruisers, many of them judges and graduates of the University of South Carolina School of Law, run the state's legal system like a private club. "Even if you have a Harvard law degree, you won't go far over there," says Buddy Dallas.

Into the morass of legal backbiting, nepotism, and personal feuding walked David Cannon. Cannon had once headed the local Republican committee that had hosted former president George W. Bush's campaign visit to Barnwell, and he had actually lunched years ago at the Edisto Beach house with the very same judge, Doyet Early, who would one day be among those who handed him his head. According to Cannon, the trouble began just days after Brown died. Several of Brown's children, led by daughters Deanna and Yamma, sued, claiming that Cannon, Dallas, and Bradley had "unduly influenced," i.e., flimflammed, their father in his later years. Tomi Rae Hynie, Brown's "widow," who was said to be three thousand miles away in Los Angeles when Brown died, and whose bill from a California drug rehab facility that year cost Brown $50,000, filed claims of her own. She appeared on the Larry King talk show shortly after Brown's death using the term "my husband" enough times to make your head spin.

The suits hit the South Carolina courts like a smoke bomb and quickly spread. The mostly white political and legal entities in South Carolina could not have been overly fond of James Brown anyway. The guy had led cops on a two-state chase and brought international spotlight and embarrassment to a proud state, with his six-year sentence drawing international calls for his release—public pressure drummed up by the Reverend Al Sharpton, who among the South Carolina legal bullyboys is probably about as popular as a can of sardines in Rome on a Friday.

In the wake of Brown's death, a weird toxic trio of good-old-boy lawyers, Brown's children, and his poor white widow battled together, using "the poor children" that Brown left most of his money to as a kind of carrot that each of the three dangled publicly as justification for their greed. The mob needed a head on a platter. David Cannon was available. They called for his head. And they got it.

Cannon sits in the back parlor of his modest Barnwell home, facing his modest yard, surrounded by antique swords and paperwork. In front of him, on the table, is a Scooter Pie and a Coca-Cola. In front of me is the same—my reward for days of grilling the poor man about events that have flipped his life upside down.

"Have a couple for the road," Cannon says of the Scooter Pies. "I got a whole box."

I saw the crate in the kitchen. That's when I knew I really liked the guy. I love Scooter Pies.

Outside, the sound of a lawnmower roars to life, and a middle-aged black man in cool-looking shades and a baseball cap roars past, waving, mowing the grass outside. Cannon calls to him out the window.

"Hey, hey," the gardener calls out.

Cannon watches him. "I've known him a long time," he says. "He wanted to buy a house. He came to me and said, 'I can't do it. I don't know how to get it done.'" The gardener knew nothing about banks. He didn't even have a checking account. Cannon opened one for him, then arranged a meeting for him with one of Cannon's friends in the mortgage business, who got the gardener a bridge loan. When the gardener had a serious operation, Cannon showed up at his hospital bed. "He was just about to go into surgery, and I was setting by his bed," Cannon says. "He was worried. I put my hand over his hand and was talking to him. The doctor came into the room and said to him, 'I see your boss is here!'"

"I'm not his boss," Cannon said. "I'm his friend."

That kind of thinking was one reason Brown asked Cannon and Dallas to join his team in the first place, and why they later became friends. They also did for Brown what several high-powered northern executives and lawyers could not do. They brought him back to prominence and cleared his $15 million debt to the IRS. It was something Brown never forgot, and when a group of northern managers and promoters sought to undermine Cannon and Dallas, promising Brown the moon if he left his southern management team and brought them on instead, Brown told them to get lost. "Mr. Brown died not owing the government a penny," Cannon says proudly. "He used to tell folks, 'Mr. Cannon told the IRS what to do.' But I didn't really."

What Cannon did was maneuver Brown out of an IRS situation with great skill over a two-year period. Brown appreciated that skill, and celebrated the trust between the two when he introduced Cannon and Dallas to thousands at the October 2006 naming of the James Brown Arena in Augusta, Georgia, as two friends who deserved credit for helping his career. As the overseer of Brown's accounts, Cannon had power of attorney to sign Brown's checks. He tried to curtail Brown's crazy spending habits by putting him on a salary of $100,000 a month, which they both agreed on. (Brown called that "walking-around money.") He and Dallas worked to keep Brown on the right side of things. Dallas's job was to "keep him out of the ditches." When Brown put a $300,000 deposit on a private plane, then changed his mind, or made an offer on the land next to his house, then walked away from it, leaving the seller incensed, or found a contractor who ruined his basement, leaving Brown ankle deep in shit, having somehow constructed the basement so that the house sewage poured into it, it was Dallas's job to handle those matters. Cannon oversaw the money, watched the deals, sometimes made the deals, and worked to keep Brown out of tax trouble. His job, he says, was to advise Brown as to options. But the ultimate decision regarding all deals, Cannon says, fell to Brown. "No one told James Brown what to do," he says.

After Brown's IRS troubles ended, Cannon and Dallas helped Brown sever ties with his old booking agent, Universal Music, and brought him over to William Morris. Rev. Sharpton marshaled his enormous capacity to push the public relations machinery in the right direction, mounting a huge public outcry for Brown's release from prison, which led to more gigs. Brown's appearance as a preacher in *The Blues Brothers* and later in a Sylvester Stallone Rocky movie had brought him new, young audiences. Things were looking up.

But his penchant for hiding money never wavered. One afternoon, Dallas and Cannon were chatting with Brown in his Augusta office and Dallas posed a question: "Mr. Brown, where do we look for your money if something happens to you?"

Brown was seated at a desk. He had a yellow legal pad before him. He scribbled one word on it and flipped it around so that Dallas could see it.

The word read: "Dig."

In his Beech Island mansion off Douglas Drive, Brown had a little red room. Nobody was allowed to enter that room. That was the money room.

Brown led Cannon into that room one day, and as Cannon watched, he opened up one of two big cardboard boxes. The box was loaded to the top with hundred-dollar bills. Cannon was stunned. "Where did you get this from?" he asked. "This is a tax problem."

Brown wouldn't say. And if Mr. Brown wouldn't say, Cannon knew there was no forcing him. He assumed the tax problem would have to be dealt with soon enough. He'd learn of its source then.

He never did. That is part of the problem. The South Carolina state court system and its bevy of attorneys that have frittered away millions out of Brown's estate as it "administers" it during these confusing court battles is still trying to deflect the blame of "lost funds" onto Cannon, claiming that Cannon "knows where Brown's money is." Cannon insists he does not know. During his tenure with Brown, Cannon could challenge Brown about his spending, but ultimately no one changed Brown's spending habits. Brown was impulsive. If he wanted to walk into a jewelry store and spend $10,000 on a necklace, or hire a private jet to fly a young lady he'd met overseas thousands of miles to visit him, or book extra gigs while touring Europe that he didn't tell anyone about so that he could bank the cash, or cart $9,000 in silver dollars into his house in a wheelbarrow, he simply did it. Despite Cannon's objections, which usually came after the fact. "I was one of the few people who could get behind closed doors and raise hell with him," Cannon says.

But that didn't change Brown's penchant for hiding money or spending impulsively. He hid and spent so freely, Cannon says, that even Brown, who could "count his money to the dollar," began to have trouble keeping up with how much he had. Particularly aggravating, Cannon says, was Brown's habit of spending through the salary they'd agreed on, then borrowing from a huge cache of cash he stored in Cannon's home safe. According to Cannon, Brown treated that safe as a bank for eight years, storing money in it, coming by to pick up thousands at a time, storing thousands more, running out, coming back to put more in, pulling out, taking in, pulling out. The problem grew worse when Brown discovered that Adrienne had taken $93,000 that Brown had hidden in the ceiling of his pool house. He ramped up his use of Cannon's safe. "At one point he had about a million dollars in my safe," Cannon said. "I told him, 'Mr. Brown, this money belongs in a bank. I'm not a bank.'

"'No, Mr. Cannon. It's fine right here.'"

According to Cannon's account, Brown ran so much money into and out of his safe that Brown himself lost track, and about a year and a half before he died, Brown called and said, "I know I don't have any money over there."

"I said, 'You got $400,000 here.'

"He said, 'No, it's yours. I want to borrow $350,000.'

"I said, 'It's your money.' I gave him $350,000 in cash." Brown put it in a plastic grocery bag and left.

"That's something no one knows," Cannon said. "They never deposed me. I've never been on the witness stand. No one knows I was keeping cash for James Brown." Brown later insisted that Cannon repay himself the $350,000 as payment for constant borrowing and storing his funds. He had offered Cannon 10, 15, even 20 percent for keeping his money in his safe over their fourteen-year relationship, and Cannon had always declined. In addition, Cannon helped Brown broker a huge bond deal with a Wall Street outfit, which advanced Brown $25 million against future royalties. Brown wanted to reward him. That was, Cannon says, the James Brown way of doing business, based on trust, friendship, and his whims. You make a big deal, James Brown rewards you in James Brown fashion. But James Brown gives you what James Brown feels you deserve—maybe more or less than you believe you deserve. It was in keeping with his past behavior, for example the way his son Terry says that Brown would buy cars for friends or trusted associates—it might be a used one, but a used one, Brown said, would do. Or the way Fred Wesley, Brown's co-composer, says he got percentages ranging from 2 to 80 percent on songs he was involved in creating or wrote outright—and for others he did not create at all. "It was all based on JB's whims," he said.

In December 2006, Brown made an appointment to see an Atlanta dentist about his teeth. When he arrived, the dentist saw that he was seriously ill and sent Brown immediately to nearby Emory Crawford Long Hospital. Cannon got word and drove to the hospital right away. On Christmas Eve, two days later, Cannon drove there intent on staying the night. Brown said, "It's Christmas, Mr. Cannon. Go home to your family." Cannon left, reluctantly. He'd never see Brown alive again.

Brown died within hours after Cannon left, at about 1:20 A.M. on Friday, Christmas day. Cannon, who wrote and signed all of Brown's checks for James Brown Enterprises, cashed a check to himself the following Tuesday, three days after Brown's death, for $350,000. The direct source of those funds, he says, was a roughly $900,000 payment to Brown's company from a routine audit that had been performed on one of the entities that collected Brown's royalty and music publishing money. The indirect source, he says, is that it was his money anyway. Brown had given it to him, based on his storing and handling James Brown's money—doing things the James Brown way.

In an estate that at Brown's death was estimated by Cannon conservatively at a minimum of $100 million—and that figure, too, is a matter of court fighting, by the way—and where millions flowed in and out and hundreds of transactions took place annually, $350,000 is not much, particularly between two partners who cut their own deals and worked with a lot of cash. Show business, Cannon points out, is still a cash business, probably second only to drugs in terms of cash moved around. Moreover, most agents who represent artists get 10, 15 percent, even 25 percent of that artist's fees and income. Overall, Cannon's take during the course of his fourteen-year stint with Brown added up, in Cannon's view, to about 15 percent. Brown likely made much more money for the various lawyers, agents, and hustlers who visited his career long before Cannon and Dallas pulled him out of hot water, and most did far less for Brown in his career than those two, which is probably why he appointed them—along with Judge Bradley—to run his education foundation at his death.

But it didn't matter. The flurry of accusations, from Brown's alleged widow and his children, came at Cannon so fast and hard they knocked him on his heels. "You can't imagine my offense," he said. "For fourteen years my job was to build his credibility."

The initial legal warring and clamor for Brown's money was so vicious that the various parties couldn't even agree where to bury Brown. After his three funeral services—one at the Apollo in New York, one in Augusta, and a private one at Brown's daughter Deanna's church—were done, Brown's body lay in an Augusta funeral home for months while the lawyers duked it out. Cannon, who had been the guy that Brown trotted out to keep away phonies, money mongers, money grubbers, and even, at times, Brown's children, now found himself on the outside with a bull's-eye on his back, targeted by everyone who had an ax to grind. Cannon initially had to pony up $40,000 of his own money to pay for Brown's funeral and was then ordered by a South Carolina court to pay back the $350,000 check that he wrote without having the chance to explain why he wrote it. As he says, he was never deposed. He never took the witness stand. No witnesses were presented against him. He was never allowed to explain—nor could he have easily explained—the doings of a man who never trusted banks, or the government, or even some of his own children. Cannon's lawyer—since fired—told him, "It looks bad. Just give it back and you won't have to worry about it." Cannon paid the $350,000 to James Brown Enterprises to help clear the decks.

But placing the $350,000 back into the JB account just made things look worse. By then the war was full-on. All the warring parties who'd been left out of the estate plan—the claimed children minus Brown's son Terry, the alleged widow, and the growing contingent of lawyers working on contingency fees of reportedly up to 30 percent, paid out of Brown's estate and eventually totaling millions—had an easy target: a white guy who had exerted "undue influence" on the Godfather. Dallas and Judge Bradley suffered terribly as well. Dallas spent $300,000 on his legal defense, barely survived a terrible auto accident, and his law practice was nearly destroyed. Bradley died, the stress no doubt helping him to an early death. But it was Cannon who took the brunt of the accusations. A newspaper article, reported from a cleverly placed "tip" from an opposing lawyer to a friendly AP reporter, plastered Cannon's name and face across the country. Readers and television snippets showing Cannon's face bore the news that old Brown had been bamboozled out of his dough. The Internet did the rest, with half facts and rumors morphing into unsubstantiated fact. The South Carolina attorney general, Henry McMaster, who planned a run for governor, marched into the mess trying to play white knight. He tossed Brown's will and rewrote it, creating a new trust mandating that half of Brown's estate be split between the widow and the kids. By then the court had tossed Cannon, Bradley, and Dallas as trustees and appointed a new lead trustee of Brown's estate, attorney Adele Pope, who was eventually ousted by the same old-boy network that appointed her when she attempted to move the estate as Brown intended. She was ousted for a third trustee.

"In nine years, the will has never gone to probate court," says Buddy Dallas. "As long as it's in state court, they can do with it what they want. It's being sucked to death."

Meanwhile, attorneys representing Tomi Rae Hynie and Brown's children kept coming after Cannon, claiming he owed millions, at one point tossing a figure of $7 million for "restitution" in the air. Why not $10 million, $100 million? The figures seemed to come out of thin air. It seemed nearly impossible to determine what the real numbers were because the judge in the case, Doyet Early, had banned discovery going back to 2007. The $7 million figure, according to Cannon, had no basis in reality, but rather came from a $7 million certificate of deposit he'd purchased for Brown, who wanted to use it to buy an airplane. Later, when court officials went to look for the CD Cannon was alleged to have "stolen," they found it in a New York bank in Brown's accounts.

"My attorney hired a forensic accountant," Cannon says. "He went through the books. He told my attorney, 'Everything that David Cannon has said has been proven in the books.' They never wanted to take my deposition. They still—today—don't want to hear what I have to say. They never wanted to talk to me. They heard only what they wanted to hear. Things they didn't want to hear, they wouldn't hear."

By the time the dust cleared, Cannon was ruined. He had lost $4 million in net worth, including an investment home in Myrtle Beach, South Carolina, and an office warehouse in Columbia. But more than the financial loss, the embarrassment of the case, which destroyed his reputation, was too much for his wife, Maggie, a delicate, dignified woman of impeccable southern manners and hospitality. Maligned by the publicity that ruined her husband's reputation and by extension hers, she tried to commit suicide twice. Believing that his wife would not survive alone if he went to jail for a long stretch, Cannon, worn down by accusations of a case that dragged on for years, worked out a deal. He agreed to an Alford plea, which basically says he would have been found guilty, and agreed to be sentenced for contempt of court. Four days before his sentencing, his son David was murdered by two young black men who broke into his house to rob him. David's mother and Cannon's first wife, Margaret Fulcher, upon hearing the news, rushed to the hospital to be by her son's side. She crashed her car into a telephone pole en route to the hospital and died.

At Cannon's sentencing, the attorney general's office that had forced him to give up his fight did not trot out one witness against him. The presiding judge, Cannon says, was so startled by that admission that he asked the lawyers from the attorney general's office twice: "You have *no* witnesses?"

The lawyer representing the attorney general's office said nothing. The judge asked him what he thought Cannon's sentence should be. The lawyer said, "I don't have any comment."

On Cannon's side, Charles Bobbit, who had known Brown for forty-one years, spoke in Cannon's favor. His testimony, in essence, was that whatever Mr. Cannon did, Mr. Brown surely told him to do it. Nobody put one over on Mr. Brown when it came to his money. Nobody ever told Mr. Brown what to do. Cannon says a former FBI agent hired by the prosecutor spent four years investigating him. After Cannon was sentenced, the agent came up to Cannon and told his family, "I investigated this man for four years. The more I investigated, the better he looked."

The judge was lenient. He reduced a ten-year sentence to time served at home, six months in county jail, and three years' house probation wearing an ankle monitor. Cannon, who had never been arrested in his life, served three months in state prison, and was sixty-eight when he was released.

Cannon's and Dallas's insistence that they never "unduly influenced" Brown was proven true. In February 2013, after seven years of hearings involving up to ninety lawyers, three sets of trustees, and several lawsuits that comprise more than four thousand pages, the South Carolina Supreme Court, in a moment of supreme decency and sane judgment, stepped in and put the case right back where it started—declaring that Brown was not "unduly influenced" by Cannon, Bradley, and Dallas when he set up his will and trust. But the court inexplicably stopped short of putting the three original trustees back in place. So the case has lumbered on, growing more heads, with the legal wrangling continuing.

Nine years after Brown's death, not a single child in Georgia or South Carolina has benefited, while the value of Brown's estate, which, according to Cannon, was easily $100 million or maybe $150 million at Brown's death, has plummeted to an unknown figure. According to Dallas and Cannon, Brown's estate is effectively ruined. It will never be worth its top value, because when an artist dies, there's a rush to buy his or her product. That rush is usually the peak of that artist's sales worth, and contributes to the overall value of the artist's estate.

Cannon, after paying lawyers $870,000 and counting, is ruined financially. His legal costs continue, as do the court efforts to seek more restitution. "The more they come after me, the more they can bill the estate," he says. Instead of an easy retirement earned after more than four decades of work, he lives on thin ice, waiting for the next expensive legal attack and hoping to live long enough to care for his ailing wife, whose medication is prohibitively expensive. He says the case "destroyed my confidence in the judicial system in South Carolina. The good-old-boy system is alive and well here."

Seven years after Brown's death, his body lies in a mausoleum in his daughter Deanna's front yard, which cost Brown's estate—paid through the state, which still controls his wealth—$100,000 to maintain in 2013. There are plans afoot by some of Brown's children to make Brown's South Beech Island home into a museum like Elvis Presley's house in Memphis. Deanna started a James Brown School of Funk in Augusta, later called the James Brown Academy of Musik Pupils, complete with corporate donations—so the little children, presumably, can learn the Funk.

Not math. Not science. But the funk. Just what poor kids need.

So here Cannon sits, in the back room of his modest Barnwell home, on a hot August afternoon in 2012, doing exactly what James Brown's last words told him to do: *Go home, Mr. Cannon. Go home to your wife.* . . . . He finishes his old-fashioned Scooter Pie and looks out at the freshly cut yard. He enjoys the grass, the birds, the hundred-year-old tree. He hands me another Scooter Pie. He takes another for himself, bites down on it.

"When I was in prison, they put me on a detail in the kitchen," he tells me. "If you're good, they'd say, 'You can take out the garbage.' Everybody wanted to take out the garbage, because you were outside then. You could see the sky. One day they asked me, 'Mr. Cannon, you don't want to take the garbage out?'

"I said, 'No, no. I don't want to go outside and see the sky until I'm free.'"

Tears fill his eyes.

"So I never went out. I never took out the trash. That was the hardest part."

He sits in silence for a moment, his blues eyes red now. He doesn't wipe away the tears, doesn't sob, doesn't dissolve into pitiful. He sits silently watching the yard. The birds. A soft, gentle wind brushes the tree branches nearby, pregnant with leaves.

"I'll tell you what. When I first got in, I was in an eight-by-ten cell with three other people. Lying on my bunk. Crying. My stomach hurt. Knowing I had six months ahead. I said, 'Lord, I can't handle this. I can't do it. Lord, you got to take it.' And you know what? I woke up the next day and I had peace in my heart."

He rocks slowly back and forth, nodding as he talks. "No matter what has happened to me, there isn't a day that I don't get out of bed and thank the good Lord for what he's done for me. I don't know anybody the Lord's been better to than David Cannon. I thank God, and I'm grateful."

"For what?" I ask him.

"For every blessing I've ever had. For my wife. For my life. I've had too many blessings to count. God has been good to David Cannon."

Chapter 14

The Hundred-Dollar Man

The old warrior sits in the parlor of his newfangled Atlanta-area home, peering out the window at his red Chevy Corvette, the one he got as a gift from the president of Gabon, the one that will be stolen in a few weeks from this very driveway. His wife would see the guy who stole the car too. How 'bout that? She would see him at a gas station just up the road, a young guy, black, standing over the red Corvette—gassing up *his* red Corvette. She'd walk over to confront him, but the thief would smell a rat, jump into the car, and speed off. The old warrior would be steamed about that. "You can't keep nothing," he'd fume.

This is what happens when you live long enough. You see everything. You work your way up to the top of the music game after eating lard sandwiches in a shack in Franklin County, North Carolina, then watch the things you worked for vanish down the road, just like that car. He worked hard for that car. He spent decades taking care of

James Brown, then left for twelve years to work in Africa, and that was no picnic. But Charles Bobbit, eighty-one, a sharecropper's son, a man who never saw his father and lost his mother at age six, didn't rise to this level and come to own this beautiful suburban house in Snellville, Georgia, being stupid. He didn't spend forty-one years as friend and personal manager to James Brown and another two years managing Michael Jackson being naïve. He worked in Africa because he liked it, but after twelve years, he came back to a music world that had changed. The old R&B had died. Disco was gone. Rap was the new world. Kids wore their pants around their behinds and their hats sideways. His friends had changed. Even the old man, the old boss, James Brown, had changed.

He remembers that day, when Brown called him up out of the blue. "Come work for me again," he said.

Bobbit stalled. He'd been down that road. The yelling, the fights, the screaming, the horrible business of falling on his sword for Brown in 1976, when he took a hit for Brown by agreeing to testify that he paid a New York City DJ to promote Brown's records, while allowing Brown to testify that he had no knowledge of the payments and didn't condone them. Payoffs to DJs, though illegal, were widespread in the record business in those days. Brown gave him two grand. Two grand for taking the bullet for Brown.

"What do you want me to do?" Bobbit asked.

"I don't want to tell you what to do," Brown said. "You tell me what to do."

Bobbit could hardly believe his ears. For twenty years, Brown had given orders, and some were brutal. Now, after thirty-five years of giving advice, of knowing everything, Brown was asking for advice.

"I'll come for a little bit," Bobbit said. He knew how clever Brown could be. It was probably a trick, he thought, to suck him in.

But it wasn't a trick. The old man was as good as his word. He wanted Bobbit's advice. Not on big things. Not money things—nobody told Mr. Brown what to do with his money. But other things, important things, like "I'm thinking 'bout squeezing an extra gig in

Japan, what you think?" or "Can you go check on Leon?" referring to Leon Austin, Brown's childhood friend who was ailing, or "What should we do about the Rev?" because they both loved Rev. Sharpton. Brown followed Sharpton's doings like a cheesehead football fan in Wisconsin follows the Green Bay Packers. Every move, every blink, he wanted to know. Whenever the Rev was in the public eye raising civil rights hell, mostly in New York someplace, Brown would follow it on television or read the newspaper and give a running commentary to Bobbit. "Why'd he do that?" he'd say, or "Mr. Bobbit . . . Listen to this. Rev's got 'em on the ropes. . . . Ha ha!"

Those were good times, the final years, watching the Rev, their prodigal son, birthed in their baptism of fire in a Brooklyn theater forty-five years ago. And talking over the old days too. The band. The women. Those were good times for him and Brown. Like when they got the news that the Rev was going to host *Saturday Night Live*. Brown was furious. "He's gonna make a joke of himself, Mr. Bobbit," Brown muttered. "He's gonna look like a fool." The two watched Sharpton host the show in a hotel room together, and when Sharpton broke into a James Brown send-up with the Saturday Night Live Band playing behind him, Brown hollered with laughter and shouted, "Call him, Mr. Bobbit! Get Rev on the line!" Bobbit got a nervous Sharpton on the line and said, "You turned him, Rev. He says you did all right." Bobbit listened to Sharpton's palpable relief on the other end, knowing that the only opinion that ever mattered to Sharpton belonged to the old man who was suddenly fighting him for the phone, trying to grab it, to tell the Rev himself, "Rev! You got a B. I give you a B on it."

But it wasn't really a B. James Brown gave no one an A but James Brown.

Even the Rev had changed with the times. The Rev had pushed off from the dock and was on his own, ferrying into the deep waters of the civil rights movement up north. Rev was a star now.

Brown's retinue was gone. He was vanishing into history as younger, slimmer black stars took center stage. Guys who had never done the chitlin circuit. Guys who wouldn't know the blues or jazz from a pair of pliers. Even as the younger stars praised Brown, they forgot him, one of the greatest American forces in modern musical history; they saw him as a guy in their rearview mirror, extolling his virtues and vanquishing him at once. History seemed to move so fast for Brown, and as it moved for Brown, so did it move for his shadow and ace man, Charles Bobbit. Brown, who was once lauded the world over, seemed to be growing smaller before Bobbit's eyes. It was horrible. There was no new music, only the old stuff, with new guys playing it at superspeed. In the old days, Brown would have slowed them down, demanded groove, and snap—"Get the band together, Mr. Bobbitt. We're going into the studio"—and Bobbit would pull Fred, Maceo, Pee Wee, Jimmy Nolen, and Clyde outta bed from some godforsaken hotel someplace and watch Brown work them until they busted loose with some bad shit that would knock out the competition. But Brown was old now, and tired.

His body was going. Bobbit could see that way back in 2000. The prostate cancer that Brown tried to hide, the swollen knees, the swollen feet. The inability to get out of bed easily. And the drugs that he did secretly, after never drinking more than an occasional beer, and rarely smoking so much as a cigarette in front of Bobbit in forty-one years. You watch the man you gave most of your life to, the guy who burned up the stage for nearly four decades, who epitomized black life for generations past and future, see him torch his own life at its end, alone, and you realize how rich you are. You realize that the one thing you are capable of, and that he was not, is what's destroying him: sharing your life, trusting somebody else. Brown knew it. He even admitted it. He confessed it to Bobbit at one point, said it outright. "Mr. Bobbit, you're the only one I let know me. You're the only man that knows I don't know how to love."

Charles Bobbit knew how to love. He loved his wife, Ruth. He loved his kids, and his grandkids. He loved his house. And he loved his red Corvette—which, he would confess later, when muttering about its theft, was just a car, after all.

Peering through the blinds of his house, he looks at the manicured lawn, the quiet suburban street, and mutters softly, "'Stay ahead.' That's what Mr. Brown would tell me. He never stayed in one place a long time. He would go somewhere, to a meeting, or whatever. He'd be there for a little while and then go. He'd say, 'Mr. Bobbit, don't ever stay nowhere for a long time. Don't make yourself unimportant. Come important and leave important.'"

The horrible slew of lawsuits following Brown's death, the dozens of lawyers, most of whom never knew Brown, sucking Brown's estate dry, the squabbling children and widowed wife or ex-wife, depending on what you believe, each trying to pick one another's pocket while claiming to love the poor children for whom Brown's money was meant, gnaws at him. Brown predicted it would happen, Bobbit says. "He told me, 'It's gonna be a mess when I die, Mr. Bobbit. A big mess. Stay out of it.'"

So he has stayed out of it. Brown planned to give $200,000 to Bobbit. He signed a $40 million deal to sell his writer's share of his music in October 2006. But he died suddenly, three months later, in December 2006, before the sale was completed. And just like that car Bobbit's peering at in his driveway, that $200,000 is gone. And it likely ain't never coming back.

"Shame what goes on in this world," he says.

Bobbit was the facilitator, the guy who made things happen. There were other facilitators in JB's life—Fred Davis, Judge Bradley, Buddy Dallas—but Bobbit cut turf on the gig during the early big years, 1965 to 1976, when Brown was on top of the world, making musical history, serving as a symbol of black American pride at a time when millions of young blacks were fighting to integrate, to go to decent schools and vote.

He was born dirt-poor in the 1932 depression that flattened rural Franklin County, North Carolina, twenty-eight miles north of Raleigh. His mother, a midwife, died when he was six. He was shuttled from one relative to the next, working the cotton fields and pulling tobacco, living without shoes, decent clothes, or a dad. None of his relatives down there, he says, wanted little Charles Bobbit. At ten, he was shipped to an aunt in Crown Heights, Brooklyn, who agreed to take him in. He lived among Brooklyn's toughs as a careful, cautious kid. He was born with an athlete's natural build, but he refused to go out for sports teams in school because he worried he might get hurt, and if he got hurt, who would take care of Charles Bobbit? He was a country boy on his own in a world of Brooklyn hustlers and con artists who grinned and slapped you on the back with one hand while picking your pocket with the other. So much hustle. So little space to move around in that tight little world. He dreamed of getting out.

By 1965, at the age of thirty-three, he'd made his way up in the world. He had a good job laying subway track on the overnight shift for the New York City Transit Authority when he met a man who served as James Brown's driver. "Julius Friedman was his name," Bobbit says, leaning back in his chair. "Imagine. A brother, with a name like that." He chuckles. He's a heavyset man, with a hairpiece, youthful looking. He could easily pass for sixty-five. "He and I got to be friends. We started hanging out together. I'd go by his house. We'd go to a restaurant and have coffee and whatnot."

Brown was living in St. Albans, Queens, at the time and had just bought a Rolls-Royce. One day, while working a show at the Apollo Theater, Brown telephoned Julius the driver and ordered him to go out to his Queens home and deliver his Rolls and an extra set of keys to him after his show at the Apollo. "Julius asked me to ride with him," Bobbit says.

When they got to the Apollo Theater, "I was supposed to sit in the car while he went upstairs to give Mr. Brown the keys. Hell, I went on upstairs too. He went through the door of the dressing room and I was behind him. I was right on his butt, boy."

They found Brown sitting in a chair before a mirror, combing his hair in a room crowded with men in $400 mohair suits and $200 alligator shoes. Bobbit stood behind them in his Sunday best, a fifty-dollar suit and an eight-dollar pair of Thom McAn shoes.

Brown spied Bobbit. He made no comment. He simply took his car keys from Julius, and then Julius and Bobbit left.

Two months later, Brown was returning from an overseas tour and found Julius—and Bobbit again—waiting at the arrivals gate. Just before he got into the car, Brown turned to Bobbit and said, "Come down to the house. I want to talk to you."

"Me?"

"Yeah."

Bobbit reported to Brown's house in St. Albans. "When I got there, he said, 'I know you wonder why I was looking at you so hard in the dressing room that day at the Apollo.'

"I lied and said, 'Oh, no, no.'

"He says—and you know his thing was always his bad English. He was always saying 'I and you.' *I and you*—whatever. He said, 'I and you are a lot alike. We had a hard way growing up. I can see that about you. I recognized you because it wasn't but two real men in that room that day besides Mr. Friedman. It was *I and you*. The rest of them bums'—he liked to use that word, *bums,* he never cursed, it was rare for him to curse, but he'd say 'bums'—he said, 'The rest of them bums was nothing. You know what I'm gonna to do with you? I'm gonna hire you.'

"I said, 'What?'

"'I'm gonna hire you. I'm gonna hire you to be the manager. I'm taking you because you don't know nothing and you ain't got nothing. I can put my ideas in your head. I can teach you and send you out. You're an educated person and I can use you to represent me in places that I normally wouldn't be able to represent myself. You're gonna be my personal manager. I'm not hiring you to be the valet or porter or this or that. I'm hiring you to be the manager. I and you gonna be together till one of us dies.'

"'Oh yeah?'

"'Yeah. You gonna take the job or not?'"

Bobbit, standing in Brown's living room, was taken aback. The great James Brown, the Godfather of Soul and Hardest Working Man in Show Business, was offering him a job.

But Bobbit hadn't asked for a job. He already had a job. A good, safe "city job," one that most workers would die for. He had a lovely new wife, and a new child. To leave that safe job to work in show business? For the rest of his life? *Till one of us dies,* Brown had said. That was, he thought, pretty scary, no matter how you sliced it.

But Charles Bobbit had always had big dreams for himself. When he was a boy picking cotton in the fields of Franklin, North Carolina, till his hands bled, thinking of his mother, the one person who had truly loved him, now gone, and what his life would have been had she lived, he would look up at the planes that flew over the cotton fields and dream of flying. He dreamed of flying places far distant from the lard sandwiches and tobacco fields of Franklin County in the hot summers when he was sent down from Brooklyn to cure tobacco and pull cotton with the cousins who threw rocks at him, the relatives who talked right over his head about what to do with him, the same ones who'd talked over his head after his mother's funeral when he stood in their shack at age six, still dressed in his cousin's borrowed suit, fresh from his mother's burial. He heard them say to one another, "I don't want that snotty little nigger. You take him." The wounds from that conversation would last the rest of his life. His mind would sometimes wander in the afternoons and he would dream of flying high over his relatives' heads, traveling across the world, vanishing into the future, until his painful past was just a dot, a small circle in his mind that would soon vanish. Charles Bobbit, a man who worked underground in the New York City subway system, had always dreamed of flying. And as he thought about Brown's offer, it occurred to him that if there was one thing that the Godfather of Soul did a hell of a lot of in those days, it was flying.

"I'm in, Mr. Brown."

"Yeah."

"I took the job," Bobbit tells me, "thinking I could fly in planes and stay in nice hotels and quit when I was ready."

Things did not happen the way he planned, of course. He did fly in planes. He flew around the world more times than he could count. He stayed in five-star hotels and ate food that his relatives never dreamed of. He met heads of state in Africa and Asia, he met the king of Morocco, and he even shook the hand of the infamous African psychotic dictator Idi Amin. He visited the White House four times, shaking the hands of four different American presidents. He flew more in one year than most people fly in a lifetime. He even took the controls of private planes as they flew over the Atlantic. But as for quitting the James Brown job, that would not happen. Because even after twenty years, when Bobbit quit the job, the job did not quit him. Nobody quits on James Brown. As it turned out, Charles Bobbit would be the last person on this earth to see James Brown alive. James Brown's prediction came true: *I and you gonna be together till one of us dies.*

When you're a fixer, your job is to make things happen, and you have to be quick. In 1968, when Brown needed thirty kids for a three A.M. recording session to shout the background chorus of "Say It Loud— I'm Black and I'm Proud," he sent Charles Bobbit to round them up from the black section of Watts. When Brown needed to fine a musician in his band for missing a hit onstage, or for scuffed shoes or an improperly tied bow tie, Bobbit collected the dough. Resolve a dispute with a promoter? Bobbit could do it. Slip a kid $500 for college? See Mr. Bobbit. Collect twenty-five or fifty grand in a cash advance for a gig—hundred-dollar bills only, please—in a stained brown-paper sandwich bag? See Mr. Bobbit. Slip a DJ a few dollars to play his records? That was Bobbit's job. In the sixties, when the James Brown Revue was a traveling show, with big acts like the gorgeous singer Yvonne Fair, the legendary comedian Pigmeat Markham, the Impressions, which included the great soul singer Curtis Mayfield, and Anna King, it was Bobbit's job to spread the catnip around. He did so with such cool that Nipsy Russell, a much-beloved black comedian who toured with the Revue, nicknamed him the Hundred-Dollar Man. The nickname stuck. Always loyal. Forever discreet. A man of a thousand faces. The Hundred-Dollar Man was a guy who could go 360 degrees: he could yak up a United States president or face down a mobster who threatened to release rats into the Apollo audience. A guy who could grab Brown's .38 caliber out of Brown's pocket when Brown flew off the handle—Brown carried it everywhere—and, if necessary, wade out into a crowd and calm the offending party himself, because he was a third-degree black belt and a former member of the Nation of Islam. There was no better soldier, no more discreet lieutenant. There was no better right-hand man than the Hundred-Dollar Man.

"I don't lie for anyone and I don't lie against anyone," Bobbit says. "That's not my nature. I don't have to. I just tell the truth. Everything I have—a lot of it—is because of him."

The Hundred-Dollar Man remembers the friend that was both a brother and tyrant, and the business that sucked their collective blood and gave them life at the same time.

"I don't normally give interviews," he tells me. "The one or two times I did, I said the same thing basically because I don't talk against him. Whatever I accomplished has a lot to do with him. Many people claim they know him. Oh, I see the books and I hear the people say they know him. It's pure bullshit. Most of them don't know him because he did not let them know him. He didn't want them to know him. When he met you, he either liked you or he didn't. There wasn't no whole long thing about it."

"Would you say you're that kind of person too?" I ask.

"Yes, because I learned a lot of that from him. I mean, hey, after all those years, I loved the man. We learned a lot from each other at the end of it all. I'd read him. I'd say, 'Let me figure out which James Brown I am talking to today, because there was about three of him—to me. He even had two or three signatures. One for contracts. One for the fans. And one for whatever. He did not believe in letting people get to know him. This is what most people didn't understand."

"Which were the three people?" I ask.

Bobbit talks in circles for a few minutes. It's a habit of an old survivor. Those old record-business guys are a different breed, they're not used to talking in straight lines. You talked too straight in that business, back in the old days, and you might find yourself lying facedown in back of a packinghouse someplace looking down on yourself from above. Finally he says, "He was a giving person. But he could go from a smile to a scream if things weren't just so. He was a complex individual. If you did something he didn't like, he would chew your ass out right then. Even if you were in front of the president. No matter who it was, he would come down on you. There was no such thing as 'We'll talk later.' He made no distinction between his housekeeper or me, the manager. Or the band. The band would piss themselves when he walked into the room. With him, you listened. You didn't debate with him. You'd be wasting your time trying to convince him of something anyway. Everybody was in the same bag with him."

"So who was the second person?" I ask.

He spins the web a bit more for a while, then says, "The other one was a businessperson. But he wasn't that great a businessperson. He admitted that. He said he was about sixty percent entertainer and forty percent business. And then the other one was he could be a demon when he wanted to be. Yeah, he could be mean and devious. He could go from a smile to a scream if things weren't just so."

He is seated at the table now, fiddling with his hands a moment, thinking. "Very complicated. But he never forgot where he was from. He'd say, 'Mr. Bobbit, don't forget where you're from.' Even when he met other entertainers on the road, he'd ask 'em, 'When's the last time you been home?'"

He shifts uncomfortably, opening and closing mental doors, running out of good stories to tell, maybe. Which doors to open? Which to keep shut? Talking to Bobbit is like interviewing a live dinosaur at a museum someplace and asking it what it ate last. It's not worried about last night's meal. It's the next meal that counts. He's part of a disappearing breed: America's soul-music wheelers and dealers. These guys—and most were guys, although Gladys Hampton, wife of Lionel Hampton, was as clever and shrewd a businesswoman as you could meet—know where every skeleton is buried. They know every secret. And they never tell. In many ways, Bobbit fits that mold to a T.

Though he doesn't sing or dance, he's named as a cowriter on several Brown songs, mostly minor hits. America's music-publishing catalogs are loaded with managerial types listed as cowriters—Duke Ellington's manager, Irving Mills, is listed as co-author on a number of Duke's most famous hits, and Mills, as far as I know, is famous as a manager—whereas the great gay composer Billy Strayhorn had a much larger hand in the creation of Duke's music. But the truth is, Duke could never have climbed the greasy pole of success without Mills, who was said to be among the first to integrate blacks and whites on the bandstand in New York going back to the 1920s. Talent is just dessert in the ear-candy business anyway. It's about who can stand the ride, the merry-go-round that forces you to toss off self-esteem, decency, and morality and pull out your gun on the competition—beat 'em down with the barrel instead of killing 'em outright, then pick them up afterward and say, "Get up, let's do it again." A life of making ear candy can kill off every dream you ever had. The old record guys in Brown's life—Henry Stone in Miami, Ben Bart of Universal Music, Charles Bobbit—are old survivors in a game of musical chairs that often doesn't end well for everyone. It's a game of unwritten rules that they all understood and cared about: Fresh fruit. Old fruit. Bad fruit. Good fruit. Sell it if you can, because if you don't, the next guy will, and if the feds come knocking asking about payola to DJs, or if some lawyer with shiny shoes shows up asking for money, just remind that joker that he's probably got a can tied to his tail, too, that will rattle from here to the FCC or some Senate subcommittee hearing if he tries to make too much noise about you. Everybody in the record business has secrets, but the most obvious one is the hardest for musicians to accept: there's talent everywhere. I remember having lunch years ago with a legendary record executive in LA, bending his ear about a great unsigned singer I knew. The guy listened, nodded, yawned, reached for his triple-decker sandwich, and took a bite. "Great singers," he said between chews, "are a dime a dozen."

In that regard, Bobbit is a blend of General Patton and Gumby. You can bend him this way and that way, stretch him like a rubber band, put him in a headlock and give him a noogie, threaten him with jail even, but he will not talk in any direction he doesn't want to. He's a witness to more black history than most will ever see. He was a member of the Nation of Islam Mosque No. 7 at the old 116th and Lenox Headquarters in Harlem in 1953, when two promising young ministers, Malcolm X and Minister Louis Farrakhan—a respected musician himself—came on board. Malcolm X was the renegade who left the Nation and was murdered on February 21, 1965, in Harlem's Audubon Ballroom. Farrakhan—a calypso singer and also violinist—remained. Bobbit knew them both and never speaks of either. He was with James Brown back in the sixties, when everyone from the Black Panthers to the mobsters tried to push in on the James Brown Revue. No dice. Brown staved them off with payoffs, favors, concerts, and a willingness to fight back with a loyal crew, of which Bobbit was both lieutenant and soldier. Bobbit even took one in the face for Brown in a 1970s payola scheme involving Brown and Frankie Crocker, a legendary DJ out of WBLS in New York City. Bobbit admitted to having given Crocker $6,500 to play Brown's records. It cost Bobbit thousands in legal fees and two years' probation to get out of what was then a widespread practice in the record business.

I am curious about that one, and I ask Bobbit, "Did Mr. Brown help you after you took the hit for him?"

Bobbit smiles. The smile drips to the floor. "That's another story for another time," he says. Another time, of course, will never come. Instead, he reels off the story of a fortune-teller who predicted his future, saying he would never go to jail after taking the hit for Brown during the trial. "Everything she said came true," he says. "Thanks to God, Allah, Jehovah. Whatever you want to call it. I came out clean."

Mention Bobbit's name to some of the old Brown band members, and the air in the room thickens. Their smiles move sideways, floating from left to right, aimless, like a drop of olive oil floating on a plate of water. They were friends. All part of the same troop. All shared the same hardship—"working for Mr. Brown"—all part of the plantation, so to speak. But Bobbit was both friend and hatchet man, jobs that in Brown's later years fell to Buddy Dallas and David Cannon. The legal case that nearly destroyed those two men also took a good swipe at the career of South Carolina attorney Adele Pope, an experienced and respected probate attorney and the only female lawyer of prominence in the case. But Bobbit, who was as close to James Brown as anyone in this world, walked away relatively unscathed. It was Brown's last gift to him. "Mr. Brown told me before he died, 'I know you wonder, out of all the things we said to each other, why I didn't make you a trustee or something like that. I'm gonna tell you: I don't want you involved in that. When I die, it's going to be a big, big mess. If you were there, they're gonna put you in the middle of it and a lot of the blame is going to fall on you. It's going to take ten years or more before they straighten it out because they don't know how. And the reason they don't know how is they don't know Mr. Brown.'"

"But who is Mr. Brown?" I ask, because after several hours, we haven't gotten any further than we did when we first started.

"He didn't want you to know him."

"Why?"

Bobbit pauses a moment, looking at his hands, then says, finally, "Fear."

"Of what?"

Bobbit, the master web spinner, spins the web awhile, then says, "The white man. He was Mr. Say It Loud, but he knew the white man owned the record business. He wasn't stupid. He wanted to stay ahead. That's what he would tell me. 'Stay ahead of the next guy. That way, you control the conversation. Don't let nobody out-talk you, Mr. Bobbit.' That was the way it was with him, even if he was wrong as hell."

He takes a sip of water, his mind reeling back to a time and place long forgotten: the Muhammad Ali–George Foreman fight in Zaire in 1974, which featured Brown and several entertainers, the famous "Rumble in the Jungle."

"They had chartered a plane for the performers. B.B. King was on it and Etta James and Sister Sledge and Bill Withers. Brown wanted to bring his equipment. I told him, 'You don't need to bring equipment. They're on a different current over there in Africa. They're 220. We're 110.' But he insisted. They had to take a lot of his stuff off the plane because it was too heavy. He held the plane up. It was so loaded it barely got into the air. Oh my God, Bill Withers was so mad. They were late getting to Zaire because of Brother Brown.

"Mobutu [the president of Zaire] was famous for giving diamonds as a gift. He sent word for all the entertainers to stay behind for a while when the music was finished. Mr. Brown said, 'I ain't staying here.'

"He come offstage, went into a room, changed his clothes, and went straight to the airport and sat there for four hours. And he could have got a bag of diamonds as a gift. But he was a man that did what he wanted to do. That was him.

"That's why I say most of these people don't know James Brown. They don't know that part of him. He let known what he wanted to be known."

He sits pondering.

"Did you feel trapped with him?" I ask.

"No," he says softly. "I loved the man."

Forty-one years after the two met, in the wee hours of Christmas Day in 2006 at Emery Crawford Long Hospital in Atlanta, James Brown's prediction about himself and Charles Bobbit—*I and you gonna be together till one of us dies*—came true. David Cannon had left a few hours earlier. Andre White, another close friend of Brown's, had come and gently massaged Brown's feet but had also departed. Brown lay on a hospital bed in the ICU, his body shutting down. His knees, his prostate, his heart, his teeth, his lungs were all giving out. The room was empty save Charles Bobbit and James Brown.

Brown suddenly sat up and said, "Mr. Bobbit. I'm on fire! I'm on fire! My chest is burning up!" Then he lay back and died.

"He closed his eyes and I felt his pulse and he didn't have a pulse," Bobbit says. "I don't know why, but I looked at the clock. It was 1:21 Christmas morning, and I felt his pulse and there was none. I felt his stomach and there was none. I picked up the phone and called the nurse's station and they all came running. They worked on him till 1:45, when they officially declared him dead. The doctor told me to leave the room, so I went and stood in the door and they were working on him, working on him. The doctor said, 'You might as well stop. This man is gone.'

"I said, 'Gone? Gone where?'

"He said, 'This man is dead.'

"Dead? James Brown is dead?"

"He said, 'Yeah, yeah. He's dead. Everybody dies.'

"Then they pulled the blanket up around to his neck. They didn't even cover him over. They just pulled the blanket up and walked out of the room."

Chapter 15

The Rag That Nobody Reads

Sue Summer wheels her battered 2010 Toyota Prius down the streets of Newberry, South Carolina, like she owns the place, spinning left, and right, then left again. She's in a hurry this hot August afternoon. Her two-year-old granddaughter Eleanor needs to be picked up soon. Eleanor is a real beauty. A southern belle in training? Not quite, because this heavyset, attractive, sixty-two-year-old grandmother is doing a lot of the raising of Eleanor. And Sue is nobody's belle. She's big-league and plays with the big boys.

She passes the old post office, built in the early 1900s. The whining gas motor hollers for mercy before the car jumps into silent mode as she glides down a hill, just four blocks away from Bubba's, the town bar where her brother Danny Davis, an ex-marine who did two tours of duty in Vietnam, used to drag his soldier friends home to meet his pretty little sister "Annie Laurie." In the old days, when he was training at Camp Lejeune, North Carolina, the next state over, Danny would call Sue and say, "I'm coming home for the weekend, Annie Laurie. Getting a lift from a buddy, Annie Laurie." *Annie Laurie*. It was a code word that meant he was standing next to some army sap, usually a Yank, who was giving Danny a free ride home, hoping to get lucky with one of Danny's pretty southern-belle sisters. The guy got lucky all right. He was lucky if Sue didn't drink him under the table and make him walk home. *Annie Laurie*. Yankees are so stupid.

She whirs past the C&L Railroad on O'Neal Street to the old mill side of town, where her mother grew up, turns, and beats it past Newberry Middle School, which lies above the hallowed field where baseball legend Shoeless Joe Jackson once played with a local ball team from the mill in nearby Greenville. Shoeless Joe is the guy from the Chicago Black Sox scandal of the 1919 World Series—he took a payoff to throw the series, but still played to win. Until he died, he denied that he had cheated. Down here they believe him.

She turns down a tree-lined street, swerves past a boy walking a dog, then hits a state highway still rolling hard. The neat homes give way to farm country, clapboard houses, trailer homes, hulks of cars lifted on cement blocks surrounded by high weeds, and tiny churches bearing placard poster signs out front like the ones I saw earlier that said, HOW WOULD YOU FEEL IF GOD ONLY LISTENED TO YOU ONE HOUR PER WEEK? and I DON'T I-PAD. I-PRAY. God is serious business down here in South Carolina. You speak foul of the Redeemer Who Spilt His Blood in these parts and you're liable to find yourself knocked upside the head hard enough to spend the rest of your life leaning like a flower a week after the rain.

She stops across the street from a humble schoolhouse near Silverstreet, a quiet country road. Then she points out the window of her old car. "That's it," she says. "That's the place."

I'm looking at the Reuben Elementary School. This is where Sue's daughter teaches. The school has a "backpack ministry," just like the one run by Sue's church at nearby Gallman Elementary. The "backpack ministry" gives out free breakfast and lunch to dozens of kids every day, but volunteers realized the need was so great that they had to give the kids backpacks on Fridays, because the kids didn't have enough food at home to last the weekend. "To give them food in paper bags would be to single out the poor ones," she said, so they gave them backpacks with cereal, soup, peanut butter, crackers, enough to last through Monday again. Many of the kids are white, whose proud working-class parents often keep cows in the garden for milk and work two or sometimes three jobs a week to make ends meet.

These are the kids that James Brown left his money to. As the lawsuits drag on and his estate plummets in value, the children of Reuben Elementary School can't afford the cost of lunch. And because so many children in Newberry County come to school without pencil and paper, a school-supplies drive was launched by volunteers—Sue's been doing that for fifteen years, too—gathering pencils, papers, and notebooks for the kids. Imagine that, in America, in the new millennium. These are the children we expect to compete with kids from France, China, Japan, Russia. And when they don't succeed, we say it's their fault. Or it's the video games. Or their parents. Or hip-hop music. Anything but the lawyers and politicians up the road, feasting on the money meant for them, fighting over an airtight will that James Brown spent $20,000 putting together.

Sue sits at the steering wheel of her car, peering through the windshield at the empty schoolyard. Without a word, she puts the car in reverse, backs up, and swivels the car around toward town.

She was lighthearted on the drive out. But now, driving back to town, her face is etched in a firm frown. She drives in grim silence. The old homes and high weeds and dilapidated houses seem to whiz past as the beaten Toyota picks up speed. I mumble something about the whole case being a shame.

She says nothing for a while, staring straight ahead. Finally she speaks. "Everybody is lying," she says. "That's what I've decided."

Sue Summer is the kind of reporter they used to teach us about back at the Columbia University Graduate School of Journalism when I was a student there in 1980. I remember those days, staggering into the big lecture hall at 116th and Broadway at eight A.M. on a cold fall morning, rubbing the sleep out of my eyes, scrounging low in my seat in the back of the lecture hall as First Amendment attorney Benno Schmidt and the mighty Fred Friendly, president of CBS News, lectured us on the importance of a free press in a democratic society. Friendly was a tall, regal figure, as kind as his name implied. He'd stalk the lecture room floor, regaling us in his booming baritone about the swinging pendulum of the Freedom of Information Act, how he used it like a baseball bat—kicking in doors, massaging sources to truth. He recalled the fights, the arm-twisting, the tension, the furious arguments that broke out in smoke-filled production rooms at CBS News just seconds before airtime as he and legendary radio and TV newsman Edward R. Murrow grappled with the network, forcing it to take aim at some loathsome public sleaze, or at some smooth crook who was paying his bills with foreign dough. I'd walk out of those classes wired, ready to jump out the window and begin preserving the Freedom of Information Act right then and there, pack it in ice, can the whole thing the way my aunt Parthenia used to can peaches back in Virginia, then lob it like a hand grenade through the window of the first enemy of the press I ran across. That's how inspired I was.

Then I had to get a job after J-School. And that was that.

But had I known that I would meet a Sue Summer, I suspect I would have paid more attention. For more than twenty years Sue has been a reporter and columnist for the financially strapped 130-year-old *Newberry Observer*. For more than three of those, since August 2011, she has been the sole journalist guarding the public's right to know, as it pertains to the James Brown court case, which has dragged on for more than nine years under the cloak of near secrecy, with forty-seven lawsuits and over ninety attorneys.

Here's the setup: Imagine a boxing ring and two fighters. In one corner, you have a sole journalist who writes for a nearly bankrupt newspaper, a grandmother who spent most of her career writing baking recipes, local jokes, and gossip but who stumbles onto a big story.

In the other corner, imagine some of the richest and most powerful music executives, and political foes you wouldn't want to meet, from LA, Atlanta, and of course South Carolina. They too have stumbled onto a story. It's a story with a pot of gold—an estate and will of a dead guy that hasn't been sent to probate court yet. If it had been sent to probate court, that would have frozen the thing and left it just as the dead guy wanted it. Instead, it's been shoved into circuit court, which means it's red meat on the table. And this is not just any will. And it's not just any guy. It's the will of a black guy named James Brown, a damned troublemaker who caused South Carolina a pisspot of trouble. And the only thing standing between them and James Brown's pot of gold is this little old lady and her little old newspaper, which one of them dubbed "a rag that nobody reads."

Well, it turns out that old Grandma knows how to throw a punch or two herself. Turns out old Grandma has Muhammad Ali speed and Joe Frazier guts. Here are some of the powerful characters spelled out in Sue's Rag That Nobody Reads, the guys in the other corner: Louis Levenson (representing some of Brown's children); attorneys Robert Rosen and S. Alan Medlin, the latter a University of South Carolina law professor, both representing Tomi Rae Hynie, Brown's female companion later ruled to be his wife; Aiken County judge Doyet Early III, who helped dismantle James Brown's original trust and whose 2015 ruling elevated Brown's female companion to the status of "widow"; Peter Afterman, an LA-based producer who represents the Rolling Stones' music catalog; Russell Bauknight, trustee of the James Brown estate, who forked over management of the catalog to Afterman in the first place; the powerful South Carolina law firm of Nexsen Pruet, which represents Bauknight, among others; and the tag team of Henry McMaster and Alan Wilson, former and current attorney general and heads of the most powerful law-enforcement body in the state of South Carolina.

These are heavy hitters. They represent money. Power. Influence. And little ol' Sue Summer just gives 'em all headaches. Why is that? Because she's tough? She's smart? She's a journalist? Which?

"I'm just a broad," she says simply.

Some broad.

The fight began within hours of Brown's December 25, 2006, death, with disputes about how to conduct his funeral and initial legal fire coming shortly after from two parties: Brown's "widow," Tomi Rae Hynie, and five of Brown's six claimed children. Both parties claimed Brown was "unduly influenced" at the end of his life by his selected trustees: Buddy Dallas, David Cannon, and Albert "Judge" Bradley. The three were jettisoned by Aiken County judge Early in 2007. Judge Early named two local attorneys, Robert Buchanan and Adele Pope, as trustees. A plethora of lawsuits and wild legal scrambling followed, including a hastily arranged auction of Brown's personal effects at Christie's in New York to raise legal fees, which netted a relatively paltry sum for some seemingly valuable items.

The fight never really came up to street level. There were hearings to determine hearings. Hearings to determine the status of other hearings. Hearings for this. Hearings for that. Two assessments of Brown's worldly items. Calculations and more calculations and hundreds of questions, posed by lawyers who, of course, billed James Brown's estate. Sue wandered into it in 2011, when she got word that there was an FOI request. The request involved Tomi Rae Hynie Brown, who had married Brown in December 2001. Brown filed to annul the marriage in 2004, after learning Tomi Rae was already married to another man. It meant, at the time of course, that Hynie, angling for a percentage of Brown's estate, was not his wife at the time of his death. Tomi Rae kept a diary that allegedly revealed pertinent information about that marriage or lack thereof. The diary was suppressed by Judge Early, who collected all of the copies of the diary, placed a 2008 gag order on it, and, seven years later, ruled that Hynie was, in fact, Brown's wife. This ruling came after untold hundreds of thousands of Brown's money was spent on attorney fees.

In the meantime, some of Brown's kids filed their own legal grievances. They're led by Deanna Thomas Brown, lead plaintiff in the children's lawsuit. Thomas Brown entombed her father in her yard—the same father she and her sister Yamma sued in 2002 for royalties on songs for which Brown gave them writing credit when they were six and three years old. The wrangling between these suing parties was so heated that the great state of Georgia, which had a 50 percent interest in Brown's education trust, walked away, leaving the South Carolinians to duke it out.

In the fracas, the net worth of James Brown's estate, which was worth easily $100 million according to his accountant Cannon, plummeted to as low as an estimated and disputed figure of $4.7 million, declared by the court-appointed trustee Russell Bauknight in 2009. Bauknight, fifty-six, of Irmo, South Carolina, has been mentioned in many of Sue's stories. He's a tiny fellow, an accountant, and the one who described the *Newberry Observer* as "a rag that nobody reads." He's also a reserve deputy captain for the Lexington County Sheriff Department, appointed by a sheriff who was convicted for his role in an alleged scheme to help illegal aliens in his jurisdictiion avoid federal detection. Bauknight's accounting firm has scarfed up some pretty sweet fees working on the Godfather of Soul's estate—$345,000 in 2013 and $315,000 in 2014—and is represented by the goliath South Carolina law firm of Nexsen Pruet, with its cadre of 190 attorneys. That firm raked in $1.6 million in legal fees from the James Brown estate for the years 2013 and 2014 combined. Bauknight, Nexsen Pruet, the South Carolina attorney general's office, and attorneys Medlin and Rosen, who represent Brown's "widow," Tomi Rae Hynie, have been key figures in Summer's more than sixty stories about the James Brown case. One result: She's been served with subpoenas three times, once in May 2012, then again six months later and again in January 2015. The subpoenas demanded notes, tapes, sources, and contacts. Sue refused. One of those subpoenas was served while Sue was at home putting her granddaughter Eleanor, who was then one year old, down for a nap. She told the server, "Come back after I put her to sleep." The guy did. She showed up at court for the second subpoena with a toothbrush, a tube of toothpaste, and an extra pair of underwear crammed in her purse for a possible jail stay. At one of the hearings, Sue brought her eighty-two-year-old mother, Ethel, along as "backup," in case her attorney from the South Carolina Press Association couldn't keep her out of jail.

Bauknight and one of his legal teams claimed that the public documents Summer posted on her Facebook page and in the *Observer* were somehow hurting the resolution of the James Brown case as it made its way to the South Carolina Supreme Court. Meanwhile a second law firm that represents Bauknight trotted out their own arguments about the case just before the South Carolina Supreme Court heard arguments about it—in an interview with Nexsen Pruet attorney David Black, which appeared in over four hundred newspapers.

There was a time, say thirty years ago, when a story that smelled this bad—lawyers and politicians wrangling money meant for the poor and kicking a sole journalist around as they did it—wouldn't last long in America. The odor of the thing would waft clear out of South Carolina and up to, say, *The Philadelphia Inquirer.* That newsroom during the 1980s was loaded with some of the greatest reporters this nation has ever known, headed by legendary editors Gene Foreman, Gene Roberts, a white southerner who covered the civil rights movement for *The New York Times,* and the late Jim Naughton, one of the greatest newspaper editors ever. The old *Philadelphia Inquirer* would pivot on a story like this with the agility of a cougar and devour it like catnip. The rats would scurry, the castle would totter, the big networks would move in to finish the job, and down it would go—and the money to educate poor kids would be freed up. But today, print newspapers are the poor kids on the block in America, as ads revenues vanish; the once mighty network news departments are like punch-drunk boxers, crippled by cuts, forced to fight off cable, which in turn is fighting off the still-developing serious digital news sites (which are, thankfully, beginning to muscle up), which are, in turn, fighting off the information chatterboxes that serve a steady diet of potato chips and cake icing as news.

In late 2014, two enterprising *New York Times* reporters, Larry Rohter and Steve Knopper, ambled into South Carolina, peeled the lid off the garbage can, and let the nation get a full whiff of the stench. Their December 2014 front-page story said essentially the same thing Sue Summer had been saying in the Rag That Nobody Reads: that the bulk of Brown's estate has not reached the children for whom it was intended, that the estate has paid millions to attorneys and creditors, and that it remains mired in lawsuits years later. The next day *The Times* of London called Sue, interested in pursuing the story. "Now," Sue says grimly, "they know someone is watching."

The sad fact is, though, that even if the greatest reporters in the world descend on South Carolina to dig out the facts, this story is knotted up so tight in history that only a local like Sue could figure it out. The case is bound by race, blood, nepotism, and feuds that reach back to slavery and the Reconstruction that followed. Only a local would understand, say, that Adele Pope, the attorney who fought against the same network of bullyboys who threatened to jail Sue, is actually a Hammond; that her great-great-grandfather is former South Carolina governor James Henry Hammond, who once owned the land where James Brown's house is. Only a local would understand that former attorney general Henry McMaster, who kicked the James Brown case into the court system for an extra five years by rewriting Brown's will in 2008, was in the midst of a failed run for governor at the time, and that McMaster was a fundraiser for the University of South Carolina School of Law—where Tomi Rae Hynie's attorney, S. Alan Medlin, is a professor, and which most of the attorneys and judges in this case attended, including Judge Early, who's done his share of kicking this carcass up the road so everybody and their brother can have a bite. Many of these guys—and they're mostly guys—know one another. They toss cases at one another. They dine together. They hire one another. "This case is a dairy farm," Sue says. "They have this political dairy they can feed off of. They keep milking it."

Sue and I are sitting in her handsome Newberry home at her

kitchen table, with its lazy Susan ("which I always took offense at," she jokes) made by her husband Henry's grandfather. I asked Sue if she knew of James Brown when she was young.

"Sure," she says, "but I grew up trying to learn how to shag." That's a Carolina dance, by the way. It's pretty complicated. I tried it and nearly fell on my face. "The shag," Sue says, "will turn you around a bit."

You poke deep into this woman's psyche and you get the same temperature every day. Cool. Determined. A deep stubbornness, a wide streak of kindness, and a long memory for the good. It runs in the family. Her mother raised three kids after a difficult divorce. Her brother Danny came home from the war in Vietnam determined to live a life of purpose. Danny was a helicopter gunner, and after the war spent his middle years with his hand draped not around the trigger of a .50mm gun but around the handle of a church hand bell. He built homes for the homeless in Mexico. He volunteered in church for whatever they asked, and served as a volunteer at the Augusta National's thirteenth hole, the tough one, one of the holes that make up what they call "the Amen Corner." That's where Danny is today. Just a bit of his ashes, snuck in there by a friend, tucked between the azaleas and the green. He reached the Amen Corner in July 1999, at age forty-seven. Cancer got Danny, not the bitterness of Vietnam.

Sue can't get Danny out of her head. He represented everything her parents wanted the Davis children to be. It's one reason she continues the fight, walking into hostile courtrooms alone, a sole reporter from the Rag That Nobody Reads, the rag that serves as watchdog for tens of thousands of needy kids who have no voice and deserve a decent shot at an education. For them, the Rag That Nobody Reads is the Most Important Rag in the World. "It's heartbreaking," she says of the whole business. "If it weren't so terrible, it would be funny." She chuckles bitterly even as she says it.

Sue takes me to the Central United Methodist Church on a balmy spring afternoon. Her granddaughter Eleanor is with us; Eleanor goes wherever Sue goes. The three of us came here so that Sue could show me the beautiful stained-glass windows. "People come from every-where to see them," she says. I can see why. The windows were crafted in 1891 by two German immigrants. They are biblical images—Jesus with his lambs, the apostle Paul beckoning to the light, Jesus in the Garden of Gethsemane comforting mourners. They're gorgeous and almost defy description. The glass pushes various light and colors into every corner of the wide sanctuary. It's like the Lord himself is stand-ing directly over the building holding a work light.

Summer points to the huge stained-glass portrait of Jesus just be-hind the pulpit, his arms outstretched, beckoning. It's one of the larg-est Von Gerichten windows still in existence, and one of her favorites. "A storm damaged it," she tells me. "The congregation raised the money to repair it."

"How much did it cost to fix?" I ask.

She picks up a hymnal and leafs through the pages. She rubs the book thoughtfully. "Half a million to fix them," she says. "The con-gregation raised it somehow. They tell us the windows are worth four million dollars at least."

"I bet that's more than the worth of the building," I say.

She shrugs and remains silent. A strange aura seems to cover the room. I look up. Those stained-glass windows cast a warm, protective glow everywhere about the room. I've never seen a church like this before—and I've seen a lot of churches.

"How often do you come here?" I ask.

She laughs and places her choral book back into its placeholder.

"If you're asking do I pray a lot," she says, "the answer is yes."

She gets up to leave, picks up little Eleanor, and slowly heads toward the door. There's dinner to make for Henry, who has stood steady at her side throughout this struggle. Her grown son is coming home to visit. And she has just lodged another written Freedom of Information request, tossed another grenade over the transom so to speak, to see where this James Brown case is being dragged, which could mean another subpoena and court date for a woman who drives a beat-up car and lives in a simple house on a simple road in a simple town in a simple state where nothing, not even a simple gift to poor children, is simple. Thankfully, two local attorneys, Jay Bender of the South Carolina Press Association and Tom Pope, whose father once represented the *Newberry Observer*, stepped into the fray on her behalf and kept her out of jail—this time. But what happens next? Only God knows.

I watch her now as she walks past the preacher's pulpit, just under the stained-glass image of Jesus in the Garden of Gethsemane that holds his arms out in welcome. He smiles warmly over her shoulder as she heads toward the door. And then she's gone. And the polished glass door of God's house closes behind her without a sound, silent, sure, and blessedly solid.

Chapter 16

Sis

She rumbles up to the beaten yellow house in Augusta's black neighborhood driving a handsome old Lincoln Continental that thunders to a stop. One tire pushes up onto the curb then plops back onto the street, and finally she halts and cuts the engine. It's a bad parking job. Across the street, a suspicious-looking black dude shuffles along the sidewalk in a loose T-shirt and jeans, peering curiously as the pretty, light-skinned black woman in a beautiful white hat emerges from her car. He lifts a hand to wave at her. The wave is heavy, slow. "Miss Emma."

"Hey, honey."

Everybody knows Miss Emma for her church hats. She's got at least a dozen of them, all shapes and sizes. She'd be hard to miss anyway, with her fine, beautiful self—they called her type a redbone down South when I was a boy. Even now, at age sixty-six, she looks twenty years younger. She's old-school gracious and old-school southern

cool, never poking, prying, never asking questions about personal
business or telling her own. Even the nosy neighbors don't know
about her back pain, and the bursitis, and the roaring pain in her hip
that knocked her for a loop for nearly a month. She's allergic to just
about every medication and also allergic to asking for help. She was
raised that way, to remember only the good, to speak well of folks, to
be kind: she recalls the days of her family's business, McBowman's
Motor Inn, which for years housed so many of James Brown's circle
for free—Maceo, Rev. Sharpton, Country Kellum, Jimmy Nolen—
those were wonderful days. They all ate cornbread and yams and
chicken at her kitchen table. Then later when she moved into this
house, many of them followed—the Rev himself stayed there. The
house is too big for her now. The kitchen counter is too long, and it's
hard for her to lift those heavy pots; the lush couches and chairs that
the musicians lounged on when they retreated to her house hurt her
back when she leans over to dust them; the beautiful white grand
piano they once jammed on into the wee hours sits proudly in the living room, and the Bible atop it has clearly gotten a lot of wear. The
guys loved that house. A lot of them have gone on to their reward
now. But they always wrote and called from around the world because
they loved Miss Emma. And they loved that house. It's a beautiful
house because Miss Emma is in it. And God is on high in that house.
God is good. All the time. He's good to Miss Emma.

She steps out of her Lincoln Continental into the warm Augusta
air looking bright and happy, wearing a warm smile, gazing up and
down at the old houses, a couple of them boarded and the others, like
hers, neatly trimmed. She gazes up and down the street with the air of
someone peering at a sandy beach on a sunny island in Jamaica someplace. She sees you standing there, looking confused. She laughs.

"Why you standing over there? You ain't got to do that. C'mon
inside the house and rest your feet."

I'm walking into the house of one of James Brown's many women.
A woman he loved. And who loved him back like no other.

A woman he called Sis.

In 2006, when James Brown began to die—his prostate cancer eating at him, his toenails clipped off, his teeth killing him, knees aching, body hurting from arthritis—one of the first people he began to call frequently while he lay in bed resting was Miss Emma, wife of his best friend, Leon Austin. There were others he would call frequently as well: Leon, Al Sharpton, Charles Bobbit, the former NFL star Al White, his first wife, Velma—he called Velma from his hospital bed as he lay dying, though he never told her where he was calling from—and his son Terry. They all understood him, saw him as he was, and asked for nothing. But Miss Emma had a special distinction. She was neither a man nor a business acquaintance, neither lover nor wife. She was a woman who knew his history, had known him, in a way, more closely than all four of his wives, with the exception of Velma ("she was always his heart," Emma says), because Miss Emma had been a witness to all three of his latter marriages and their attendant troubles. She grew up in Augusta, met Brown in 1966 after she married Leon, and was the one female friend who talked straight to him. And in 2006, that last year of his life, he'd call Sis at all hours, almost every day when he was home, and sometimes from the road as well, especially when Leon was sick. At two A.M, the phone would ring: "Hey Sis, you sleep?"

"Not no more, Mr. Brown."

"How's Leon?"

"He's sleep, Mr. Brown. But he's feeling better. Thank you for asking."

"Tell him don't play no more funerals. The next one might be his own."

"All right, Mr. Brown."

Click.

The next day at noon the phone would ring again. "Hey, Sis, you know I can't stand a dirty house. What you clean your kitchen with?"

"I ain't the one to ask, Mr. Brown. I can't clang two pots together."

"You cook that vegetable soup!"

"That I can do."

"Can you make me some? I'll be home by 'bout six."

"All right, Mr. Brown."

The next day at eleven P.M.: "Sis, what you doing now? You reading? What you reading? You see them hollering on the gospel quartet show today? Lord, they put it together, didn't they. . . ."

It occurred to Miss Emma in that last year of Brown's life that James Brown, who she always knew was one of the loneliest people she'd ever met, was far lonelier than he'd ever been.

You put a man in a house. You smother him with material things. You call him a star for forty-two years, then tell him he's through, he's an oldies act, he's outlived his own revolution. And then he falls. The fall is long, painful, and there is no one to catch him on the way down. Brown had money. He had fame. He had made a great comeback. But he was short on friends and trust, and he owed everyone. He owed his ex-wives for his behavior. He owed his kids and grandkids for not being the father and grandfather they needed. He owed his out-of-wedlock kids for the horrible way he denied some of them. He owed the cadre of women he'd slept with and abused. But Miss Emma, a woman with a soft heart and a bright outlook, a former employee of his radio station, who nursed his best friend, Leon Austin, toward his own gracious date with death, he owed nothing to, and so those calls to her were free.

"Sis, I might get some work done on my teeth."

"Didn't you do that before, Mr. Brown?"

"Gonna do it again."

"Don't hurt yourself, Mr. Brown."

"I'm all right."

An hour later, the phone:

"Sis, I might get my toes worked on too."

"Well, you should get that done, Mr. Brown, if they're bothering you."

An hour later:

"Sis, you busy?"

"Not really . . ."

He never called to ask a favor. He just called to talk. He'd talk for hours, about everything from Inca Indians to Bible passages. She'd nod off and wake up and he'd still be talking. Sometimes Leon would answer and Brown would talk so long into the night that he'd hand the phone to her and say, "Emma, you got this." Then Brown would burn thirty more minutes gossiping about Leon. But favors? Never. He was too proud. The closest he could come would be to imply, and she would understand.

"Sis, when's the last time you made that vegetable soup of yours? I know I asked before and I guess you forgot."

"Funny you should ask, Mr. Brown. In fact, I might stir up some today. I'll bring it by."

"All right, Sis."

And off she would go to cook up her soup and bring it to his house in Beech Island, the one that was supposedly locked up tight, from which his fourth wife had been banished, sent off to LA to drug rehab, the house at which his kids would have to make an appointment to see him, the one he built on sixty acres in the middle of nowhere, within sight of the mighty towers of the nuclear bomb plant. She knew about Brown's paranoia in his later years, had heard what he'd told Adrienne, his third wife, and Mr. Bobbit about those radio towers—how the government had planted microphones in his teeth so they could hear everything he said. She paid it no mind. That was loneliness, she understood.

When she came to the house, they'd sit in his den while he watched television and they'd chat about the old days, about the old Augusta they longed for, where black businesses thrived and black children didn't have to be forced to be in school, but rather wanted to learn, and wore their clothes straight and didn't wear their pants around their asses; an Augusta where folks were poor but where drugs weren't rampant, and parents stayed home and looked after their kids, and if your neighbor spanked a child for doing something, they didn't have to worry about going to jail or getting shot for doing it. She'd earned her way into that kind of talk with James Brown. Because she was old-school Augusta herself.

Together, they'd seen their world change. She knew he wasn't the father he could have been, nor the man he should have been. She'd worked as Brown's personal assistant for several years, back when he owned his Augusta radio station, WRDW, and later as a popular DJ at the radio station. She'd traveled with him, even to Africa. She knew the wives, the longtime girlfriends, the short-term lovers, the one-nighters. In the old days, she'd book the girls in hotel rooms when Brown traveled: one girl on the second floor, the other on the fourth, another on the third, five of them altogether at one point, Brown running between them all. She got fed up with the whole business after she became friends with his second wife, Dee Dee. "I can't do this anymore," she announced to him. She expected Brown to hit the ceiling and holler, "You're fired!" He did that at his station all the time. He'd hit the ceiling over some small infraction and holler to some poor soul, "You're fired!" He did that to her a couple of times, but she paid it no mind, because the next day the phone would ring at her office and he'd be on the line saying, "Sis, ummm . . . what's the name of that promoter in Milwaukee? You know the one. . . ." and off he would go, chatting about how maybe he'd like to get his memory together so it'd be as sharp as hers, both of them knowing he had a mind like a bilge pump and could recall the names and the phone numbers of two or three dozen promoters without a blink. It was his way of apologizing, saying everything was cool, and sometimes during the conversation he'd even throw in the whole bit about books, because he knew she loved to read, because she'd been a college girl, a Fisk girl, saying "Sis, what you reading these days?" and then hearing about it and piping out, "I'ma read that book too," and adding if she wouldn't mind dropping that book by the house later, why, he just had his house man, Mr. Washington, run by that restaurant downtown, the one with the rice and beans that Leon liked, she could pick some of those rice and beans up and bring them home to Leon—just chatting on as if nothing happened. As if *him* calling *her* at his office and *her* answering *his* phone after he'd fired her the day before was just a normal thing. She didn't mind. The fact is, she never stopped working when he fired her. She'd finish her day and come back the next. She knew how he was. She could quit that job anytime she wanted. He knew it too.

Some outsiders never understood that. Danny Ray did, though. He was an insider too. Good old Danny Ray, the great MC for Brown, was the guy whose main job for forty-five years was to place Brown's cape on his shoulders onstage during his "Please, Please, Please" routine and help him offstage, the one who at the top of each show would say, "Ladies and Gentlemen, introducing the star of our show, Mr. Dynamite himself. Soul Brother Number One. The Hardest Working Man in Show Bizness! Mr. . . . Jaaaammmees Brown!" Danny Ray, skinny as a rail, who back in those days was as lush as a bowl of cherries and the sweetest man who ever tipped a cup of joy juice to his mouth—poor Danny Ray got fired like it was lunch at the post office. He got axed in Brown's radio station one time for some offense— some long-forgotten transgression, something stupid—but he hit Brown's hurt button somehow and Brown let him have it: "You're fired!" he yelled. Danny Ray turned to leave, and Brown said, "Where you going, Danny Ray? Ain't nothing out there for you. You got to stay here with me."

Danny Ray turned around to stay, only to hear, "You're fired!"

Then, "Where you going?

"You're fired!"

It was madness. Many at the radio station could not take it—the bounced paychecks, the drunk station manager, and Brown's rages and constant calls. DJ Youngblood, a well-known, thoughtful radio voice from Atlanta, scored his first major job out of college at WRDW, and recalls, "James was a conflicted man. His drive and determination was good and admirable. He liked me. He did appreciate and respect education. But the pay was embarrassing. The way he handled people was horrible. He'd fire people for simply asking for their money. If you saw him on the left side of the street, go to the right side."

That was the flip side of the coin, the side for those who weren't let in. But behind the looking glass, behind the bluff and the ranting, the rages, the hollering, and the shouting, was a man who was so torn by conflict that he snuck off to smoke cigarettes so that no one would see him. Here was a man who rarely drank or cursed or let down his guard in public—which meant in front of people, in front of anyone, period; an incredibly lonely, overwrought, and sensitive man. A man who lived alone inside himself.

Miss Emma understood him because she understood his best friend. Leon Austin always dreamed big, but when his dreams fell short, he took it with a shrug. "What difference does it make?" Leon would say. "We're together, you and I. We're the whole world, you and I." That meant everything to her. And that was something Brown did not have. He would complain, "I can't walk two feet down the street in Japan without getting mobbed, Miss Emma. But here in my hometown . . ." and he'd trail off and say nothing. She understood: He never felt big at home. Never felt appreciated in his hometown. Watching Augusta decline as a metropolis was, for Brown, like watching the air hiss out of a balloon. What's wrong with us, Sis? Brown would ask. There was no easy answer. When a black man's dream is deferred, when he fails in the matter of the heart, when he watches a town he gave so much to fall away to pieces by forces beyond his control, who can he blame for that? Drugs? Crime? When his dream fails or is deferred, where can he be allowed to show hurt, show the pain in his heart, show his own suffering when the stage lights are gone and it's dark and he's alone, and the very town he loves seems to reel beyond seeming repair and is unable to repay him for what he gave?

"I've never met anyone in my life," she says, sitting in her parlor cradling a cup of tea and carefully pondering the memories, "that worked harder to hide his true heart. Mr. Brown worked at that very hard. He had a sensitive heart. If you knew that about him, there was not much else you needed to know."

It's a dangerous business trying to show the yawing valleys and pre-cipitous peaks of a man's life in these Internet-happy days. All it takes is one bozo to get on the Internet and say, "I slept with him," and the whole of a man's respectability and reputation topples onto itself like a house of cards. The gossip machine of the Internet can destroy the life of the most anonymous of citizens. Imagine what it did to Brown—a wounded child who became a superstar and later a man in hiding. Michael Jackson, who adored Brown, suffered similarly. In the six months I covered Jackson for *People* magazine, I was the only writer, by dint of circumstance or coincidence, allowed to watch him rehearse his band. He was meticulous in his rehearsal, attentive to every detail. The musicians left those rehearsals exhausted. I'd never seen a guy rehearse so hard. Yet in those years, Jackson was seen as a freak, a wannabe white man. He was far deeper than people ever knew, and compassionate to a fault. I met his mother, a sharp, kind, deeply religious woman, and after meeting her I saw where he got it from, saw why a man so private and tender, so kind and talented, had to hide the private person he was. Jackson, like Brown, left millions to children. Like Brown, he felt deeply misunderstood and wounded.

James Brown hid everything, and in the game of instant informa-tion he lost big-time, because the information machine turns a truth into a lie and a lie into the truth, transforms superstitions and stereo-types into fact with such ease and fluidity that after a while, you get to believing, as I do, that the media is not a reflection of the American culture but rather is teaching it. As long as James Brown was selling records, he let that craziness run. He didn't care. The media worked in his favor and helped fuel his success. But it killed his public reputa-tion, and once the success was gone, once the head disappeared, the body followed.

Instant information turns the cauldron of race and class into a con-coction of doublespeak, and if you reach in and try to make sense of it, you'll yank your hand out holding nothing but air and the resolve not to use the n-word again. Big deal. Whether you decide to use the dreaded n-word changes nothing. In the instant-information Internet age, every truth contradicts another truth: Brown was crazy. Brown was a genius. Brown was a woman basher. Brown was abused by gold-digging women. Brown was cheap. Brown would give away his last dime. Stick your finger in the dike to cover one lie and water bursts out of another hole. You have to choose what to believe. And therein lies the real story of James Brown, who was more southerner than he was black or white, more sensitive artist than he was superstar.

Miss Emma peers through the blinds in her window, out to the rough tundra of what once was a booming middle-class community. The smell of low country, the freight-train whistles howling in the distance, the abandoned slaughterhouses, the old smell of the canal, the dangerous, deserted rail crossings near Walton Way—Augusta is a foreign country now to the blacks who remember it from the forties and fifties. If you're a yuppie looking for a Starbucks, Miss Emma's side of town will make you feel about as lonely as a Hong Kong bartender on a Sunday. Almost every street is spotted with homes that are boarded up tight. There's a vacant old school building around the corner, a half-empty strip mall up on Gordon Highway, a closed Winn-Dixie, a dollar store, a Mr Cash pawn shop. They rent furniture for today and sell futures in church for tomorrow in places like these. At the convenience store down the street, I saw two black guys in line each wearing the uniform of a different security-guard outfit. The poor guard each other down here. This is the real Augusta, not the one they show on ESPN every spring, the city of the sparkling Augusta National shows and Tiger Woods—the guy who, blacks snicker, forgot he was black until he got into trouble and then found out he was black after all. This is James Brown's Augusta. Miss Emma's Augusta. And to some degree, the Augusta of us all.

Miss Emma lowers the blind and takes a seat on her couch. "It would break his heart to see what Augusta has become now."

I point out that they built a statue for him. They named an arena after him. The mayor knew him. The folks here liked him. They still have his Thanksgiving turkey giveaway, and the Christmas toy give-away.

"Charity was not Mr. Brown's stripe," she says simply. "He despised it." He wanted to help poor children, she explained, not by giving them something but by educating them. By giving them a reason to work. "He wanted his money to help poor children be something. He said that many times. Not to be tied up in court someplace."

"But he's famous here," I argue.

She shrugs and looks away, sadly shaking her head. It was Brown's dream to bring jobs and joy to this town. His vision was to see children happy. But he could not account for lack of business acumen, relatives who would slice his money up, a cousin's son who would burn his office to the ground, his radio stations going belly-up, the divorces, the business ideas gone to pot, the women who tired of his abuse, the bands who quit. Everyone wanted more and he had no more to give. "He carried so many people," she says. "And so few people wanted to carry him. He always moved with the best intentions. And when it didn't work, it hurt him. He hid that from people. Because people used him. And after a while, he didn't know who to trust. If Mr. Brown let you in his inner circle, it meant he'd trust you with his life," she said. "If you didn't form an opinion against him; if you kept an open mind, no matter what he did—and no matter what you did—you were a trusted ally."

The door knocks. A young guy enters bearing cold Coca-Cola. I realize with a start that it's that strange-looking fella I just saw walking aimlessly down the street when she pulled up. Miss Emma smiles at him and his face lightens into a shy grin as he drops two Cokes onto the coffee table. She thanks him and discreetly slips him a few dollars.

I grab a Coke. I pop the lid and lift the can to my lips.

Without a word, Miss Emma vanishes from the sparse living room. She returns with a glass. She picks up the Coke can and pours the drink into the glass.

Mr. Brown smoked cigarettes, she said. "He never wanted people to know he smoked. He didn't want young people seeing that. Would never let young people see him drink. He was not much of a drinker anyway. He was a proper man."

But what about the drugs? And his relationship to women? The beatings, the cruelty?

She thinks a long moment, her brown eyes staring at me thoughtfully. She takes a deep breath. "Even at my age," she says, "I'm embarrassed to shame my parents. And they've been dead for many years. I was taught you don't talk low on somebody. Especially if they're dead. A lot of people have said a lot of things since he died. And some of those things, a lot of them, are not true. Or exaggerated."

I say, as gently as I can, that it doesn't change the facts. The man had four wives. He reportedly slept with some of his female singers. Had all kinds of fights with women. I'm told his treatment of Motown singer Tammi Terrell was terrible. He was charged with rape, and he had at least four outside children besides the six he claimed—I've heard as many as thirteen. This kind of bad news ain't the same as stealing your best friend's lunch money.

"Mr. Brown," she says, "thought a woman should be changed." Shaped, she says. Treated like a pet. Molded into his ideal, with minks, and plastic surgery, and new cars. With money. "He was part of that generation," she says. "A lot of men from his era thought that way."

I argue that while Brown spent thousands on his wives, on plastic surgery, drug treatment, liposuction—according to Buddy Dallas, he spent $50,000 on Tomi Rae's drug rehab and replaced thirty-two of her teeth—that still didn't give him the right to treat his wives cruelly.

"I can't speak to all his business," Miss Emma says. "The things that happened between him and all those women is over my head. But I'll say this. His wives, the ones I knew, were good women. Except," she adds drily, "I can't speak for that last one. I didn't get to know her very well."

Part III

Quit It!

Chapter 17

Say Goodbye to the King

It was nearly lunchtime on December 29, and funeral director Charles Reid of Augusta was sitting in his office trying to stay awake. James Brown had been dead for four days, and the circus that surrounded his death—the media blitz, the howling of the relatives who began squabbling, and the hundreds of details involving his memorial services—had beaten Reid to near senseless exhaustion. He hadn't slept in four days.

He was about to place his head on the desk and close his eyes for five minutes when the phone rang again. He picked up. A voice on the other end said, "Michael Jackson wants to come see James Brown."

"When?"

"Tonight. We're leaving LA by jet in about an hour."

Reid hung up the phone and moved from his desk. He was bone tired but there was still much to do.

The chaos surrounding Brown's death, up to that moment, had

been like nothing Reid had ever experienced before. Brown died on Christmas Day. The next day his family, including Al Sharpton, gathered to plan his memorials and decided to hold three: the first at the Apollo in Harlem, the site of the recordings of Brown's great live albums; the next a private one on December 29 in South Carolina for the family; and the last on December 30, a public one in Augusta at the arena, newly renamed in Brown's honor.

Reid was exhausted from the harrowing blitz of preparation for three separate funerals, and getting the casket in place was the worst professional nightmare he'd ever experienced. The family had ordered a gold-plated casket at a cost of $25,000. Reid had to special-order it from an outfit in Nashville. The casket was scheduled to arrive in Augusta at 6:30 P.M. on December 27, the day before the Apollo memorial eight hundred miles north in New York City. Initially, they had planned to fly Brown's body to New York in a private jet with the family, but that night, Reid had called Sharpton and explained a major problem.

"The casket is too heavy for a small jet. You'll need to find me a bigger plane."

Sharpton suggested a commercial plane.

"It won't work. The casket doesn't arrive here till six-thirty tonight," Reid said. "The last big jet leaves Atlanta about eight. We don't have time to get the casket, move the body into it, and get it to Atlanta in time. You'll need to find me a bigger plane."

Sharpton called everyone he knew. An attorney in Florida had a big jet, but it was out of commission. New York mogul Donald Trump said he would be happy to send his plane, but he was having it fixed out in California.

Sharpton called Reid, exasperated. "I can't find a plane."

"I don't know what we're going to do," Reid said. "It ain't gonna work."

"Are you sure the casket's going to get here at six-thirty?" Sharpton asked.

"Yeah, it's on the way."

Sharpton hung up and came to the funeral home. The two men tried to figure out solutions while they waited for the casket to arrive. Reid, normally a cool customer, used to the kinds of crises that accompany death and burial, when families are flustered and dismayed, was flummoxed. It wasn't just the logistical problem of getting Brown's body to New York, or his phone ringing off the hook nonstop with calls and requests from all across the globe that bothered him. This was a personal issue. He'd known James Brown most of his life. His father, Charles Reid, Sr., a civil rights advocate and one of the most successful black businessmen in Augusta's history, had been a friend of James Brown for nearly fifty years. The two men were once business partners, co-owners of a popular Augusta club called Third World, which was mysteriously burned to the ground in October 1973 by a suspected arsonist who was never caught. Reid had presided over the funerals of Brown's father, Brown's third wife, Adrienne, and many of Brown's friends and employees. This wasn't a job. This was a duty to a loyal friend.

He racked his brains as Sharpton, usually not at a loss for words, sat in glum silence. Finally Reid spoke out. "I'll tell you what I'm going to do. You told me the viewing in New York is eleven A.M. I'm going to put his body in the back of the van. I'll get me a driver, and we'll just ride it up there. We can get there in twelve to fourteen hours."

Sharpton said, "You think you can make it?"

"We'll leave at nine o'clock tonight. That'll get us there by eight or nine in the morning. You go up by jet with the family. I'll meet you at the Apollo."

"All right," Sharpton said.

Sharpton departed and Reid called two drivers, one of them William Murrell, James Brown's longtime driver. Then he rushed home, showered and shaved, and grabbed a suit from his closet and threw it into his car. He drove back to the funeral home and waited while Miss Ella Overton, Brown's longtime hairdresser, styled Brown's hair one last time. She had tears in her eyes as she combed his hair with the big rake combs that only Brown used and only Brown knew where to obtain. When the old woman was done, Reid carefully prepped and dressed Brown, gently placed him in the heavy gold-plated casket, then hauled the casket into the van. "That thing was so heavy," Reid said later, "it dropped the back of the van down several inches. The front was sticking up in the air."

The lopsided van was about to roll out of the funeral home when the door opened and Al Sharpton walked in.

"I thought you were flying back to New York," Reid said.

"If you're gonna ride to New York, I'm gonna ride," Sharpton said. "I'm gonna stay with him all the way. Mr. Brown would have never left me." Sharpton placed his suitcase in the van, patted Brown's coffin, and said, "I'm ready."

They rode all night, four of them: Reid, Sharpton, Murrell, and a second driver, Sharpton's hand resting on the casket for most of the journey. They stopped for gas only. At a rest stop in North Carolina in the middle of the night, two of the store clerks, teenage black girls, saw Sharpton emerge from the odd-looking van with its back end nearly touching the asphalt and put two and two together. One of them grabbed her cellphone and ran out to take a photo. Sharpton erupted. "What did you do that for?" He did not want them taking a picture of an awkward-looking, hopped-up van sitting at a gas pump in the middle of the night, bearing James Brown's body. Brown would never have allowed it. James Brown, who had never stepped out in public unless he was decked out, who had his hair done before and after each show, whose house was so clean you could eat off the floor—Brown would never be caught in public in a shoddy way. The man made an entrance. *Come important and leave important, Rev. Kill 'em and leave, Rev. Kill 'em and leave.*

"You will not take that picture tonight," Sharpton said.

A hasty compromise was reached. The girls took photos with Sharpton and the drivers, but not of the van. Then the van motored on.

By the time they hit the New Jersey Turnpike just outside Manhattan, dawn was breaking and the word had spread. "We started seeing people in the tunnel," Reid says. "I don't know how so many people found out. Rev. Sharpton didn't call a soul." The plan was to stop at Sharpton's apartment building near Sixtieth and Madison Avenue and discreetly move Brown's casket from the van to a hearse, then head uptown to place his body in a horse and carriage, which Sharpton had arranged at his National Action Network office at 145th Street, to march Brown to the Apollo, twenty blocks south, on 125th street. But by the time they got uptown to Sharpton's headquarters, thousands had gathered, and many followed the horse and carriage on foot as it made its sad procession down Lenox Avenue, with hundreds gathering on the sidewalks of Lenox Avenue for twenty blocks, waving, some holding Brown's picture, some sobbing. By the time they reached 125th Street "we could hardly get the horse down the block," Sharpton said. "People were everywhere." It was December 28, just before New Year's Eve. The rich and famous were out of town. It was mostly the people of Harlem who crowded the sidewalks for blocks in both directions, just as they did in the old days when Brown performed. At one point Sharpton leaned over to the casket and said, "Mr. Brown, you did it again. You sold out the Apollo one last time."

Reid, meanwhile, was exhausted from the drive.

"When I got to the Apollo, they had no place for me to take a bath or change into my suit," he says. "I fell asleep in the greenroom. When I woke up, someone had brought out a buffet. I got up and put a hurting on that buffet. Yes sir, buddy. I was hungry." But the scene was chaos. "Nobody knew where anything was. They asked me all kinds of questions." Reid did his best, organizing an impromptu massive memorial with thousands of mourners in a venue he had never seen before. At one point Sharpton sent for him and said nervously, "Charlie, Mr. Brown's sweating!"

Reid came out to take a look at the body. "It's all these lights on him," he said. "This lanolin fluid, it's got to come out."

He laughs, recalling the look on Sharpton's face at the mention of the preservative. "I think he thought Mr. Brown was coming back."

When they finally closed the doors of the Apollo—which they had held open for hours overtime—there were still several thousand people waiting for a chance to see Brown's body, but Reid had to rush it back for the family's private memorial the following day. He drove fourteen hours back to Augusta, straight to his funeral home, dressed the Godfather of Soul in a different suit, and got him to the private service in time. Then he took the huge heavy casket back to his funeral home for a third time and changed Brown again.

"I changed him three times," says Reid. "James was tired, and I was too."

That's when the phone rang. Michael Jackson was coming to Augusta that night.

Reid took Brown's body into a plush waiting room. He prepped him, tidied him, then fluffed and tidied the casket. Just like Sharpton, he would make sure his old friend was ready and proper, in good form to meet his visitor.

Later that night, the phone rang again. This time it was Michael himself asking if he could come see Brown.

"Come on. We'll be here when you come."

Just past midnight, a caravan of four SUVs pulled into the parking lot. Several silent, grim-looking men in bow ties and suits, bodyguards from the Nation of Islam, got out, and behind them, emerging from one of the SUVs, tall and silent, was Michael Jackson himself. He was wearing a simple shirt and slacks, and his hair was wrapped in a kerchief. No fancy clothes. No fancy entourage.

Reid led him to James Brown's body, lying in a plush room in cream-colored satin. Michael stared at it. He gently touched James Brown's face. He stood there silently for ten minutes. A half hour. An hour.

After an hour, Reid left the room.

Michael Jackson had a lot in common with James Brown. He often told friends that his dance moves were influenced by Brown's. He recalled his mother awakening him when he was six to see Brown perform on TV. Also, the military precision of Michael's music was a Brown specialty. Even the early Jackson 5 bands were tight units. When I watched Michael rehearse his band at SIR studios in LA for several weeks back in 1984, before his Victory Tour, he was meticulous, working his musicians till they were worn to a nub. At one point he hung them up for hours rehearsing just one hit, a hit on which he had a one-kick dance move. It was just one hit. An ensemble smash—bang—and the dance move with it. But it wasn't big enough or tight enough for Michael. He tweaked the sound technicians and the exhausted players, among them the talented drummer Jonathan "Sugarfoot" Moffett, originally of New Orleans, and the late David Williams, a fabulous guitarist out of Virginia, until they were red-eyed tired. That was a James Brown specialty as well, working his band to the bone, till it sounded tight as a drum.

Jackson and Brown shared more than just a similar approach to music and dance. Michael, like Brown, was competitive. He wanted to beat every other guy. Brown, during his biggest years, was bent on crushing the opposition—Isaac Hayes, Little Willie John, Jackie Wilson, and the entire Motown machine. But beneath the competitive edge was a deep respect for his competitors. Sharpton told me that in the late seventies, after soul star Isaac Hayes went bankrupt, Brown visited Hayes's Atlanta apartment unannounced and knocked on the door. Hayes answered and his face lit up. He said, "James Brown!" Brown handed him $3,000 and said, "Isaac, don't tell nobody I helped you out. You don't ever want people to know you needed a handout. When we was rivals, I wanted to beat you. But I want you on your feet when I beat you again." Jackson was the same: Prince, the Stones, the Beatles, Bruce Springsteen—these were competitors that he respected and admired. Also like Brown, he was a fanatic about being seen at his best. He would never allow himself to be caught with his shirt off in one of those horrible *National Enquirer* photos, or pictured lying on a beach, tummy exposed, or blowing bubbles in Santa Fe someplace. He was religious, though he kept quiet about it, as was Brown. Near his home area of Ellenton, Brown spent thousands rebuilding St. Peter church, where he was baptized and which he visited on Sundays without fanfare, even occasionally singing with the choir. Jackson was raised a devout Jehovah's Witness, something his mother passed on to her children. At the height of his success, during the Victory Tour, he'd venture out in various cities wearing a fake beard and hat, accompanied by a security guard, knocking on doors, making the missionary visits that Jehovah's Witnesses undertake. The press had a ball with that, by the way; they talked to folks who answered the knock on their door and practically fainted when they recognized the world's hottest superstar standing before them in fake beard and hat. I looked the other way when Michael did that kind of stuff, rarely passing that kind of juicy tidbit on to *People* magazine, which likely would have gobbled it up.

Michael, like James Brown, had few friends outside of his family. Those two were public property. They were two dinosaurs who walked alone. Two black superstars. And each knew the abject loneliness of the other.

In 2003, when Michael was facing seven counts of child molestation, Al Sharpton was living in New York, sipping civil rights soup by the gallon, when his cellphone rang. He picked it up. It was Brown. "Rev, where you at?"

"I'm in New York."

"You ought to be out there in California helping Michael out."

"Well, Michael's in trouble."

There was a pause for a moment, and Sharpton could feel Brown gathering steam. "Oh, s'cuse me," Brown said. "I'm sorry. I got the wrong number. I got the American Legion. I thought I called the civil rights headquarters. That's what you're in business for, handling people in trouble, right? Pardon me, sir. I forgot who I called."

He hung up. Sharpton called him back.

"I didn't say I wasn't gonna help," Sharpton said.

But Brown was already giving him a mouthful. "Didn't Michael come to your headquarters in Harlem when you had a problem?" Brown asked.

"Yeah."

"So a man comes to you. And you're going to leave him."

"I didn't say that, Mr. Brown."

"I didn't raise you for that," Brown said. "You go where the rest of them ain't got the guts to go. The reason they ain't going to Michael is because they think he's guilty and they're scared. I never taught you to be scared."

"Yes, sir."

Sharpton hung up the phone, packed his bags, and got on a plane to California. After the verdict was announced, when Michael was exonerated, I watched on TV as Michael was rushed out of the court-room to the clicking of photographers' cameras. Michael stood there, tall and ever thin—people forget how tall he was—and next to him, with the trademark James Brown hair, combed with the giant rake comb that his adopted father James Brown had given him, was Rev. Al Sharpton in a suit, the jogging outfit and gold medallion long gone. As the cameras clicked and the tapes whirred, Michael said nothing, but Sharpton, James Brown's adopted son, said plenty. He said everything James Brown himself wanted to say and would have said if he could have, which amounted to, "I knew it all along. I told y'all. Y'all hung him out to dry without even knowing who he is."

Three hours into Jackson's visit, Reid found himself giving the King of Pop a tour of his facility. Most people shy away when it comes to death, Reid noted, but not Jackson. He asked pointed and thoughtful questions. He asked about the preparation of the body, a subject people usually avoid. "He wanted to know how it was done," Reid said. "What types of fluid do you use?" Michael asked.

"He wouldn't ask a question unless he thought about it," Reid told me. "That's how precise he was. Whatever he asked, he was very interested in. 'Do we freshen it up?' he asked about James Brown's body. He asked if we were going to change his outfits. He wanted to know had his hair been done, how it was done."

Jackson toured the casket room, and Reid showed him the various models. "Who requested Mr. Brown's gold-plated casket?" Jackson asked.

"Well, it's the family's decision."

"Is that something Mr. Brown wanted?"

"Entertainers, they always say solid gold," Reid said.

Michael laughed and they returned to the chapel.

Jackson spoke of his love for Brown, the influence Brown had had on his childhood. He was there for five hours. Not once did Jackson sit down.

Back in the chapel, Reid stood in the back of the room as Jackson lingered over Brown one last time, touching his face, then tidying his hair. Reid looked at his watch. It was 5:30 in the morning. James Brown's service at the arena bearing his name was scheduled for later that day. But that was later. For now, they were just two men, the Godfather of Soul and the King of Pop. They had lived their fantastic lives alone, on the third rail of fame and fortune, even as they electrified and changed the world. One lay in a gold-plated coffin; in less than three years, the other would be lying in his own. It would be the end of an era. And black America has never been the same.

Chapter 18

The Dream

William Forlando Brown, age twenty-seven, stands at the practice tee at the Heritage Golf Links, a public course in Tucker, Georgia. He pulls his club back with ease and swats the ball mightily. You watch it soar into the air, four hundred feet if it's a foot, and there, in that instant, as the ball is pitched against the clear blue Georgia sky, you see the old man's dream:

They'll gather at his house like they do at Christmas dinner. All the suspects. The whole family. The ex-wives Velma and Dee Dee, and Tomi Rae—loving mother of James, Jr., whom Brown nicknamed Little Man, and all the rest of the kids and the grandkids, including Teddy's daughter. And they'll eat. They'll eat what he eats because he eats good food. "Food that's got grease in it, grease you up, make you limber and strong," he used to say: rice, beans, smothered steak, chicken. Then, when they're done, they'll head over to Barnwell, to St. Peter church in Elko, not far from old Ellenton, where the family got started. Old St. Peter, the renovated church that he gave thousands to, that looks better than any other church in that area, with new wood beams and a new roof and acoustic ceilings and new instruments and a freshly paved parking lot. On Sundays in his last years he'd slip off to St. Peter to sing with the choir, sing his favorite song, "God Has Been Good to Me," and open his Bible to his favorite verse, the same verse they found it open to at his bedside the morning after he died, the book of Psalms 37:1, "Fret not thyself because of evildoers, neither be thou envious against the workers of iniquity." He'd walk in and say hi to his old friends, the minister, his aunt Saree, and his good friend Ruth Tobin and her children—Ruth, whom everybody called Mutt except for him. He called her Sis. He called her every month or so, saying "Sis, what you doin'? You praying for me? I'm praying for you. Pray for me, Sis." And she did. And to this day, still does.

They'd sing and pray a while and thank God for everything that he's gifted them with. And after they're done, the family—his family—they'll get back in their cars—his cars. He's got thirty of 'em, and none has more than five thousand miles on it. They'll jump in his cars and ride back to Augusta, head over to the Augusta National Golf Course—a white man's golf course, a golf course that might as well have been on Mars when James Brown was a little boy, and they'll watch his grandson William Forlando James Brown play a round of a white man's game. And he'll say, "I don't know what he sees in that. But he does it good."

Back in Atlanta, William Brown, tall, slim, athletic, with a serious face, dressed in a smooth jogging outfit and golfer's shirt, watches keenly, his club still held high, as the ball lands about ten feet from its appointed hole. He frowns. "I'm pulling my head too far to the right," he says.

If he's pulling too far to the right, I can't see it. William is the man James Brown would have been had he been educated. The old man was proud he had a grandchild in college. William Brown and his father, Terry, were the only ones of Brown's claimed offspring who largely refused to participate in the massive deluge of early lawsuits filed against Brown's estate by his children and widow. Terry was so disgusted with the lawsuits that he handed all his rights to his son and said, "You handle it." William, for his part, has followed his father's path, mostly keeping clear of the legal fray, insisting that Brown's millions go to the kids exactly as Brown intended. In September 2015, his father—and William, as his father's representative—was offered a "settlement" of $2 million to essentially capitulate and join the morass of suing parties who wanted to settle the mess by rewriting Brown's will and spreading Brown's money around among the children, Tomi Rae, and the education trust. They refused. They want the money to go as Brown intended. Says William, speaking for himself and his father, "Why would we want to go against Grandfather's wishes? He worked and danced for that. He sweated for it. He wanted poor kids to have a chance to educate themselves. It's real simple."

From the time William, or Flip, as Brown called him, entered college at University of West Georgia as a political science major, Brown, who paid for his education, checked his grades, grilled him about school, and admonished him no end to finish college and do well in school. The old man laid criticisms on him that set the kid's teeth on edge at times, but still, the kid could take it. When Brown walled himself off from the world and announced that his kids would have to make appointments to see him, William said, "The hell with that." He climbed the fence and showed up in his grandfather's living room.

"What you doing here?" Brown asked.

"I'm here to see you. I don't need an appointment."

Brown loved that kind of moxie. He made the kid work harder in school. He indoctrinated the kid in his ways. One day, while the two were sitting on the porch of Brown's Beech Island house, he handed the kid a broom. "Sweep that grass," he said.

William swept. For an hour. Two hours. In the hot sun. Three hours. He was exhausted. But he wasn't going to quit in front of the old man. Finally Brown said, "Okay, quit it."

William was furious. "What's the point of that?" he snapped.

"If you don't have an education, that's the kind of job you gonna have," Brown said.

So the kid listened. And he did well in school. And when he neared graduation at University of West Georgia and started thinking about his future, he decided to do what his grandfather did.

He decided to chase a dream.

His dream was to be a professional golfer. He bought a golf club. Then another. Then a set. Then he got a job in a golf store. He sought out golf fanatics, and golf coaches, and finally pros. He read books. He studied the game. He practiced on public golf courses—no private clubs for him, he didn't have the money. Over the course of the next eight years, his game evolved. By 2014, he'd worked himself to the outskirts of the PGA. This is a guy who didn't even make his high school golf team, who was an all-county trumpet player at Stephens County High School, not a golfer. The thought among his teachers was that William would become a musician, or a lawyer, but even back then, he'd already decided, he didn't want to be the next James Brown. He liked the trumpet, but he loved golf. He loved being outdoors. He loved the air, the space. He loved the competition. Today, the kid who couldn't make his high school squad is one of the most promising young golfers in the southern region.

It's been a difficult road. Golfers need professional coaches, private golf courses, and practice times with tutors. Which means, of course, money, of which the struggling athlete has very little. Every cent he's earned on odd jobs—cutting grass, selling golf gear—has gone to golf training. He's getting old for the game. He knows it. But not too old. Not yet. Law school, maybe grad school—that's down the road, that's in his future. He knows that too. Why? Because he's a Brown. He knows that education is everything. But for now, he likes this dream.

He holds his club at his side as he peers at the shot he just made. "Golf is an honest game," he says. "Either you can do it or you can't. The ball rolls where you put it. You can't magically make it go there. Hard work. That's what this game is. That's what Grandfather taught me."

He does the things Brown would have done. When Nafloyd Scott died at age eighty, in 2015, and Scott's family was short on funds to bury him, William Brown was one of those who stepped forward to help pay for Scott's funeral. He speaks the way Brown wishes he could've talked. "You speak the language," Brown told him. And he looks the way Brown probably wishes he could have looked: a tall, cool, almond brown. He's a strikingly handsome young man. And he plays the game the way Brown would have. Fair. And hard. He could, if he wanted, walk over to that nice shot and putt the ball right into the hole. Ten feet he can do with his eyes closed. He can putt with the big boys most days. But he's here today to work on his long game. The other golfers in this park are mostly amateurs, making shots to look good. William is at this public golf course to work.

He lines up another ball. The wind blows. He waits until it stops. He brings the club back and sends it forward with a powerful *whack!*

The ball goes high, high, even higher than the first one. And as you follow it, high into the Georgia sky, you see the dream again . . . there it is. . . .

Epilogue

Sister Lee

In 1955, my parents founded a church called New Brown Memorial Baptist Church. It's at 609 Clinton Street in Brooklyn, in the Red Hook housing projects where I was born. It was in New Brown that I first heard an organ swing. The lady who swung that organ was Sister Helen Lee.

The first time I heard Mrs. Lee play was the first time I actually saw someone read music. I couldn't have been older than seven or eight. The act of reading notes on a page seemed so impressive. What's more, if someone in church stood up to testify—to tell about the good that God had done for them—and began to sing, Sister Lee would close her music book and just play along with them. She operated that organ as if it was a spaceship. She pulled knobs. She mashed buttons. She worked pedals. She changed its sound. She swung like crazy. Every quarter note was swinging while her feet danced on those pedals and her hands flew over the keys.

I got married in that church in 1991. I still have a picture of Sister Lee at my wedding, sitting in the sanctuary, smiling. She was a fabulous musician, and a wonderful friend to everyone in the church, including my mother. She was a firm woman. She didn't make small talk. She said what she felt. The kids in her children's choir used to think she was hard on them, because she was. She wanted them on time. And prepared. She didn't tolerate excuses. She came to every service on time and ready to play, and she expected them to follow suit in their own lives. She told one of them, "If I didn't care about you at all, I wouldn't say a word." They loved her.

She was the consummate professional, who played organ in that church for more than fifty years, always showing up on time in rain, snow, or sleet, to play at hundreds of funerals and services. She got sick in 2009 but still came to church every Sunday. At New Brown, Sister Lee was never, ever, short for a ride—to church or anywhere else. That same year, the longtime minister of the church died and was replaced briefly by a rascal who decided he didn't need an old organist in his church. He wanted the new gospel music—the kind that sounds like every other song you just heard. He played CDs in the church service and even sold a few out of the trunk of his car. They tell me he placed Sister Lee and her mighty organ in a corner behind the pulpit.

I got word of all this and went to see her in a Brooklyn hospital in the summer of 2011. She was pretty ill. It was the first time in my life, in more than fifty years of knowing her, that I had ever seen Sister Helen Lee without her wig. That's a big thing for the older generation of black women in church, to be seen without their wig—it's like being seen without clothes. James Brown was the same way. He'd sit under a hair dryer for three hours before he let anyone outside his circle see him. But Sister Lee was glad to see me. I brought her some chocolate cake. "I know you're not supposed to eat this," I said.

"Get me a fork," she said.

We laughed and ate cake, and I asked her about music. She talked about songs, and approach, about growing up in Fonde, Kentucky, near the Tennessee border, how her parents paid a neighbor twenty-five cents to teach her, and how that teacher talked about quarter notes—how important they are and how to swing them, the use of triplet octaves in your right hand at the very top of the keyboard for drama and emphasis; how to play the bottom part of the piano to add rhythm to the music, because when she was a child, her church didn't have a drummer. The congregation clapping their hands and stomping their feet were the drummer; the pianist's left hand added rhythm and bass so you didn't really need a drummer. I had never talked about music with Sister Lee before, but I was smart enough by then to know, at that moment, that she was giving me something special. I would never, from that day to this, hear much more of her style of playing. With the exception of a few young masters like the late Moses Hogan of New Orleans, Joseph Joubert and Shelton Becton of New York, and Fred Nelson III of Chicago, who today conducts for Aretha Franklin, I personally don't know many pianists today who can play like that. I'm sure there are a few. But a lot of American church music has become like Broadway shows, all cowboy hat and no cowboy, lots of lights and sound, the drummers basically conducting the thing from beginning to end, with massive choirs hollering lyrics you can't understand. It's a lot of puff and smoke. That old-time gospel swing, played by musicians like Sister Lee who, when the spirit would hit her, would close her eyes, throw back her head, and lift those old spirituals toward Heaven something fierce, they're disappearing.

Shortly after that, on August 11, 2011, Sister Lee died.

New Brown nearly fell apart then. It was a bad time. But the church righted itself, thank God, and tossed that scoundrel preacher that same month and got a good, strong, intelligent minister who everyone loves. And slowly the church began to come back.

I started a music program there for kids from the housing projects in Sister Lee's memory. We've been meeting every Thursday night going on three years. The kids are ages eight to fourteen. We started with fifteen kids playing plastic buckets with drumsticks. I teach piano and music history, and added a second teacher, a fellow Oberlin alumnus.

For the music-history portion of our class I downloaded twenty-five artists on my iPad. I have it set up so you just hit a number button and an artist plays: for example, Maria Callas is number 3, Ennio Morricone is 7, John Coltrane is 4, John Lee Hooker is 9, and, of course, James Brown has a number. He's button number 14 on my list.

It's tough and involved, teaching kids after school, when they're hungry and tired, and it takes a lot—dedicated parents, patience, pianos at home for the kids. It's a headache, and at times, there's been some heartache. I have one student, a beautiful African American girl, eleven, who lost both her parents in the last five years. I played her father's funeral two months ago. He was a wonderful father, Vincent Joyner was. When I first organized my program three years ago, Vincent was the *only* father there. About two weeks before he died, Mrs. Vivian Miles, who helped me start the music program, who often picked up the kids and brought them to church and sometimes even kept them overnight, *she* died. These were special people. And those were heavy losses.

Sometimes I feel overwhelmed by the whole bit. The music program feels like an exercise in shouting; the repetitiveness, the expense, the banging away at discipline that requires patience and tedious practice is frustrating—for the kids and for me—in a world where they can conjure up 3D wizardry on a twenty-dollar cellphone in seconds. I force them to listen to music. I show them how much I love it, and wonder if it rubs off. Sometimes during lessons I get so tired of hammering away at scales and harmony, I turn off the pianos, dim the lights, pass out cookies, and go straight to a music-history quiz. I pull out my iPad and announce, "The winner gets three dollars." And the kids shut up and say, "Let's go!" They're ready to make that money. I start punching up various selections.

I play song number 3 (Maria Callas) and the yells come from everywhere, all guesses.

"*Rosetta Tharpe!*"

"*Celia Cruz!*"

"Nope, nope, nope . . ." I say. "Quit guessing. You're a long way off."

I play the next song, number 9 (John Lee Hooker).

"*B.B. King!*"

"*Rubén Blades!*"

"*Willie Colón!*"

"Nope. Nope. Nope," I say. "Forget it. Y'all are terrible."

But there's no guessing when I play song number 14. Their hands shoot up. Their faces light up. They hear hollering. They hear the scream. They hear the groove. They hear the tightness. And you say to yourself, *They will remember him. He will make them remember him. He's hollering from the back of the bus of history, just so they'll know who he is. So Vanessa will know him. And Cecil. And Maddy. And Laura. And Helen. And even little Ni Ni and the twins Malcolm and Malik. And in knowing who he is, maybe they will one day know who they are.*

And in that moment, just in that moment, as they holler his name, all is right in the world.

"James Brown!"

Acknowledgments

This book could not have been completed without many people, and I'd like to thank them all. But I can't remember them all. Here's the ones I can remember:

My research team: especially Faith Briggs, whose deep talent and sweat is all over these pages, and who created the chapter summaries. Also thanks to Georgette Baker and Margaret Saunders for their solid reporting, and Monica Burton for hours of transcribing.

The musicians. Especially Alfred "Pee Wee" Ellis and Fred Wesley, who created more of James Brown's sound than any two musicians in the world. Thanks to their respective wives as well: Charlotte Crofton-Sleigh and Gwendlyn Wesley.

Thanks to William Forlando Brown, who first invited me to the party, and his dad, Terry Brown, and Dahlia Brown, altogether a family of grace and courage. Thanks to Sue and Henry Summer for their tireless fight on behalf of needy children of South Carolina. Deepest gratitude to Mrs. Velma Warren Brown, and Mrs. Emma Austin, whose prayers and friendship have enriched my life, and whom I will never forget.

Thanks to my sister Helen McBride Richter and brother-in-law Dr. Gary Richter, for all their loving hospitality. A nod of respect and gratitude to David and Maggie Cannon, and to Buddy and Denise Dallas, for their courage, and willingness to carry on what James Brown asked them to.

A special thanks to Mr. Charles Bobbit and his dearly departed wife, Ruth Bobbit, for their insight and kindness.

I am grateful to the United House of Prayer of Augusta; James and David Neal of Toccoa, Georgia; Joya Wesley of Greensboro, North Carolina; and Andre White of Atlanta.

A special nod to the Reverend Al Sharpton for sharing his insights on James Brown.

Thanks to Carol L. Waggoner-Angleton, special collections assistant at the Reese Library in Augusta, Christine Miller-Betts, executive director of the Lucy Craft Laney Museum of Black History, and Michelle R. Austin, manager of the Toccoa-Stephens County Public Library. Also my gratitude to George Wingard and the Savannah River Archaeological Program.

Deep thanks to Edgar Brown of Blackville, South Carolina, who opened the door to Brown's history, William Murrell & Associates of Augusta, and Mr. William F. and Sherly Guinyard of Guinyard & Sons Funeral Home in Barnwell, South Carolina.

Thanks to Charles Reid of the C.A. Reid Sr. Memorial Funeral Home in Augusta and to his late father, Charles A. Reid, Sr., as well.

Thanks to Tony Wilson, James Brown impersonator extraordinaire, and appraiser Tom Wells; also a deep thanks to Joe Thomas and the Thomas family, and a special thank-you to Ruth "Mutt" Tobin and the members of St. Peter church in Elko, South Carolina.

Also to other Brown band members and "musical family," I extend my thanks, including John "Jabo" Starks, manager Kathie Williams,

Clyde Stubblefield, Nafloyd Scott, and the deeply talented Sweet
Charles Sherrell and his entire Dutch family.

Thanks to Greta Reid, Alan Leeds, Brenda Kelly, and violinist/mu-
sical director Richard Jones of Philadelphia, who, with Sylvia Med-
ford, Marlon Jones, and Vivien Pitts, were James Brown's first string
section. Thanks to pianist and musical pioneer Geneva Woode of Cincinnati, Ohio, who began her long and impressive musical career as a
studio backup singer with James Brown while still in high school.

To Mrs. Iola Brooker and Perry Lee Wallace of Brooker's Restaurant in Barnwell, South Carolina, I extend my gratitude. They were so
hospitable and kind and I am grateful.

Deep gratitude to CR Gaines of Barnwell, South Carolina;
Shelleree Gaines of Barnwell, South Carolina; Desai Ewbanks, and
Duane Ewbanks.

I am deeply grateful to former Brown sidemen and trumpeters Joe
Davis and Joe Dupars, as well as pianist George Caldwell, saxophonist
Patience Higgins, drummers Damon Due White and Dwayne Broad-
nax, and my New York roommate of two decades, Bill Singer, saxophonist repairman extraordinaire, for their insights on James Brown
and music in general.

Deepest thanks to Howard L. Burchette of the Burchette Media
Group for his priceless radio interviews of members of the James
Brown world.

Thanks to Jay Bender of the South Carolina Press Association, and
a special thanks to my NYU Journalism Department colleagues
Charles Seife and Pam Newkirk, whose insights into investigative reporting helped me through many a difficult moment in the reporting
of this work. I also extend my gratitude to my Oberlin friends Chesley
Maddox-Dorsey, bassist/composer Leon Lee Dorsey, and David Stull,
former dean of the Oberlin Conservatory, who actually got this ball
rolling.

And finally, thanks to my inner circle, those who know me best:
my agent Flip Brophy, who has minded me and kept me straight for

decades; editor Cindy Spiegel, whose work on *The Color of Water* launched my literary career, and whose friendship and generosity of spirit I will remember the rest of my life; thanks to New Brown Memorial Baptist Church for their prayers and love, thanks to my siblings for always being there, and finally thanks to Azure, Jordan, and Nash McBride and my niece Kawren Scott-Logan for putting up with a busy father and uncle who, despite everything, still loves them to pieces.

James McBride
Lambertville, New Jersey

JAMES McBRIDE is an author, musician, and screenwriter. His memoir, *The Color of Water* (Riverhead), is an American literary classic that has been translated into more than sixteen languages. His novel *The Good Lord Bird* won the 2013 National Book Award for fiction. His novel *Miracle at St. Anna* became a 2008 Touchstone Disney film. His novel *Song Yet Sung* was the One Book, One Maryland choice of 2010. He has written screenplays and teleplays for film icon Spike Lee (*Miracle at St. Anna, Red Hook Summer*) and television pioneer David Simon (*Parting the Waters*). McBride is a former staff writer for *The News Journal* (Wilmington, Delaware), *The Boston Globe, People,* and *The Washington Post* Style Section. His work has appeared in *The New York Times, Rolling Stone, Essence,* and *National Geographic*. He is the recipient of the 1997 Anisfield-Wolf Book Award.

McBride holds several awards for his work as a musical theater composer, including the American Academy of Arts and Letters Richard Rodgers Award, the ASCAP Foundation Richard Rodgers New Horizons Award, and the American Music Theatre Festival's Stephen Sondheim Award. He has written songs (music and lyrics) for Anita Baker, Grover Washington, Jr., Gary Burton, Silver Burdett music textbooks, and for the PBS television character Barney. He served as a saxophonist sideman with jazz legend Little Jimmy Scott. McBride was born and raised in New York City and attended New York City public schools. He studied at the Oberlin Conservatory of Music and holds a master's degree in journalism from Columbia University. He was elected to the American Academy of Arts and Sciences in 2015, holds several honorary doctorates, and is currently a Distinguished Writer in Residence at the Arthur L. Carter Journalism Institute at New York University. McBride still tours with his Good Lord Bird band, playing gospel music.

jamesmcbride.com
Facebook.com/JamesMcBrideAuthor

For literary discussion, author insight,
book news, exclusive content,
recipes and giveaways, visit the
Weidenfeld & Nicolson blog and
sign up for the newsletter at:

www.wnblog.co.uk

For breaking news, reviews and exclusive competitions
Follow us 🐦 @wnbooks